Modern Business Correspondence

Fifth Edition

Modern Business Correspondence
A Text-Workbook

Donna C. McComas

Former Business Instructor
Arkansas State University
Jonesboro, Arkansas and
East Arkansas Community College
Forest City, Arkansas

Marilyn L. Satterwhite

Business Division
Danville Area Community College
Danville, Illinois

GREGG DIVISION

McGraw-Hill Book Company

New York   Atlanta   Dallas   St. Louis   San Francisco
Auckland   Bogotá   Guatemala   Hamburg   Johannesburg   Lisbon
London   Madrid   Mexico   Montreal   New Delhi   Panama   Paris
San Juan   São Paulo   Singapore   Sydney   Tokyo   Toronto

Sponsoring Editor: Edward E. Byers
Editing Supervisor: Mitsy Kovacs
Design and Art Supervisor: Meri Shardin
Production Supervisor: Priscilla Taguer

Interior Design: Suzanne Bennett & Associates
Cover Design: Sulpizio Associates
Technical Studio: Burmar Technical Corporation

Library of Congress Cataloging-in-Publication Data

McComas, Donna C.
  Modern business correspondence.

  Fourth ed.: Modern business correspondence / Marjorie
Hunsinger, Donna C. McComas. 4th ed. c1979.
  Bibliography: p.
  Includes index.
  1. Commercial correspondence.   I. Satterwhite,
Marilyn L.   II. Hunsinger, Marjorie. Modern business
correspondence.   III. Title.
HF5726.M425   1987   651.7'5'0711   86-757
ISBN 0-07-044840-X

MODERN BUSINESS CORRESPONDENCE,
Fifth Edition

1 2 3 4 5 6 7 8 9 0   SEMSEM   8 9 3 2 1 0 9 8 7 6

ISBN 0-07-044840-X

CONTENTS

PREFACE

Letters, memorandums, and informal reports are the primary means of sending and receiving written information in business. These forms of communication permit an exchange of ideas, facts, recommendations, and proposals. Without this exchange, modern business could not operate efficiently and productively. Because written communication is vital to any organization, the ability to write effective correspondence can enhance one's chances for a successful career in business.

The primary objective of *Modern Business Correspondence*, Fifth Edition, is to help develop the ability to write successful business letters, memorandums, and informal reports. The materials have been carefully selected to present the fundamentals of business writing logically, clearly, and completely. The topics covered in the previous edition of the text-workbook have been expanded and reorganized to ensure coverage of all essential subjects. Also, the materials have been updated to reflect currently accepted business practices. New examples, illustrations, and worksheet problems have been added.

Modern Business Correspondence, Fifth Edition, has been designed to keep the student involved in a natural learning process from the beginning of the course to the end.

The text divides the elements of business writing into four major parts. Part 1 (Units 1–7) introduces the general principles of good writing, including how to plan and outline correspondence and how to dictate, edit, and proofread. Part 2 (Units 8 and 9) provides practice in formatting and writing effective memorandums and reports. Part 3 (Units 10–19) teaches how to format and compose many types of business letters. Finally, Part 4 (Units 20 and 21) discusses employment communications and helps the student to prepare a résumé and letter of application, as well as other employment-related correspondence.

The worksheet following each unit contains exercises correlated with the material in that particular unit. Each worksheet provides comprehensive practice in handling realistic communication problems. The instructor will assign several problems from each worksheet; the number will depend upon the length of the course as well as upon the emphasis the instructor wishes to place on the various topics.

The Reference Section beginning on page 241 provides a concise, illustrated summary of the rules of grammar, punctuation, capitalization, number expression, abbreviation usage, word division, spelling, and revision. It supplements the text discussion of these topics and provides you a convenient source of information for use throughout the course.

Donna C. McComas
Marilyn L. Satterwhite

Part 1

PRINCIPLES OF GOOD LETTER WRITING

Writing better business correspondence is a many-sided challenge. Both planning and composing effective messages require that you put the principles and techniques in Part 1 into practice. At first you will have to use them consciously and with much thought; later (sooner than you think) you will master them and use them with ease.

Every business writer should be able to produce a structurally complete letter. But the real test of a good letter—one that achieves its purpose quickly, clearly, and effectively—is the total effect it has on the reader. In Part 1 you will learn several steps that will help your letter make a favorable impression on the reader and accomplish its purpose.

You are not expected to master all these techniques at once, but you will quickly see that writing is a combination of things going on at the same time, not a disconnected series of "things to do in a certain order."

The Total Effect on the Reader

Most people respond favorably to a letter's naturalness, courtesy, friendliness, and sincerity. Picture your reader receiving your letter. Will he or she be receptive to its message and respond favorably? Follow your reader's reactions in reading the letter. A reader who will stiffen at the sentence "We give every request full consideration" will relax when met with the sentence rewritten, "You may be sure that your request will be given full consideration."

The total effect on the reader determines whether he or she will do what you want or react the way you want. If your letter has done its job properly, the reader's response to each of the three questions below will be positive. You will then have taken three important steps toward successful communication.

Will the Reader Understand the Message?

Writing must be simple if it is to be clear. The simple sentence is the most useful tool in business correspondence. It is made up of a single clause containing one subject and one predicate. Resist the temptation to join a single idea to another idea with one of these links: *and, but, nor, or*. Use sparingly, in the interest of simplicity, such conjunctions as *therefore, moreover, however,* and *accordingly*.

Avoid using complex and vague words. Don't try to impress the reader with your knowledge by using fancy words. Using simple words your reader will easily understand (without consulting a dictionary) will help the reader quickly grasp the intended meaning of the whole message. Be correct and natural in your use of words and construction of sentences so that your writing flows smoothly. Your reader will understand you and be grateful to you as well.

The highest compliment a reader can pay you is to say that your letter was simple, clear, and easy to read. This reaction tells you that you have done your job well—and your letter has done *its* job.

Is the Tone of the Letter Positive?

How you say what you have to say may influence your reader just as much as *what* you have to say. Your letter will appeal to the reader if you develop a conversational, informal writing style; stress positive rather than negative ideas; and emphasize a "you" viewpoint throughout the letter. The friendly tone of your writing should suggest that your attitude is positive, that you are interested in the reader, and that you sincerely want to help. Naturalness, courtesy, friendliness, and sincerity are all essential to good tone in a letter.

Will the Letter Do Its Specific Job and Also Build Goodwill?

The qualities your letter possesses will cause the reader to react favorably or unfavorably. One of the main objectives of all business correspondence is to encourage the reader to react favorably. The easy readability and friendly tone of your message attract and impress your reader. But the letter must do its specific job and, at the same time, increase goodwill. You can't always do all that the reader wants, but you can almost always convince the reader that you understand his or her problems and that you want to do something about them.

The Impact of a Unified Message

As you write, you must think in terms not of one attribute, one principle, or one attitude, but of the unified effect of the whole message. Overlooking even one quality that is important to the reader may weaken or destroy the effectiveness of even the most carefully composed letter. You should take time not only to determine the important points to include in a particular letter and the best method of organizing and presenting them but also to review and improve what you have written. The reader's positive response to your message will prove your success. When you succeed, you will know that you understand how to make a good impression and promote goodwill through effective business letters.

You can write letters as good as the ones in this book (some of the examples were written by students!). If you keep practicing and follow the general suggestions given in Units 1–5, you *will* write successful letters. To help you further, Unit 6 will show you how to plan and prepare letters that communicate clearly and effectively. In Unit 7, the final touches will be added as you learn to dictate, edit, and proofread your correspondence.

Unit 1

THE CHALLENGE OF MODERN BUSINESS CORRESPONDENCE

Higher education is an investment of your time and money, but what better place can you invest them than in yourself? You are involved in a series of courses designed to provide you with the necessary background and skills to enter the business world and achieve success. Your business correspondence course is designed to help you develop one skill which may be every bit as important as all your other skills combined.

The Importance of Writing Ability

It is not enough to possess job skills without having the ability to communicate with supervisors, customers, and fellow employees. Obviously, employers wish to attract business workers with top skills; consequently, they screen job application forms for evidence of the applicant's knowledge and experience. More and more job application forms include essay-type questions designed to test an applicant's ability to write effectively.

Employers will usually choose from near-equally qualified candidates for a job or a promotion the individual who best demonstrates skills as a business communicator. The ability to communicate effectively is a skill included on almost every list of attributes possessed by the successful executive. This skill is also included on most lists of areas in which employees need to improve. Whatever path your career may take, from entry level to the highest executive level, your written communication skills are vital to you. Whether or not you get a job or receive a promotion may well hinge on how extensively you have developed these skills.

No matter what field you enter, the ability to communicate effectively will serve you well. Communication is a vital part of our world today. You may be a very intelligent person, but if you can't successfully transmit your ideas to others, you will be perceived

as someone less intelligent than you are. Ideas are commonplace, but the ability to communicate them is sometimes more valuable than the ideas themselves.

Written Communications—The Lifeline of Modern Business

Letters, memorandums, and reports are the primary means of sending and receiving written information in business. These forms of communication permit an exchange of ideas, facts, recommendations, and proposals. Without this exchange, modern business as we know it could not exist. Maintaining the flow of written information is essential to modern business. Business correspondence is functional, useful communication. A modern business letter, memo, or report is simply a good business conversation transferred to paper. The impressions customers and business associates form of you and your organization are important and lasting—and many of them are based solely upon your written communications.

Business letters typically attempt to build or retain goodwill, which is a priceless commodity, hardearned and easily lost, that a business never has too much of. Good letter writers recognize this purpose in their writing and strive to sharpen their understanding of psychology as well as English composition. Because the exchange of written communication is vital to business and essential for promoting goodwill, the art of producing effective correspondence will help ensure your success in business.

Your Communications Are Your Trademark

The memos, letters, and reports you write demonstrate your ability, or lack of ability, to communicate. Whether you like it or not, many people judge your ability and intelligence by the quality of your writing—

which includes the accuracy of your spelling, punctuation, and grammar. Your written communications are a permanent record of your ability to write. People who read your communications form an opinion of you and your organization. You and the executives of your organization will be concerned that this image be a positive one. Presenting yourself well in writing means that you will project a favorable image of your organization as well as promote successful business operations. Your communication skills will have a significant impact on both internal and external operations.

You will also find that the techniques presented in this book can be applied to your personal-business affairs. Everyone must write business letters in dealing with retailers, banks, insurance companies, and other businesses. Letter-writing skills facilitate effective communication in all aspects of life.

Advantages of Written Communications

The business letter has several advantages over other types of business communication. For one thing, it is frequently much less expensive than a personal visit or a telephone call. And, of course, a letter will get into an office when a telephone call may not be accepted; even the executive who travels a great deal or is too busy to be reached by phone will eventually read his or her mail. One of the main advantages is that people seem to attach greater importance to a letter than to a phone call. Also, the business letter provides a written record of a transaction and becomes a document that may be legally acceptable as a binding contract or as evidence in a court of law.

Business letters are confidential, since they are usually read in privacy. The reader will most likely be able to concentrate on the message without interruption. Therefore, material that might be unsuitable for a telephone conversation can be communicated in a letter (especially if the envelope is marked "Confidential" and "Personal").

Technical data and other enclosures can be transmitted with the letter. And if you need to send the same information to a number of individuals, sending a letter is a fast method that ensures you are giving exactly the same information to all.

Written communications provide an opportunity to say in writing what you might wish you could spend more time thinking about if you had to say it in person. Business writing allows you to spend more time on the content of your communications and word your messages in the most advantageous and persuasive way.

Modern Business Correspondence Is a Writing-Oriented Course

Simply reading good business letters or reading about how to write good business letters won't teach you to write. By comparison, listening to a concert will not teach you to play the guitar, nor will strolling through an art museum teach you to paint pictures. So, to develop your writing ability, you must analyze good and bad examples of communication and then practice writing business letters, memos, and reports. This course will offer you many opportunities to compose effective business correspondence in response to realistic communication problems.

The Five Tests of Effective Correspondence

To communicate easily and effectively with your reader, apply the following "C" principles.

Courtesy

Successful writers take careful measure of the words they use, avoiding words to which they themselves would react unfavorably. In short, they try the words out on themselves before writing them to others.

Many times you've heard the expression "It's not what you say, it's how you say it." The people who read your letters will judge you and your organization by your friendliness and courtesy. It is friendly to be informal and write in a natural, conversational style. It is courteous to conserve the reader's time and effort by expressing yourself with words that are easily understood.

An attitude projected through your writing that focuses on the reader—the "you" attitude—should show that you are genuinely interested in communicating. The tone of your letter should also show your sincerity and desire to be of service. You should be as helpful, pleasant, and courteous to the reader as possible.

Clarity

Clear writing is easy to understand. It demands short words. There should be no doubt in the reader's mind of the shade of meaning intended by the writer.

Here are a few phrases that are the enemy of clear writing:

    acknowledge receipt of
    at an early date
    at the present writing
    attached please find
    due to the fact that
    for your information
    in due course
    in receipt of
    regarding the matter
    regret to inform
    this is to acknowledge
    we are pleased to note

Forceful writing is obtained through the use of active verbs—those that are used in the *active voice* as opposed to the passive voice. In the active voice the subject of the sentence performs the action described by the verb. In the passive voice the subject receives the action described by the verb.

The active voice creates the illusion of movement; the passive voice limits movement. For example:

PASSIVE: The proposal was approved by the general manager.

ACTIVE: The general manager approved the proposal.

Another thief of forceful writing is the participial phrase. When introduced by such words as *assuring, hoping, believing,* and the like, the participial phrase is the weakest verbal construction in the English language.

The most obvious advantage of clear writing to the reader is that it helps the reader to grasp the essential message quickly. Make your writing coherent by using link words and phrases as transitional devices to join the parts in each message. Clear structure also aids reader understanding and retention. It isn't enough to write so that your message can be understood—you must strive to write so that your message *cannot* possibly be *misunderstood.*

A plan or outline of content will also help ensure adherence to organization and purpose. Other keys to clarity include logical arrangement, specific instead of general terms, directness, consistency, balance, comparison and contrast, and unification.

Completeness

Completeness is closely related to clarity; a message may be unclear because essential information has been omitted. When you are replying to an inquiry or request, be thorough in answering all questions asked, and even anticipate the reader's reaction by providing relevant information. Formulating and expressing a complete message will show your genuine interest in the reader and your wish for a favorable reaction. It will also save you the embarrassment and expense of a follow-up message.

Conciseness

Conciseness doesn't necessarily mean brevity or curtness. It is saying what you have to say in the fewest possible words—which may mean two words or hundreds. Conciseness is achieved when you pare down your letter to essentials, stripping it of superfluous words.

Teaming up two or more words of the same or similar meaning robs letters of conciseness. For example:

We are *grateful* and *appreciative* . . .

We stand *ready, willing,* and *able* to be of *assistance* and *service* . . .

We *look forward* with *anticipation* to . . .

Being concise means saying all that needs to be said and no more. Do not omit important facts, but do increase communication effectiveness by omitting irrelevant details and by combining complete, pertinent information with few words.

Correctness

After you have determined that your message is courteous, clear, complete, and concise, you must be sure that it is correct. A small error in a date or an amount of money, for example, may result in loss of time, money, or goodwill—or all three. Verifying your facts and paying attention to accuracy of details is time well spent.

Reasons for errors fall into two categories:

1. Typographical. Wrong letters, strikeovers, errors in spacing.

2. Failure to check reference sources. Misspelled words and names; errors in word selection, dates and figures, capitalization, and punctuation; and incomplete information.

Unit 7, "Dictating, Editing, and Proofreading," Unit 10, "Letter Format and Letter Styles," and the Reference Section will help you check each message to ensure that it is correct.

Summary

When the message you write passes the five tests of effective correspondence, you will have reached your goal of informing, persuading, and positively influencing the reader.

The techniques of composing business correspondence discussed in this text will clear up misconceptions you may have and help you to produce letters, memos, and reports that achieve their purpose.

ASSIGNMENT: To make sure you understand the importance of learning to write well, complete Section A of the Worksheet for Unit 1. In Section B you will have an opportunity to apply the five Cs.

Unit 1 Worksheet

THE CHALLENGE OF MODERN BUSINESS CORRESPONDENCE

A ANALYZING THE IMPORTANCE AND TECHNIQUES OF MODERN BUSINESS CORRESPONDENCE

1. List six advantages a business letter may have over a personal visit or phone call.

   a. _____
   _____

   b. _____
   _____

   c. _____
   _____

   d. _____
   _____

   e. _____
   _____

   f. _____
   _____

2. Name three ways your writing skills can make you valuable to a prospective employer.

   a. _____
   _____

   b. _____
   _____

   c. _____
   _____

3. Give five techniques you will use to improve the clarity of your writing.

a. _____

_____

b. _____

_____

c. _____

_____

d. _____

_____

e. _____

_____

B APPLYING THE FIVE Cs. *Each of the following sentences lacks one of the "C" qualities. On the line provided, write the word or phrase that improves the italicized word(s).*

1. *We are in receipt of* your check for $59.

_____

2. The personnel manager reviews all the impressive résumés and calls *them* for interviews.

_____

3. Please *advise me as to the date on which* you plan to make delivery.

_____

4. We *demand* payment now.

_____

5. The supplementary forms should be mailed in a *seperate* envelope.

_____

Unit 2

CHOOSING THE RIGHT WORDS

Have you ever thought of writing as a matter of building? The writing process is complex, yet simple: the writer takes several steps to compose a message, but many things are actually happening at the same time. To understand how writing takes place, let's do what a writer does. A writer:

1. Chooses words.
2. Assembles them into phrases.
3. Connects the phrases to form sentences.
4. Groups the sentences into paragraphs.
5. Organizes the paragraphs into a coherent message.

To attempt to describe writing in the way the process really takes place would be difficult. So let's start with the simplest parts of language and proceed to the more complicated. We'll try to explain why some of these activities are necessary and how they relate to writing and the job it strives to do.

Let's start with the basic tools of writing, the words we use to communicate. Each word has one or more *denotative* meanings, or definitions as listed in dictionaries. Usually one meaning is commonly used; the others are less frequent.

In addition, words may have *connotative* meanings, or the subtle and often emotional meanings that we associate with some words. Because the emotional overtones, or connotative meanings, of words may vary from person to person, they are especially difficult to control. These connotations are often the result of the reader's intensely personal bias, and unless you enter into each reader's mind, you can't be sure how the reader will react. With groups of readers, however, you can often foresee that a particular word will evoke a negative image in those readers' minds. You can then choose another, less antagonizing word that has the same denotative meaning but does not have a negative connotation.

The study of the meanings of words is called *semantics*. There are many books on the subject that will help you understand this interesting and important aspect of our language.

Before we look at how words are used in writing, let's look at how they work in reading and listening. When a person reads or hears a word, the word goes into his or her "word bank," or memory, that part of the mind where all the words the person has ever heard or read in all their contexts are stored. The reader or listener matches the new instance of hearing or reading a word with all the other instances stored in memory and from the context picks the meaning most likely to be the one intended by the writer or speaker.

Let's take *remote* as an example. It's not a commonly used word, nor is it exotic. It means "far away," right? As in *a remote country*. But it also can mean distant in time, as in *the remote future*. It can also mean having only a slight relationship, as with *a remote cousin*. And it is also used to mean aloof or distant, as in *a remote manner*. Add *control* and you get *remote control*, meaning control (usually electronic) from a distance. This is one of the strengths of English: that we can give multiple, though necessarily related, meanings to a word and so extend our language without making it impossibly cumbersome.

Suppose, however, that *remote* didn't fit your needs precisely or that you had just used it in the previous sentence and didn't want to repeat it. By using a dictionary or a thesaurus you could find synonyms like *distant*, *removed*, and *far*. And this is another strength of our language, that many words can have the same meaning or closely related meanings. As an example, a student once counted over 220 meanings of *get*!

Maize means only "corn"; it has no other meanings. Between *get* and *maize* lies the difference between familiar and unfamiliar words. *Maize* is one of those words that one seldom hears or reads. If you

Choosing the Right Words **9**

think of it, you have no other uses to compare it with, so you are unable to attach another meaning to it. For *get*, you have an abundance of meanings to choose from, depending on the context in which it is used.

Here is a principle to keep in mind when you are writing. Generally, the more familiar a word is to your reader, the more meanings he or she will know for it and the more likely he or she will be to attach to it the meaning you intended. The more unfamiliar a word is, the fewer meanings the reader will know for it and the less likely he or she will be to give it the meaning you have in mind.

Most of the common words you use in everyday speech are short, one- or two-syllable words. Using short words helps to keep the message readable. To communicate easily and effectively with your reader, use common, short, familiar words whenever it is possible.

You can make your writing clearer and your reader's job easier by using:

1. Simple words that the reader will understand.

2. Concise words that do not waste the reader's time.

3. Conversational words rather than trite expressions.

4. Appropriate words for conventional business usage.

5. Correct words instead of inaccurate words.

6. Specific words that make your writing more precise.

7. Positive words instead of negative words.

Simple Words

Short, familiar words make your writing easy to read and to understand quickly. They are far more effective in business writing than complex words that the reader may understand only after rereading the sentence or paragraph, or even consulting a dictionary. The reader's attention is shifted from the message if he or she must guess at the meaning of some of the words or reach for the dictionary. The reader is much more likely to listen comfortably and understand easily if you use words that are familiar.

Short words have more force and clarity than long words. When simple words will convey your meaning quickly and clearly, use them in preference to longer, less familiar words.

Simple words are not always short ones, however, and high-sounding words are not always long ones. *Displeasure* and *irritation,* for instance, are used more often in conversation than *pique* is used. As a rule, though, choose longer words only when they express the meaning more clearly or more naturally than their shorter synonyms.

You can see how short, familiar words can make

reading easier if you contrast the following paragraph with its revision:

> Consideration of your request leads us to believe that of several alternative courses of action open at the present time the maximum effect will accrue if standard procedures are amended to permit actualization toward optimal realization of the goals of our mission.

Here's the revision:

> I agree we'll do better if we change our standard procedures.

Below is a list of complex words and phrases and their simple, direct translations. Most of these formal-sounding, complicated words, often found in business letters, are perfectly good words. The point is that each has a more familiar substitute that usually does a better job of communicating.

Instead of These Complex Words . . .	. . . Choose These Simpler Words
a substantial segment of the population	many people
affords an opportunity	allows
approximately	about
are fully cognizant of	know
ascertain	find out
assistance	help
commence	start
consummate	complete OR finish
converse	talk
effect the destruction of	destroy
encounter difficulty in	find it hard to
endeavor	try
gratuitous	free
hold in abeyance	delay
I wish to assure you that it has been a great pleasure to be the recipient of your gracious generosity	thank you
interpose an objection	object
interrogate	ask
it is requested that	please
negligible	small OR slight
numerous	many
peruse	read OR study
procure	get
pursuant to your request	as you asked
render services	serve
remuneration	payment
subsequently	later
sufficient	enough
take under advisement	consider OR think over
terminate	end OR finish
utilize	use
unavoidably detained	delayed

You can add many others to this list, for your reference. Look for complex, unfamiliar words and phrases in your writing and try to replace them with familiar words which will make the reader's job easier.

Concise Words

Every word you use that does not contribute to the effectiveness of your message wastes the reader's time and weakens interest. Strive for *conciseness* in your writing—using only as many well-chosen words as you need to convey your message. Each word in the message should help make the meaning clear or the letter friendly. By using only as many words as you need for what you want to say, you help the reader in two ways: you save the reader time in reading and understanding, and you make the letter more interesting to read.

An average of 3 out of 10 words in the typical letter are not really needed, according to recent estimates. A reader is likely to lose all interest in a message if he or she must wade through wordiness to get to the main point. You want your reader to listen comfortably. Why use two or more words when one word will do the job well?

Let's look at this sentence from a business letter:

In reply to yours of recent date, I wish to advise you that Mr. Jeffrey Isaacson, about whom you inquired, was terminated from his employment at Shelbourne's on August 31, due to the fact that he frequently did not appear for work at the appointed hour.

Two-thirds of the words in the sentence can be eliminated and the message stated concisely:

Mr. Jeffrey Isaacson's employment at Shelbourne's ended on August 31 because of excessive tardiness.

Notice that none of the necessary information is omitted and the message is actually clearer and easier to read.

Here are some examples of how word economy saves the reader's time and effort.

Instead of These Time Wasters . . .	. . . Choose These Time Savers
arrived at the conclusion	concluded
at a later date	later
at the present time OR at this moment in time	now
costs a total of $50	costs $50
due to the fact that	because
during the year of 19—	during 19—
first of all	first
five in number	five
for the purpose of providing	to provide
held a meeting	met
I want to take this opportunity to tell you that we are grateful to you	thank you

I wish to say OR permit me to say OR may I say . . . that we are glad	we are glad
in a manner similar to	like
in the amount of	for
in the event that	if
in the near future	soon
in order to	to
in possession of	have
in this day and time	today
inasmuch as	since OR because
is a matter of	is
is responsible for selecting	selects
it is the opinion of many	many believe OR many think
it is probable that	probably
long period of time	long time
made the announcement	announced
may or may not	may
put in an appearance	appeared
self-addressed envelope	addressed envelope OR return envelope
take appropriate measures	do
until such time as you can	until you can
venture a suggestion	suggest
whether or not	whether
with the exception of	except
with regard to safety precautions	for safety
within the course of the next week	next week OR within a week

Avoid repetitive words. In the following redundant expressions, the italicized words are unnecessary and should be omitted.

absolutely free	*meet* together
adequate *enough*	over *with*
as to whether	*past* experience
at about	*personal* opinion
attached *hereto*	*quite* unique
basic essentials	refer *back*
both alike	repeat *again*
continue *on*	right-*hand* turn
cooperate *together*	*same* identical
customary practice	seldom *ever*
finish *up*	*still* remains
first began	*true* facts
kind courtesy	*up* above
later *on*	*up* until
lose *out*	*very* latest
maroon-*colored*	*vitally* essential

A doublet is formed when two words with practically the same meaning are joined by *and*. Avoid the following doublets by using either the first or third word and omitting the other two.

basic and fundamental	help and cooperation
belief and opinion	pleased and delighted
each and every	prompt and immediate
fair and equitable	ready and willing
first and foremost	wish and desire

Writing concisely, then, means transmitting only necessary, meaningful words to the reader.

Conversational Words

Many expressions that were fashionable in business letters of years ago sound lifeless, insincere, and even boring when used in today's correspondence. If a message is filled with worn-out words, the reader probably feels that you were neither thinking of nor talking to him or her when you wrote it. The letter sounds mechanical, like a record that can be played back for anyone listening, not like a personal message to the reader. Since fashions in words change, correct usage should be current usage. Don't go to out-of-date business letters to find the words to use in a letter today. Use only those words that educated business people normally use in well-planned communications.

Not only do old-fashioned expressions need to be kept out of your letters, but many modern expressions as well have lost their effectiveness because of overuse. For example, *contact* as a verb meaning "to get in touch with" has been worn out by overuse, as has *check* as a verb. They have become trite—meaningless.

The trite expressions in the column at the left too often appear in business communications. As you study them, notice how simply and naturally the suggested conversational words convey the same meanings.

Instead of These Trite Words . . .	**. . . Choose These Conversational Words**
acknowledge receipt of	thank you for
agreeable with your desires in the matter	as you suggested
are in receipt of	have
as per our conversation	as we discussed
at the earliest possible date	as soon as (you) can
at the present writing	now
at your earliest convenience	when you have time OR when you are ready
enclosed herewith OR enclosed herein OR enclosed please find	here is OR here are
give the matter our early attention	take care of this soon
in accordance with your request	as you asked
in view of the fact that	because

kindly advise me OR kindly inform me	please write me OR please call me
of recent date	of April 3
please do not hesitate to	please
regret to inform you that	am sorry that
take the liberty of sending you	send you
thanking you in advance	I shall appreciate
the writer OR the undersigned	I OR we
under date of	on
under separate cover	separately
we will thank you to	please

Clichés are well-known phrases that you must be careful of using in business correspondence. Language experts differ on the use of clichés in writing. Some say never use them—think of something original instead. Others say sometimes it's a good idea to use a cliché.

Our view is that a business letter filled with clichés will not be effective. However, the occasional use of clichés is good if it gives your reader a comfortable feeling. But use them sparingly—only when you're sure they are the best way to express your intent.

Here are some of the more popular clichés you should decide when and where to use.

all things being equal	in no uncertain terms
break the ice	in a nutshell
business as usual	in a word
by leaps and bounds	keep the ball rolling
by rule of thumb	lay the cards on the table
down to the last detail	light at the end of the tunnel
draw the line at	
few and far between	missing link
finishing touch	needle in a haystack
for better or worse	needs no introduction
from A to Z	step in the right direction
from bad to worse	unwritten law
from start to finish	ups and downs
give and take	wishful thinking

Avoid these worn-out, overused expressions in your writing:

all in all	last but not least
bare minimum	leave no stone unturned
beat around the bush	lion's share
crystal clear	needless to say
dragging one's feet	nipped in the bud
drastic action	pose a challenge
fact of life	powers that be
far and away	stands to reason
goes without saying	strike while the iron is hot
honest truth	turn the corner

In addition to these examples, many other trite expressions are still being used. To keep your letters alive and human, avoid using such expressions in your writing.

Appropriate Words

By using the right word for every circumstance, you help the reader understand exactly what you mean. You also build the reader's confidence in you and your ideas. Errors that might pass unnoticed in conversation are far more noticeable in written messages. If you use the "wrong" word, or one that is not "just right" for the context, you may imply a meaning that you do not intend. The reader may misinterpret your intended meaning because of your poor choice of words.

Errors often result from the confusion of *homonyms,* words that sound alike but have different meanings, such as *there, their, they're* and *here, hear.* Even more confusing are *pseudohomonyms*—words that are similar in sound but different in meaning, such as *adopt, adept, adapt* and *affect, effect.* And probably most confusing are *synonyms,* words that are similar in meaning. Here it is important to choose carefully the word that says exactly what you want to say. For example, *the balance of your shipment* is not quite accurate, since *balance* usually refers to an amount of money. *Remainder* or *rest* would be more appropriate. Similarly, *You can get the information from Corinne* is more appropriate than *You can secure the information from Corinne.*

To avoid confusing your reader, choose carefully among the following groups of words that are often confused. Use the dictionary to verify the exact meaning of any word you are in doubt about, or a thesaurus to help you choose the word that best conveys your meaning.

accept—except
access—excess
adapt—adept—adopt
addition—edition
advice—advise
affect—effect
allowed—aloud
altar—alter
among—between
amount—number
appraise—apprise
assistance—assistants
attendance—attendants
balance—remainder
beside—besides
canvas—canvass
capital—capitol
cereal—serial
cheap—inexpensive
choose—chose
cite—site—sight
coarse—course
complement—compliment
confidentially—confidently
correspondence—
    correspondents

council—counsel
dependence—
    dependents
eligible—illegible
eminent—imminent
farther—further
fewer—less
fiscal—physical
formally—formerly
graft—graph
hear—here
human—humane
instance—instants
intense—intents
its—it's
later—latter
lean—lien
leased—least
leave—let
lessen—lesson
lesser—lessor
loose—lose
miner—minor
moral—morale
partly—partially
party—person

passed—past
patience—patients
personal—personnel
practicable—practical
precede—proceed
presence—presents
principal—principle

respectfully—
    respectively
right—write
stationary—stationery
suit—suite
than—then
their—there—they're
to—too—two

In choosing appropriate words, you must consider also your reader's experiences and interests. Every occupational or professional group has its own technical vocabulary, or jargon. Remember that technical words that are "everyday" to you will be the right choice when writing to a specialist in your area, but they will be useless to nearly everyone else. Use special terms with care, or you may create rather than solve a communication problem. The successful business communicator learns and uses words that fit the reader's vocabulary.

Another important check for proper business language is the use of bias-free words. There is an art to choosing alternatives to gender-specific terms—for example, *business person* or *business worker* instead of *businessman,* and *sales representative, sales agent, sales associate,* or *salesperson* instead of *salesman.*

The following list offers other substitutes for such terms:

Instead of These Gender-Specific Words	. . . Choose These Bias-Free Words
chairman	chair, chairperson
fellow worker	coworker OR colleague
fireman	firefighter
housewife	homemaker
insurance salesman	insurance agent
landlord OR landlady	owner
mailman	mail carrier
newsman	newscaster OR reporter OR journalist
office boy	messenger OR office helper
policeman OR policewoman	police officer
spokesman	spokesperson
weatherman	weather reporter
workman	worker

Also, be careful to avoid using stereotypes and discriminatory language in your writing. Do not use terms that could evoke negative images of minority groups or disabled people.

Correct Words

Careful business writers are aware of the skill involved in using words correctly. The first skill is to avoid using words that do not exist. For example, *irregardless* is not a word; choose instead *regardless* or *irresponsible.*

Some of the nonexistent words that are frequently used erroneously in business writing are a result of mispronunciation, as in *revelant* (*relevant*), *irrepairable* (*irreparable*), and *relator* (*realtor*).

In addition to these examples, errors of many other types occur in business writing—for instance, grammatical errors, in the use of prepositions and conjunctions, and of adverbs, adjectives, and articles; mistakes in spelling; errors in abbreviations and contractions; and errors in number expression.

Look over the following list of words and phrases that are often misused. Are any of them mistakes you make? If so, learn to recognize and avoid them.

Instead of These Frequently Misused Words . . .	. . . Choose These Correct Words
all but I	all but me
a lot of	many OR much
and etc.	etc.
anywheres	anywhere
between us three	among us three
between we two	between us two
between you and I	between you and me
dep't	dept.
different than	different from
don't have but	have only
equally as good	equally good OR just as good
had less errors	had fewer errors
if you will	whether you will
inside of	inside
insight of	insight into
irregardless	regardless
irrepairable	irreparable
like I do	as I do
long ways	long way
might of	might have
neither . . . or	neither . . . nor
one thousand two hundred tickets	1200 tickets
person which	person who
real pleased	really pleased OR very pleased
relator	realtor
revelant	relevant
the reason why . . . is because	the reason . . . is that
these kind	this kind OR these kinds
try and	try to
two pair	two pairs

You can add many other errors and their replacements to this list for your reference.

Specific Words

You can make your writing more *precise* by using specific words rather than general words. Specific words are those that present a clear, sharply defined picture to a reader's mind. General words are those that present a hazy, indefinite picture to the reader.

Suppose we say to you "car." What do you see in your mind? Now suppose we make it "blue car." Has the picture in your mind changed? Let's be even more specific: "light metallic-blue RX7." What do you see in your mind now, and how does it differ from what you thought of when we said "car"?

Making the reader "see" what you are describing requires imagination as well as creativity. A thesaurus is a gold mine to the business writer! Even if you don't immediately find the "right" word, some other word or words will usually spark an idea for conveying your thought.

As just illustrated, sometimes the more specific you want to be, the more words you must use. In writing, though, being specific means finding the balance between extra words with broad, general meanings and only the words necessary to paint a precise, accurate picture in the reader's mind. Being specific in your writing is the result of practice and experience. It is often a matter of choosing one word over another, finding the word that will create just the right image in your reader's mind. Whenever you can supply an exact fact, figure, or description to make your writing more concrete and convincing, do so.

Instead of These General Words . . .	. . . Choose These Specific Words
fair response	22 percent response
fast	in one hour
for the full amount	for $973.59
gigantic loss	$6.5 million loss
great month	very profitable month
high proportion	5:1 ratio
low rating	C rating
said	exclaimed OR protested
sizable distance	48,000 miles
small number of votes	76 votes
soon	on or before November 6

When writing, you must constantly consider your choice of words. You can write concretely by choosing vivid, image-building words rather than vague, general words.

Positive Words

Positive words create a pleasant aura around your message. That is why the effective business writer knows and deliberately uses warm words that pave the way for stimulating desired action on the reader's part.

The following words help to produce this desirable psychological effect.

Use These Positive Words

advantage	enjoy	progress
agreeable	fortunate	satisfaction
benefit	generous	success
comfortable	pleasure	valuable
encourage	profit	welcome

Just as some words carry positive meanings, others connote negative ideas. If you want your reader to feel goodwill toward you and to do what you would like him or her to do, you'll be careful to avoid negative, unfriendly words.

One type of negative words is those that are negative in almost any context, such as *complain, disappointing, inferior,* and *unfortunately*. No matter how you use them, you'll probably convey a negative meaning to your reader. Learn to substitute words like *cooperation, service,* and *sincere*.

The second type of negative words includes those that are negative because of the context they appear in. For example, *neglect, blame,* and *error* do not bring a negative response when you write "We neglected to tell you . . ." or "We take full blame for the error." Yet when used with *you* or *your,* they arouse anger: "You neglected to . . ." or "Your error caused . . ." or "You are to blame for . . ."

Here are some words and phrases that should be used with caution—if at all. They are likely to make the reader feel you are criticizing him or her and cause the reader to become angry with you.

Avoid Using These Negative Words

abuse	discomfort	neglect
alleged	dissatisfied	problem
apology	error	refuse
blame	failure	regret
broken	guilty	sorry
cannot	impossible	suspicion
carelessness	inability	trouble
claim	inadequate	unable
complaint	inconvenience	unfair
criticism	inferior	unfavorable
defective	insinuation	unfortunate
delay	loss	unwilling

Be sure to refer to the lists of words and phrases in this unit as you begin writing sentences, paragraphs, and messages. Paying close attention to the way you express yourself in writing now will help you develop good writing skills instead of bad writing habits.

ASSIGNMENT: Test what you have learned about word choice by rewriting the sentences in Section A of the Worksheet for Unit 2 and improving the clichés in Section B.

Unit 2 Worksheet

CHOOSING THE RIGHT WORDS

A PRECISE WORD CHOICES. *The following sentences contain complex words, excess words and phrases, trite expressions, inappropriate words, too-general words, incorrect words, and negative words. On the lines below, rewrite the sentences simply and concisely, substituting friendly, conversational expressions.* **NOTE:** *You may assume any information necessary to make your revisions clear and direct.*

1. I would like to order a tin of your popcorn.

_____

_____

_____

_____

2. Jared's resignation has had a negative affect on employe moral.

_____

_____

3. Mark your reply and send it to the writer.

_____

_____

_____

4. As I read this report I found myself much interested in it and I want to say here and now that I appreciate you sending it to me.

_____

_____

_____

_____

5. We plan to be there at the appointed time.

_____

_____

_____

6. I am coming in Febuary. I would like to see you all about our new film.

_____

_____

_____

_____

7. Contact me if you are unable to handle this situation. I am here every day.

_____

_____

8. I am doing a paper on word processing so would like to have any information you have on said subject.

_____

_____

_____

_____

9. We are sorry to have to inform you that it is our policy that we cannot assume responsibility for defaults.

_____

_____

_____

_____

_____

10. I advise you to except the position by the end of the physical year.

_____

_____

_____

11. Every effort will be made to expedite delivery as per our agreement.

_____

_____

12. If you can loan me the money, please contact me, and I shall come for it irregardless of the time of day.

_____

_____

13. We have received and read your communication of March 27 and wish to say that there is truth in each and every statement you make and that we fully understand your position.

_____

_____

_____

14. Many people attended our most recent monthly meeting.

_____

_____

15. Since you claim you didn't get the merchandise we sent, we'll have to investigate and find out the story behind the alleged delay.

_____

_____

_____

_____

_____

B _AVOIDING CLICHÉS. You are writing to a former coworker about a new position that has been created in the company you now work for. No ads have been run yet, and you feel that your friend should "strike while the iron is hot." Write a sentence that conveys your meaning without using the cliché._

_____

_____

_____

_____

_____

_____

Unit 3

WRITING SENTENCES AND PARAGRAPHS

Words alone do not communicate; they must be put together in the right order, according to a careful plan. You must:

1. Construct sentences by selecting and phrasing words carefully.

2. Join your sentences to form paragraphs.

3. Fit the paragraphs smoothly into a unified letter.

Constructing Sentences

A sentence is a grammatically correct arrangement of a group of words that expresses one complete thought. How well you construct your sentences plays a very important part in determining how well you communicate with your reader. Your goal is to present ideas so that the reader understands them with the least possible effort.

The "rules" about constructing sentences are not so very complicated. Of course, you should observe the principles of written English; otherwise, you will distract your reader. If you know these principles, you'll be able to use them to achieve the effects you want in your writing.

Generally, sentence construction in business letters is somewhat more conversational than in formal writing. (Ungrammatical usage is never justified, of course.) You will be wise, therefore, to choose a style that is closer to speech than to, say, a college textbook. Remember that communication takes place more efficiently when the reader is thinking about content and not about the manner in which it is expressed.

1. A Sentence Should Contain One Complete Thought

A sentence must express a complete thought. If a group of words gives merely part of an idea, it is a sentence *fragment*. Sentence fragments, such as those in the following example, split *one* thought into *two* parts:

WEAK: To update your records and actively reflect Rohm Manufacturing's economic standing in the community. We submit the following statistics on the company.

In this quotation from an actual letter, *To update your records and actively reflect Rohm Manufacturing's economic standing in the community* is not a complete sentence. It starts an idea that is not completed until the sentence that follows. The two statements should be joined to express one complete thought:

STRONG: To update your records and actively reflect Rohm Manufacturing's economic standing in the community, we submit the following statistics on the company.

The next quotation, also from an actual letter, illustrates another sentence fragment:

WEAK: The brochure describes some of the more advanced techniques of making sound investments. Including a candid analysis of the strategies and risks involved.

Including a candid analysis of the strategies and risks involved expands the idea expressed in the first sentence but is not a complete sentence in itself.

STRONG: The brochure describes some of the more advanced techniques of making sound investments— including a candid analysis of the strategies and risks involved.

Sentence fragments, usually introduced by prepositions or participles, are frequently found as opening and closing ideas in business letters. They are particularly feeble in either of these spots because *the first few words and the last few words are the most emphatic of the whole message.*

WEAK OPENING: Realizing that an insurance company must make fast, fair adjustments. The Springsteen Insurance Agency pledges to you the best service available in the Destin area.

WEAK OPENING: With reference to your suggestion. I appreciate this information and will follow up within a week.

You can make these openings acceptable by substituting a comma for the first period in each of them. But you can make them much stronger by rewording the sentences as follows:

STRONG OPENING: An insurance company must make fast, fair adjustments. The Springsteen Insurance Agency knows this and pledges to you the best service available in the Destin area.

STRONG OPENING: Your suggestion concerning our refund policy is welcome. Within a week I hope to have a solution to this problem of refunds.

Notice how much more effective a strong closing is than the following trite expression, which is also a sentence fragment:

WEAK CLOSING: Thanking you in advance for your courtesy and cooperation in this matter.

STRONG CLOSING: I shall appreciate your cooperation.

Sometimes a deliberate sentence fragment can be very effective. It can be made to express a complete thought if an exclamation point or a question mark is placed after it:

That's right—*lifetime protection!* Worldwide, 24 hours a day. And how?

Tonight! Our special Sundown-to-Sunup 40%-off Sale—don't miss it!

In these examples, using sentence fragments successfully tends to make the writing breezy and chatty. This informality may be useful in writing a sales letter or an advertisement for use in direct mail, where it is necessary to establish quickly both friendliness and a feeling of trust in the reader. In general business correspondence, however, such breeziness may backfire. The reader may think you are being flippant or insincere. To a reader who is angry, worried, or fearful over something, a very breezy writing style is especially unwelcome. Your letter may convince the reader that you don't care.

Sentence fragments may be used effectively, but sparingly, in business letters. Be sure you know what you're doing when you use them and that your reader will not consider the fragment a grammatical error.

2. A Sentence Should Contain Only One Idea

Just as sentence fragments do not express a complete thought, sentences that contain more than one idea weaken the message. Most readers are accustomed—and rightfully so—to encountering a single thought in each sentence. Too many ideas written without a pause tend to run together in the reader's mind.

WEAK: Thank you, Miss Polito, for your letter of April 30 complimenting the *National Business Report*, and beginning with the June issue your next three copies will be sent to your summer address.

In this opening sentence, the writer is trying to do two things: (1) thank the customer for her letter and (2) tell her that her request will be taken care of. Neither idea stands out, because the two are run together in one sentence. A simple change will stress both ideas.

STRONG: Thank you, Miss Polito, for your letter of April 30 complimenting the *National Business Report*. Beginning with the June issue, your next three copies will be sent to your summer address.

The following sentence, taken from an actual memo, contains three ideas:

WEAK: Your ideas don't have to be typed, if possible though they should be written in outline form and please be prepared to discuss them at the meeting.

This sentence could be confusing even if it were correctly punctuated (it isn't). Notice how much clearer it is when split into three ideas:

STRONG: Your ideas don't have to be typed; if possible, though, they should be written in outline form. Please be prepared to discuss them at the meeting.

Try giving more emphasis to an important idea by dividing it into two parts and expressing each part in a separate sentence.

WEAK: We promise to "try harder" in the future, and please let us know of any way we can serve you better.

Here is a more effective closing:

STRONG: We promise to "try harder" in the future. Please let us know of any way we can serve you better.

3. Sentence Length Should Be Moderate and Varied

For quick, clear, easy reading, all your sentences should be short and simple, right? Wrong! The length of the sentences can make the message easy to follow or hard to follow. Sentences averaging around 17 words in length are considered about right for fast reading. This means, of course, that good sentences can be longer than 20 words, or as short as 4 or 5 words, for variety and emphasis. Imagine the monotony of a message in which each sentence is exactly 17 words long. It might put the reader to sleep rather than persuade him or her to respond.

Varying the length of your sentences can enliven your writing style. A short, short sentence sandwiched between two long sentences emphasizes the thought of the short sentence. A few very short sentences help to give the message "punch." But too many short sentences one after the other make the letter choppy. If you ask your reader to keep jumping from one short statement to another, you may soon lose the reader.

> CHOPPY: We received your shipment of February 18. It contained sixteen No. 104H Klausen dresses. There were four each in Misses' sizes 8, 10, 12, and 14. But we ordered four each in Junior sizes 5, 7, 9, and 11. You can see this on the copy of the order which is enclosed.

> STRONG: Your February 18 shipment of sixteen No. 104H Klausen dresses—four each in Misses' sizes 8, 10, 12, and 14—arrived today. However, the shipment should have consisted of four each in Junior sizes 5, 7, 9, and 11, as shown on the enclosed copy of the order.

A short, choppy sentence is seldom as irritating to a reader as an extra-long sentence that rambles on and on, as though the writer couldn't stop. The writing fault that hinders readability the most is probably the long, rambling sentence.

> RAMBLING: In reply to your letter of August 1, we desire to enter it upon the record that, out of our commission to be paid to us by the Callicotts for making sale of this property for them, we agree to pay you a commission of 2 (two) percent of the sale price, amounting to $3,000, as a service to you and as compensation for the work and expense of closing the sale, and we further agree that no portion of this charge shall be assessed against or paid by the purchaser.

This string of words shows that the writer has lost sight of the thought unit. How could the reader possibly make sense out of such a statement? Isn't the following much easier to read?

> STRONG: I want to put on record the terms of the agreement you asked about in your August 1 letter.
> Our commission is to be paid by the Callicotts for selling this property. From our commission we agree to pay you a commission of 2 (two) percent of the sale price, amounting to $3,000, as a service fee for closing the sale. We further agree that no portion of this charge shall be assessed against or paid by the purchaser.

Two careless writing habits are frequently the basic cause of too-long sentences.

The "And" or "And So" Habit. The "and" habit, which leads to run-on sentences, is illustrated in this excerpt from a business letter:

> WEAK: We presently employ 93,466 persons at 11 sites in the greater Denver area, and this makes us the third largest private employer in the area, and we hope you will see fit to include these figures in your brochure, and we thank you for your cooperation.

You can usually correct this kind of error by eliminating some of the *ands* and dividing the run-on sentences into several sentences. Sometimes rephrasing the ideas or putting them in the form of a clause makes the new sentences more varied and interesting. Don't you like this better?

> STRONG: Since Mason Manufacturing employs 93,466 persons at 11 sites in the greater Denver area, we are the third largest private employer in this area. We would appreciate your including these figures in your brochure.

Instead of *and so*, use transitional words like *therefore*, *consequently*, and *accordingly* to connect clauses.

> WEAK: Our warehouse in Des Moines stocks the X-14 filter, and so the manager there has agreed to ship one to you.

> STRONG: Our warehouse in Des Moines stocks the X-14 filter; therefore, the manager there has agreed to ship one to you.

The "Dependent-Clause Chain" Habit. Chains of dependent clauses produce confusing sentences. Series of overlapping clauses, each hanging on to the one before, introduce new ideas and expand previous ideas so fast that the reader can barely grasp one before the next one arrives. Notice all the clauses introduced by *which* in this long sentence from a memo.

> WEAK: Ms. JoAnne Haas will take Air Pacific Flight 190 at 4:15 p.m., which should arrive in Seattle at 6:10 p.m., which means that you should plan to meet her and transport her to the tennis awards banquet, which begins at 7:30 p.m.

> STRONG: Ms. JoAnne Haas will arrive in Seattle at 6:10 p.m. on Air Pacific Flight 190. Please plan to meet her and transport her to the tennis awards banquet, which begins at 7:30 p.m.

4. Sentences Should Be Concise

Whether a sentence is long or short, it should be concise. *Concise* is not the opposite of *long*; it is the opposite of *wordy*. If your sentences are concise, they contain no wasted words.

You have already studied the wisdom of avoiding needless repetition and of using concise words and phrases. You learned not to use three or four words to say something you can say just as well—or better—in one or two words.

Now go a step further. Learn to make *sentences* concise.

Eliminate Useless Words From Sentences. Organize sentences to eliminate words that do not help make your meaning clear or your tone courteous. As an example, the beginnings *It is*, *There are*, and *There were* generally add nothing to sentences except words. They also tend to lead you into stiff, artificially formal writing and passive constructions. When you have used one of these expletive beginnings, try rearranging the sentence to strengthen it and thereby achieve conciseness.

WEAK: There are two choices open to you.

STRONG: You have two choices.

Don't Repeat Ideas Unnecessarily. The only reason for restating an idea, once it has been said clearly and forcefully, is to gain emphasis through repetition. This way of emphasizing ideas has a danger: if you overuse it, you will bore the reader. People get restless when you repeat yourself without a purpose. They dislike even more your repeating an idea because you failed to state it clearly the first time.

WEAK: Is the lasting beauty of your copper cookware equal to its durability? That is, will it retain its color and brightness after long use, or will water or food acids spot or mar the surface in any way, making necessary more care and upkeep on it than on most other cookware?

Isn't the repetition in the above excerpt from a letter useless? Isn't the question more forceful when asked only once?

STRONG: Will your copper cookware retain its color and brightness after long use, or will water or food acids spot or mar the surface and make more care and upkeep necessary on it than on most other cookware?

Don't Tell Your Reader Something He or She Already Knows. If you agree that concise writing helps your letter accomplish its purpose, then you will also agree that it is wise to omit facts the reader already knows. When you tell your reader the obvious, you waste words and risk offending the reader by implying that he or she is not aware of it or has forgotten it. You also appear forgetful or thoughtless by telling the reader what you should realize he or she already knows.

Obvious statements in business letters usually appear at the beginning. Writers who use obvious statements instead of direct beginnings simply admit that they can't solve the problem of how to begin. They do not take advantage of the most effective position in the letter, the opening sentence. Too many writers begin by telling the reader that they received his or her letter, which they are answering, or by restating what the reader said in the letter. This is lazy writing. If you are answering the reader's letter, your answer is evidence that you received the letter. Why waste the important beginning of your letter telling the reader "In reply to your letter of March 23, . . ." or "In your letter of May 7 you stated that . . ."? The reader knows he or she wrote the letter and what it said! If the reader doesn't remember all the details, a quick glance at the file copy will refresh his or her memory. Your job is to give the reader an *answer*, not to echo the reader's letter.

The best way to begin a business letter is usually by answering the reader's question. We'll discuss in a later unit a few situations when you should not begin the letter with the main point.

WEAK: I am in receipt of your letter which is dated September 19. You wanted to know the current prices of our Peyton ceiling fans; so I am enclosing our latest price list, which will cover all this information.

STRONG: Here is our current price list for Peyton ceiling fans.

WEAK: I am replying to your letter of October 9. With this letter you enclosed a check for $101.23, the total amount due since August.

STRONG: Thank you for your check for $101.23, which clears your account.

As with beginnings, writers often have trouble ending a letter. After answering all the reader's questions and giving explanations where needed, a writer may then fall back on trite phrases:

Thank you again for your interest in our product. If you need further information with regard to this matter, or if we may assist you in any way, please don't hesitate to contact us.

If thanks has been given once, that's usually enough; say it twice and you will appear gushy. The best expression of gratitude is to do what the reader wanted. To offer further information or assistance may appear courteous, but it really means that you aren't sure you have told the reader everything he or she should know and you hope that the reader will remind you of anything you have forgotten. Isn't it safe to assume that if the reader needs more information or help, you will hear from him or her?

Deleting foggy endings, like avoiding obvious beginnings, usually improves the letter. Take this actual business letter as an example:

Dear Mrs. Romanov:

SUBJECT: GRAPHIC PRINTING PLATES

Thank you for your recent request for further information on the Graphic printing plates advertised in the June issue of Office Products.

We appreciate your interest in Graphic printing plates. Enclosed is literature which gives complete descriptive data and specifications—and we are asking our dealer in your area to get in touch with you. The dealer is:

Mr. Anthony Leshure, Manager
General Printing Equipment Co.
3961 Cumberland Avenue
Terre Haute, IN 58392

Phone: (492) 713-3800

This dealer is equipped to give you excellent service and will be able to answer questions about the Graphic printing plates and to show you how they will prove their value to your organization in many ways.

Meanwhile, if we can be of further help to you, just call on us. We'll be glad to assist you in any way.

Sincerely,

Suppose you took out the first and last paragraphs of this letter. Is the letter weakened? No, not really. Actually, the reader may assume that the last paragraph means you think it will be some time before the dealer contacts the reader. Omitting these two paragraphs would make the letter concise and clear. A letter is concise when everything in it contributes to the job it has to do and nothing can be taken out without lessening its ability to communicate.

5. Strong Sentences Use the Active Voice

The passive voice is probably the worst culprit in dull and weak writing. Although the passive has its uses, such as softening a negative statement, what it does to your writing should warn you to use it sparingly.

Why does the passive voice hurt readability? Consider this example:

Brian typed the letter.

This is a simple sentence in the active voice. The picture it should arouse in the reader's mind is of Brian typing. This is true of active-voice sentences; they emphasize the action, the "doing" that the sentences describe. Now let's put our example into the passive voice:

The letter was typed by Brian.

Some changes have taken place. Extra words have appeared. The extra words, *was* and *by*, signal the reader that the violation of normal English word order is intentional. In the passive version, it takes six words to tell what four told in the active. The first drawback to using passive constructions is that *they require more words without adding to the meaning*.

The second drawback is more serious, and it's what makes passives so weak. In our example look how the emphasis has shifted. The mental picture is of a typed letter. No Brian, no typing, just a typed letter. *The action is gone, and the person who did the acting is gone too.* It is precisely this shift of emphasis from "someone doing" to "the thing done to" that robs passive sentences of their interest and clarity and makes them poor forms of communication.

Avoid passives by watching for them in your writ-

ing and changing them to actives. Make people the subjects of your sentences whenever possible, and write in the active voice, so that the reader sees a picture of the subject performing the action. People doing things and saying things are interesting, not what they *have* done or said. Stress the "people" element in your writing; after all, a human being will read what you write.

6. Sentence Structure Should Be Varied

We have already seen that a long string of very short sentences makes for choppy writing, that a sequence of very long sentences makes reading difficult, and that sentences all the same length make a letter boring to read. Just as these faults will affect the reader's reaction, so do identically constructed sentences become monotonous and even seem to talk down to the reader. Besides varying the length of your sentences, you need to think about varying their structure and pattern.

Monotonous writing makes for monotonous reading. A reader who becomes bored will soon stop paying attention. One way to vary your writing is to use different sentence beginnings. Since the way you begin a sentence almost always determines the pattern for the sentence as a whole, concentrating on beginnings is the logical way to control patterns.

You can also vary the structure of your sentences by utilizing simple, compound, complex, and compound-complex formations.

A *simple* sentence contains one independent clause:

First impressions are lasting impressions.

A *compound* sentence contains one or more independent clauses:

We prepared the copy layout, but the logo didn't fit.

A *complex* sentence contains one independent and one or more dependent clauses:

When Mr. Salvemini joined Kruger-Brent Ltd., he was assigned to the Internal Audit Department.

A *compound-complex* sentence contains two or more independent clauses and one or more dependent clauses:

Since Miss Davenport has not completed her report, I shall speak with her about it; and I shall then set up another meeting to discuss it with her.

7. Sentences Should Fit Together Naturally

Just as the words in a sentence should be arranged for smooth reading, so should the sentences in the message. Each sentence should follow the one before it and flow naturally from one thought to the next.

In writing sentences that fit together properly, you

will find it often helps to (1) refer in some way to the preceding sentence or (2) use connectives (transitional words and phrases). Here are some examples of such bridging expressions:

also	for instance	otherwise
as a result	however	previously
consequently	in addition	similarly
for example	in this way	therefore

POORLY CONNECTED SENTENCES: Your proposal has a great deal of merit. There are a number of questions to be answered. A comprehensive market research program should result in an appropriate solution.

IMPROVED: Your proposal has a great deal of merit. Although many questions must still be answered, we should be able to come up with an appropriate solution through a comprehensive market research program.

POORLY CONNECTED SENTENCES: We agree with many of the suggestions in your report. We shall put some of them into effect immediately. We shall delay action on the remainder and get reports from other sales representatives.

IMPROVED: We agree with many of the suggestions in your report and shall, therefore, put those into effect immediately. After we have studied reports from other sales representatives, we shall decide what to do about your other suggestions.

POORLY CONNECTED SENTENCES: You were right when you suggested that your March statement was not correct. A payment you made on February 28 had not been credited to your account.

IMPROVED: You were right when you suggested that your March statement was not correct. Your statement did not reflect a payment you made on February 28.

8. Sentences Should Be Punctuated Correctly

Writers generally have more trouble with commas than with any other punctuation mark. A comma, when it is out of place or otherwise misused, frequently fogs the meaning of a sentence. Commas are misused in three ways: they are inserted where they don't belong; they are omitted where they are needed; or they are shifted to a wrong position in a sentence. In each case the result is usually damaging.

One mistake is to omit one of a pair of commas:

INCORRECT: Rosemary Fitzgerald, editorial assistant called while you were out of the office.

CORRECT: Rosemary Fitzgerald, editorial assistant, called while you were out of the office.

A comma may be incorrectly inserted between a subject and its verb:

INCORRECT: Analyzing the data and presenting recommendations by November 4, will be difficult.

CORRECT: Analyzing the data and presenting recommendations by November 4 will be difficult.

The thought of a sentence may be interrupted with misplaced commas:

INCORRECT: The most important, and also the most frequently discussed topic, was the discount rate.

CORRECT: The most important, and also the most frequently discussed, topic was the discount rate.

Let good usage and common sense be your guides to correct punctuation. If you do not follow accepted rules in punctuating, will your reader know what your punctuation marks mean? Maybe not. Review the punctuation rules in the Reference Section.

9. Sentences Should Be Grammatically Correct

Basic English errors in your sentences may make your reader think you are ignorant or careless—or both. What is good English, and what are the rules of good English? The "rules" are conventions or general agreements among the users of English on how the language should be used to achieve certain goals under various circumstances. Your goal is to recognize the level of usage adhered to by the majority of skilled writers and speakers in the business world.

Carelessness is a major contributor to grammatical errors in writing. Frankly, it is much easier to be a sloppy writer than it is to be a careful writer. But once you accept sloppiness in your writing, it soon becomes a habit—a habit you will find very hard to break. A good habit to develop is to edit each sentence until it is mechanically correct.

How do you know what is correct, or standard, English usage? Reading, listening, writing, speaking, and studying and practicing the rules of grammar—all these have helped and will continue to help you develop a "feel" for correct English usage, an ability to know almost instinctively whether something is correct. The ability to recite the rules of grammar, punctuation, and so on, will not necessarily give you the ability to write without making errors. It is much more important for you to develop your language sense to the point where you can instantly recognize your own errors and then turn to a reliable reference manual or English handbook for the rules you need to apply to correct your mistakes.

You will find a brief summary of grammar, punctuation, and other rules in the Reference Section at the end of this text. Review the rules and examples until you are confident that you can apply the rules correctly. In addition, you may wish to buy and use one of the many comprehensive English-usage handbooks that are available. And like every other writer—even the most competent one—you will want to own and make constant use of an up-to-date, reliable dictionary.

Developing and Arranging Paragraphs

After choosing the words and combining them into sentences, the next step in "building" a letter is grouping the sentences into paragraphs. Paragraphs are used mainly to facilitate reading. They deserve the same care you give to words and sentences.

Business letters usually deal with one major subject or have one major purpose. This major subject is made up of several items or parts, and each of these items is developed into a paragraph. Writing a business letter, then, is a matter of identifying the major subject or purpose and deciding on the items that make it up. How to organize the items—the paragraphs—in the best order is the next job.

Even when a letter deals with more than one major subject, as sometimes happens, its organization should not be too difficult. Begin by identifying each of the major subjects, then the items or parts within each subject; and finally put everything into logical order—the order most likely to achieve your purpose.

Here are some suggestions for paragraphing business letters.

1. Each Paragraph Should Contain One Part of the Major Subject

An effective paragraph consists of a closely related group of sentences dealing with one major topic—one set of thoughts related to a particular subject. It contains a topic sentence, or topic statement, and the sentences that develop the idea.

When you introduce a new topic, start a new paragraph. Beginning a new paragraph lets the reader know that a new idea is coming up. A paragraph containing unrelated ideas confuses the reader. By starting a new paragraph, you prepare the reader for the shift from one phase of the subject to another.

2. Paragraph Length Should Be Varied

The length of paragraphs is perhaps more important in business letters than in any other written communication. Most people are so busy that they simply don't have time to wade through a series of long, rambling paragraphs; consequently, they may merely skim the first couple of lines in each paragraph.

Short paragraphs can, as a rule, be read faster than long paragraphs. Also, most readers like the breaks that "white space" provides. A paragraph as short as one sentence—or even one typewritten line—may be effective. But remember that too many short paragraphs—just like too many short sentences—give a choppy effect. At first glance, the reader may feel that the page is crammed with ideas.

Do break a short letter into two paragraphs, even when the letter is only two or three sentences. A one-paragraph letter rarely looks attractive, and it may give your reader the initial impression that you didn't care enough to write more than a few lines.

Vary the length of paragraphs in a long letter. One-sentence and two-sentence paragraphs tend to stand out in a letter, especially if longer paragraphs precede and follow. They attract the reader's attention and signal "This is important." Use these very short paragraphs to emphasize important ideas.

If any paragraph runs over eight lines, you should usually consider breaking it into two or three short paragraphs. Think of "reasonably short paragraphs" in a business letter as varying from two to eight lines, with an average length of four or five typewritten lines.

Use longer paragraphs when, after editing, you decide that the last sentence of the paragraph is still on the same topic as the first sentence and that breaking the paragraph into two or three paragraphs would destroy its unity.

3. Opening and Closing Paragraphs Should Be Shorter Than Average

The most important location in a letter is the opening. The second most important is the closing. Usually, brief opening and closing paragraphs give the letter a brisk, businesslike appearance and make it easier and more interesting to read. Since a reader hesitates to wade into a long, solid mass of words, a short opening paragraph is especially important. A two-, three-, or four-line paragraph invites the reader to start reading.

> Yes, Mrs. McDaniels, you are entitled to a 3 percent discount on your first order.

And you can often stress the one idea that you want to leave with the reader in a short closing paragraph like the following:

> To get your copy of our free brochure, just fill in the enclosed postpaid card and return it.

4. Paragraphs Should Fit Together Smoothly

You have learned the importance of smooth movement from one sentence to the next. For ease in understanding a message, the paragraphs in the letter must also fit together so that the reader will be led naturally from the opening paragraph to the closing paragraph without having to reread. Sometimes you can show the relationship of paragraphs more clearly by numbering them or by using connective and transitional words, phrases, or sentences.

Let's look first at a business letter that is poorly paragraphed and then at an improved version.

INEFFECTIVE PARAGRAPHING: Six years ago, when the Gems brand first appeared in our Annual Brand Preference Survey, it was at the bottom of the list—in 13th position, to be exact. It didn't stay at the bottom for long.

Every year since, Gems' brand preference rating has risen. In this year's survey, it *zoomed!* Gems is Number 2 in brand preference.

It has passed Fischer and Neilson—and it's closing in fast on Number 1 Harlin! Gems should be Number 1 by next year.

From 0.47 percent brand preference six years ago to 16.9 percent today is a growth history unmatched by any competitor in the industry! Gems has been a major advertiser in *The American Dream*. While we won't take all the credit for Gems' accelerated brand preference, we, too, have helped!

MORE EFFECTIVE PARAGRAPHING: Six years ago, when the Gems brand first appeared in our Annual Brand Preference Survey, it was at the bottom of the list—in 13th position, to be exact.

It didn't stay at the bottom for long. Every year since, Gems' brand preference rating has risen.

And in this year's survey, it *zoomed!*

Now Gems is Number 2 in brand preference. It has passed Fischer and Neilson—and it's closing in fast on Number 1 Harlin!

At its present growth rate, Gems should be Number 1 by next year. From 0.47 percent brand preference six years ago to 16.9 percent today is a growth history unmatched by any competitor in the industry!

And during this period Gems has been a major advertiser in *The American Dream*. While we won't take all the credit for Gems' accelerated brand preference, we, too, have helped!

You can see that effective communication is achieved through the unified structuring of the paragraphs in the letter. A letter is said to have unity when all the paragraphs fit together in an organized, cohesive manner. Check the paragraphs you write to see that they are related to each other and to the central theme of the letter. Then polish the letter until the entire message flows smoothly.

ASSIGNMENT: Unify the letter in Section B of the Worksheet by applying the suggestions for effective paragraphing you have just studied.

Unit 3 Worksheet

WRITING SENTENCES AND PARAGRAPHS

A IMPROVING WEAK SENTENCES. *These examples from business letters include both sentence fragments and awkward, choppy, two-idea, or wordy sentences. Write your revisions on the lines provided.*

1. To get the best results, the instructions must be carefully followed.

   _____

   _____

   _____

2. When you receive our catalog, which should be within the week, you will notice our wide selections and reasonable prices, which are listed inside the back cover, and we hope you will then talk with Bob Tenbrun-sel, who represents us in your area, who will help you in every way he can, or send us an order direct, whichever you prefer.

   _____

   _____

   _____

   _____

   _____

   _____

   _____

   _____

   _____

   _____

3. In the event your choice has been sold out. Your check or money order will be cheerfully refunded.

   _____

   _____

   _____

4. I should appreciate it very much if you would examine the endorsement on that particular check and if possible forward the check to us and of course we shall return it for your files upon verification.

   _____

5. I am enclosing the only literature that we have which will be of interest to you, and I have turned your request over to the Chamber of Commerce, which will probably have more literature and booklets which will enable you to complete your project which sounds so worthwhile to all of us who are engaged in this work.

_____

_____

_____

_____

_____

6. Thank you, Mrs. Kennedy for the information you sent me, on urban renewal projects, in Chicago.

_____

_____

_____

7. You were always a regular customer, and it was a pleasure to fill your orders; so now, as you haven't placed an order for quite some time, we're wondering if we did something of which you did not approve, and, if we are to blame, we're sorry to lose your business and we want to begin serving you again soon.

_____

_____

_____

_____

_____

_____

8. Please make the changes as quickly as possible and the report should be ready by next Tuesday.

_____

_____

_____

9. You should use the order forms at the back of the catalog, which we are sending you along with our latest price list, as you requested us to do. Whenever you wish to make a purchase just use these convenient order forms.

_____

_____

_____

10. Home health care benefits have been increased, and so we can now offer you better service.

B *PARAGRAPHING A LETTER. In the following letter, the writer blurred the general effect and destroyed the emphasis by using too many short paragraphs and by omitting needed transitional expressions. Improve both the effect and the emphasis by grouping some of the ideas into longer paragraphs and by adding transitional words and phrases to introduce sentences and paragraphs as needed. Supply any needed details, and correct any grammatical or punctuation errors. Write your revised letter on page 32.*

Dear Mrs. DeZonia:

Five little words, ''Add it to my account,'' will now work magic for you at Starr's.

You as a member of our Easy Payment family are entitled to a special ''add on'' privilege.

Without a down payment you may order anything we sell and add many items to your account without increasing your monthly payment.

You may increase your balance to $300 and still pay only $20 a month. You will make proportionately higher payments on larger amounts.

Even though you may be short of cash at the moment, you can buy the things you and your family need.

You won't disturb your budget. And you can meet your payments from regular income.

You will find an immense variety of quality merchandise at money-saving prices in our new catalog.

Whatever your needs, wearing apparel, piece goods, toys, appliances, furniture, you can buy them at Starr's.

You'll enjoy shopping Starr's easy, timesaving, catalog way.

Stop in or phone or mail an order soon. Take advantage of the magic of our Easy Payment Plan.

           Sincerely yours,

Unit 4

PROJECTING A POSITIVE TONE

The words you use and the way you put the words together into sentences, the sentences into paragraphs, and the paragraphs into a letter play a large part in the impact your letter will have on your reader, as you learned in Units 2 and 3. The tone of a letter may influence the reader as much as the words themselves. The tone is conveyed by the words, sentences, and paragraphs and by the *spirit* behind them. All these together form the impression that the message makes on the reader—the reader not only reads the words and sentences but also "sees" what's between the lines of the letter. The spirit in which you write must be warm and friendly. It should also be sincere, for most people quickly discover the hollowness of fine words that lack sincerity.

The "you" attitude gives a business letter a desirable tone and shows sincere interest in the reader.

Project a "You" Attitude

Your attitude is influenced by your frame of mind at the time you are writing. If you are worried, frustrated, or angry, your attitude may color the tone of the letters you write. Everyday matters—personal or business—may affect your attitude and can actually determine what you write and the way you write it. You would be wise to put these distractions aside and concentrate on representing the organization you work for and satisfying the reader.

The attitude projected by the tone of your letter, then, should be one that shows the reader that you care, that you are looking at things fairly, and that you are genuinely interested in communicating.

Avoid writing from a selfish point of view. If the tone of your letter shows a "me" attitude—that is, if the letter is slanted toward you and your own organization—the reader will see that the message is one-sided. Instead, make the "you" attitude, or emphasis on the *reader*, evident throughout your letter.

One way to show the "you" attitude is to use *you*

and *your* often in your writing. But remember that writing *you* and *your* does not always give the letter a "you" attitude. For example, which sentence has the better tone: "*Your* error caused the delay, and *you* alone will be responsible for the extra charges on *your* bill," or "*We* are sorry about the delay and will have *our* shipping department look into it; *we* will, of course, accept responsibility if *we* are at fault in any way"?

Nevertheless, it is not a good idea to overuse "we" words and project a "we" attitude, as you can see in the following excerpt:

> We have been pleased to sell fine automobiles for more than two decades. We supply the finest imports to customers from all over the United States. We are proud to be the only dealer in this area for both the Jaguar and the Alfa Romeo. We are proud of our record of at least a 10 percent increase in sales volume every year since Continental Cars was founded in 1965.

The ideas are good, but they are expressed so selfishly that they don't focus on the reader at all. Notice the greatly improved tone when the same ideas are expressed with "you" words and a "you" attitude, as the writer brings the reader into the picture:

> It is our privilege at Continental Cars to serve as your exclusive Jaguar and Alfa Romeo dealer. Our showroom is stocked with an array of beautiful and desirable automobiles, to satisfy your discriminating taste. You will find the luxury car you have always dreamed about—the kind that has kept loyal customers coming back to Continental since 1965. You can depend on our reputation and experience to provide the selection and service you deserve.

Your letters will have a "you" point of view if you take this advice from a correspondence supervisor: "The letterhead takes almost one-fifth of the page, and the closing and signature lines take another one-fifth. Let's give the reader the other three-fifths!"

Show Sincere Interest in the Reader

If you are genuinely interested in the person to whom you address a "written conversation," write to show your respect for that person's intelligence, judgment, opinions, and preferences. Avoid making statements that are distasteful to the reader, statements that will have the opposite effect from the one you intended.

Avoid a Formal Tone in Your Writing

Your letters can show warmth and friendliness if you write with an informal, conversational style. Remember that formal English seems stiff and unnatural to the reader. As you learned in Units 2 and 3, a simple, personal style is much more appealing.

Stiff, formal writing reads like this:

In accordance with your request of recent date, in which you expressed concern about the damaged merchandise you received on May 18, I have reviewed your case and have reached the decision that full restitution should be made to you.

In view of the circumstances, I am sending to you today the replacement shipment of merchandise. If you will please send the damaged merchandise back to us at your earliest convenience, your cooperation in this matter will be appreciated.

Please accept our most sincere apologies for delivering damaged merchandise to you, and we deeply regret the delay and inconvenience which you have suffered.

If this message were written naturally, it might read like this:

The new shipment of aerobic dancewear should reach you within five days, Mrs. Nichols. So that you will be able to display the suits in your store as soon as possible, our driver will deliver them and pick up the damaged suits.

We are sorry for the slight delay, but we will do our best to see that the latest exercise fashions are on your racks and ready for your customers by the end of the week.

Do you see how much more friendly a message is when written naturally?

Don't Talk Down to the Reader

A person new to letter writing often talks down, or "preaches," to the reader. A condescending tone communicates lack of respect and will surely arouse resentment. You will get better results if you share ideas or make suggestions instead of writing to the reader as a subordinate and trying to force him or her to accept your views. Like most of us, your reader would rather be treated as an *equal* and would appreciate being *asked* rather than *told*.

Would this letter persuade *you* to go to Carrington's back-to-school sale?

Now is the time when all smart shoppers are taking advantage of the special money-saving buys at Carrington's, while our Back-to-School Sale is in progress.

School will be starting soon, and crowds of shoppers are trying to buy their children's clothes.

Why not come in now while we offer the lowest prices of the year and a pleasant shopping atmosphere.

When a reader is told that everyone else is doing something, the implication is that the reader is out of step if he or she is not doing it too. In this letter, the writer is telling the reader that "all smart shoppers" are coming to Carrington's. Does this mean that the reader is lacking in intelligence if he or she does not come to Carrington's? Better be careful! The reader already knows that "school will be starting soon"; and writing that "crowds of shoppers" are in the store may make the reader want to go elsewhere! Wouldn't it be better to stimulate the reader's interest by giving examples of specific sale items and then letting him or her decide that "now is the time" to shop at Carrington's?

Keep in mind that the reader, like everyone else, prefers to think and act independently and is more likely to respond favorably if you make your appeal through sound reasoning. You will guard against talking down if you put yourself in the reader's place and imagine *your* response to the letter you have written.

Don't Exaggerate

Exaggeration in the form of bragging, gushiness, flattery, overhumility, and unlikely promises makes a letter sound insincere.

Bragging. When describing your products and services, avoid bragging—be prepared to back up everything you say. Overstatements and superlatives such as *the best, outstandingly superior,* and *incomparable* seldom sound convincing to the reader unless you give evidence to back up your claims.

The unreasonable claims made in this boastful message make it sound absurdly insincere.

In your wildest dreams you have never pictured bargains in furniture like those in our showroom today. They are truly the ideal buys of the century! Competitors envy—but never approach—the magnificent choices and prices and the unbelievable service we offer. They are aghast at the fabulous deals we make to move our furniture out.

Visit us today during our Labor Day Sale to select your living room, dining room, or bedroom suite of matchless beauty fit for a king at a price a peasant could afford!

Make your letter believable by telling the reader *specifically* what your product or service can do for him or her. If you have a reasonably good product or service, you won't have any trouble finding specific points to make about it. If your product or service has no reasonably good features, there won't be much you can say—and you won't have the problem of finding something to say about it for very long.

Gushiness. Gushy language in business letters indicates that the writer is insecure about the product or service and is trying to overcompensate by using flowery words and too many strong adjectives and adverbs.

Excessive politeness makes the following letter confirming a repeat reservation sound insincere and inappropriate. The overlong paragraph and the repetition of the reader's name within it are also unbusinesslike. Using the reader's name once in the body of the letter personalizes the letter and confirms the reader's importance. However, you may lose the effect if you use it more than once.

> Yes, indeed, Mrs. Anderson, we shall be more than happy to reserve a suite for you and your daughter at the Mountain View Resort for the first two weeks in June. You certainly are remembered from last summer. How could we forget two such extremely vivacious, glamorous—and altogether charming—ladies! It will be marvelous to have you and your daughter with us again, Mrs. Anderson. We appreciate to the utmost your desire to return for another delightful visit and are even now waiting—eager to welcome you on June 1, Mrs. Anderson.

The gushy language that makes this letter sound insincere can be eliminated, and the message can become a simple but personalized confirmation:

> We appreciate your desire to return to the Mountain View Resort and are happy to confirm your reservation for June 1–14.
>
> Your daughter Lauren will be glad to know that since your last visit, riding stables have been added to our recreational facilities. Also, we have just completed construction of an indoor recreational facility which includes an olympic-size swimming pool, a sauna, and a whirlpool.
>
> A brochure of Mountain View Resort's June activities for our guests is enclosed. Your suite will be ready for you on June 1, Mrs. Anderson.

Flattery. Flattery can be more damaging than gushiness. There is nothing wrong with giving a compliment that has been earned, but subordinate it to avoid embarrassing the reader with outright flattery.

Does this opening paragraph of a request sound sincere?

> Since you are an authority on life insurance, I am sure you can help me. Twenty years' experience as a successful insurance agent should qualify you to answer all of my questions.

The writer flatters the reader and then implies that the reader may not deserve the compliments if he or she cannot answer all of the writer's questions!

Overhumility. Overhumility merely shows the reader what little self-respect the writer has. If you apologize to the point of degrading yourself and your organization, you are destroying the reader's faith. What effect would this message have on a reader?

> Please accept our deepest apologies for the thoughtless error we made in sending you a second bill for your November 14 order when you had sent us your check two weeks earlier.
>
> Our accounting department is extremely embarrassed and sorry, as are all of us here at T. J. Rochford and Sons, Inc. We need your business, and we hope you will forgive us this time. From now on we are dedicated to serving you better, and you can be sure that we will check all records before billing you again in the future.

There's nothing wrong with saying you're sorry, but don't beat that subject to death. You have more important things to say to a reader, and excessive apologies aren't among them if you have taken steps to remedy the problem.

Unlikely Promises. If you make promises like "We will take care of each order the minute it comes into our office" or "Just a telephone call and our technician will be right there," your reader may take a skeptical attitude toward *everything* you say in your letter. And as with other forms of exaggeration, you must guard against making rash promises you may be legally held to.

You know that no legitimate lending company can promise instant solutions to everyone's money problems. Don't try to entice the reader with promises that do not sound plausible, as this writer did.

> Whether your unpaid bills are many or not so many, Famous Finance Company will SOLVE ALL YOUR MONEY PROBLEMS in the batting of an eye! A moment's chat in one of our friendly offices . . . a confidential personal payment plan . . . a Famous Finance check . . . and you can jauntily bid all your financial worries goodbye!

Don't Show Doubt, Irritation, or Indifference

Negativism and doubt destroy the sincere tone you want your letters to have. Be careful in your writing not to imply doubt about your reader. Referring to "your claim" or saying "we are surprised" about something the reader said or did implies that you do not believe the reader. Do you detect the tone of disbelief in the following example?

> We have not overlooked the $35 payment on your account that is two months past due. We received your explanation of your failure to pay on time a month ago, and we are still waiting for you to pay.

Revealing that you are irritated does not help you accomplish your purpose. It merely arouses the reader's indignation at your lack of respect. Notice how this message irritates and belittles the reader:

> We have investigated your complaint about your McKenna hedge trimmer and found that you neglected to charge the battery. We charged it for you and trust that in the future you will take care to check the battery before making unfounded claims about defective merchandise.

A letter such as this would surely make the reader vow never to buy again from the organization that wrote it.

One reason retail stores lose customers is indifference. Whether the store's employees actually display an attitude of indifference or whether the customer imagines it—if that's the way the customer feels, then the customer will take his or her business elsewhere. A major concern of retailers today is to convince their customers that they really care about them.

Do you think that Schumacher, Hart & Co.'s customer relations could be improved by revising this cold and indifferent form letter, which was sent to a customer who complained about a topcoat he bought?

> While Schumacher, Hart & Co. attempts to ensure that every customer will get the highest-quality merchandise available, our enormous volume makes it impossible for us to achieve this goal 100 percent of the time.
>
> If you will bring your garment in, we will have someone look at it to ascertain whether we are responsible. Should Schumacher, Hart & Co. accept responsibility, satisfactory arrangements will be made.

The errors in the tone of this letter are obvious, from the poor excuse that the store's "enormous volume" makes the reader unimportant, to the ending which leaves the reader asking, "Satisfactory to whom?"

Avoid the Temptation to Criticize, Argue, or Be Sarcastic

When you talk with someone face to face, you usually do your best to keep the conversation pleasant. You try to put the other person at ease, and you avoid sounding critical or saying anything he or she might resent.

When you are tempted to criticize, argue, or make a sarcastic remark, remember that in a written message you can't soften the tone by smiling or listening to the reader's side, as you can face to face. The reader can only read the words you have written, harsh as they may be, and can't talk back.

Would you agree that the writer of this letter gave in to the temptation to be sarcastic and critical?

> I received my order today, after waiting over two months for it. Needless to say, I had to go elsewhere to buy the sprayer-compressor because you were unbelievably slow in sending it. After examining the sprayer-compressor, I found that it was not the high quality which I demand anyhow. So I'm sending it back, and you can keep it for someone who is not in a hurry to use it.

Sarcasm is more likely to wound the user than anyone else. Even when the temptation to "needle" a reader with sarcasm is great, giving in to the temptation can hurt. There is no way to take the sting out of a written sarcastic remark as there is in speech.

How would you feel if you, a supervisor, received this memo from your boss?

> Congratulations to you and your staff, Donald, on the new XL Copier III brochure. You people must really have put in some overtime to get it out to our sales representatives only three months after they started selling the product.

Remember that an effective letter will persuade or convince rather than criticize, argue, or be sarcastic. You will learn more about the persuasive approach in Unit 6.

Never Show Anger in Your Writing

Showing anger in a letter provokes the reader's hostility and makes it impossible to transact business. Even though your anger may be justified, *never* show it in a letter. Remember that it pays to be courteous, not to burn bridges behind you.

The best advice is to wait until your anger has passed and you can see the situation clearly and calmly. Then sit down and approach the reader logically with a good, psychologically sound letter that will make him or her see your point. "Keeping your cool" when writing is important to effective communication.

How would you describe the mood of the writer of this letter, which was addressed to the president of a large organization?

> Did you really think you could get away with taking my cash register back to "fix it" and not refunding my money? This piece of junk has never worked right, and I don't want it "fixed," or a new one—I want my money back so I can buy one that works. Is this plain enough for your dense employees?

How is the organization going to feel about this customer in the future?

Focus on Positive Ideas

The reader is more interested in what you *can* do than in what you *can't*. True—you can't always answer "yes" to a request, but you can say "no" with a friendly tone if you show consideration for the reader by stressing the positive and playing down the negative. By doing this, you will make your letters sound as friendly and helpful as possible and encourage the reader.

Why write, "We are sorry that we can't deliver your furniture by December 1"? The customer would rather hear: "We will deliver your furniture just as soon as it arrives from our Chicago warehouse. We expect it to arrive during the week of December 7."

While the tone of the entire letter should be positive, the *beginning* of a letter sets the mood. It is very important, then, that the beginning contain something positive and pleasant to the reader. In a "bad news" letter, however, it should *not* lead the reader to believe that you are going to say "yes" in the next paragraph. Try to stay optimistic while you write the bad news, using as few negative words as possible. How many positive ideas can you find in the following letter?

> It is my unpleasant duty to inform you that your application for a research grant was not approved. Only five grants were awarded. Unfortunately, the selection committee placed your application sixth on the list, which means it is not eligible for reconsideration until next semester's grants are awarded.

What a depressing letter! But what if it were rewritten to stress the good news that is almost hidden among the many negatives?

> Your application for a research grant placed sixth on a list of 200. Since only five grants were available this time, Miss Jung, the Selection Committee invites you to renew your application when next semester's grants are considered.

The difference in these two letters is a matter of attitude and tone. Each tells the reader that she was not awarded a grant this semester, but the second letter softens the blow by telling her that her application was close to the top and may be renewed for consideration next semester.

A letter may sound negative or unpleasant if the tone is not one of pleasant conversation. If it contains negative words, the overall effect on the reader is negative, as you read in Unit 2.

Notice the negative implications in this letter:

> We were sorry to receive your letter stating that there is something wrong with your Venus stereo component system. It is too bad that this merchandise was found to be unsatisfactory. Just ship it back to us, and we will send you another one just like it.

Let's take the message apart and see if we can find out what gives it such poor tone.

"We were sorry to receive your letter . . . ." Should you ever tell anyone that you are sorry to receive his or her letter? Is the writer sorry to receive the letter, or sorry that the merchandise wasn't just right?

" . . . there is something wrong . . . ." This negative clause implies that the reader may be at fault.

"It is too bad . . . ." The writer may have felt sincere regret. But does the writer regret that the reader is not pleased, or that the organization has to make an adjustment?

" . . . merchandise was found to be unsatisfactory." Isn't the writer giving the customer a negative suggestion that the organization's merchandise is unsatisfactory?

"Just ship it back . . . ." Isn't this a rather cold way to take care of a customer?

And do you think the reader wants "another one just like it"? Or does the reader want one that works properly?

Here's the way the letter might have been written if the writer had been thinking of the reader.

> Thank you for writing us about the Venus stereo component system we sent you recently. We are sorry that it is not working properly.
>
> We have instructed our carrier to deliver a new system to you next week and to pick up the system you have now.
>
> I'm sure your new Venus system will give you many hours of listening pleasure.

These two letters contain the same facts—but do you *feel* the difference in tone?

Our language helps us to think and write positively; all we have to do is choose words to which people react favorably. Good letter tone depends on positive statements, a "you" attitude, and sincere interest in the reader.

ASSIGNMENT: Practice applying the suggestions you have studied in this unit by rewriting and improving the tone of the sentences and paragraphs in the Worksheet.

Unit 4 Worksheet

PROJECTING A POSITIVE TONE

A REWRITING SENTENCES TO IMPROVE TONE. *Each sentence below projects a poor tone because it lacks sincerity, uses negative words, or shows a "we" attitude. Write your positive-tone version on the lines provided.*

1. We know from experience that our fiberglass tennis racket represents the best quality as well as the best value.

   _____
   _____
   _____

2. Rest assured that your complaint about not receiving the kerosene heater is being thoroughly investigated.

   _____
   _____
   _____
   _____

3. Do us a favor: Renew your subscription now, before we drop your address plate from the computer.

   _____
   _____
   _____

4. In 25 years of doing business, our company has never sold one-drawer file cabinets.

   _____
   _____
   _____

5. If you will accept our deepest apologies, we will never again be caught making such an error.

   _____
   _____
   _____

6. We must know immediately what type of rooms are to be reserved for the convention.

B *REWRITING PARAGRAPHS TO IMPROVE TONE. The writers of these messages forgot to plan their opening paragraphs with the reader in mind. Study the problems carefully. Then below each paragraph write your version, improving the tone. Supply any necessary details.*

7. I am sorry to tell you that the Hallford golf bag Model D109W you asked about is temporarily out of stock in our warehouse, just as Mr. Burns of our Birdie Avenue store informed you. We should get some in by next month and have them available in the Birdie Avenue store, if you can wait that long. Just check back with them in six weeks or so.

8. Your request is one of many we receive from management majors asking for data which we are too busy to assemble and send out. We should probably use a form letter suggesting that all you students phone a floor manager for an appointment to visit the store and see for yourselves how we handle these matters.

9. It's a depressing fact that the rising cost of a really good family vacation adds to the strain on today's family budget. Farmington Acres has a solution to this problem. We will give you and your family lodging at reduced rates. In addition, we will provide superb recreational facilities at a nominal charge. And all we ask in return is that you take a personally conducted land sales tour of the area. No gimmicks, no strings, no obligation to purchase a single thing!

10. Did you really think you could get by with a coupon two weeks out of date? Both the ad and the coupon stated conspicuously that the half-price offer was good only until July 31. When you sent your order and check for $6 on August 15, you undoubtedly knew that the price of the subscription had reverted to the full $12.

_____

_____

_____

_____

_____

_____

_____

_____

_____

_____

_____

_____

11. We want you to know that we do appreciate having you as one of our Parmley Equipment catalog customers. We have decided that we can make catalog shopping a lot easier and a lot more convenient by issuing credit cards. With these cards, we can take orders by phone as well as by mail.

_____

_____

_____

_____

_____

Unit 5

BUILDING AND MAINTAINING GOODWILL

Every business is concerned not only with selling products or services but also with selling itself. Goodwill is the favorable image customers have of a business. Other terms for goodwill are *public relations, customer relations,* and *business promotion.* Goodwill is an intangible asset to a business—that is, a quality that is difficult to measure in dollars and cents.

How can you as an employee help to build and maintain goodwill for your organization? You can project genuine interest in the customer, fairness, courtesy, and friendliness through your business letters. Every letter you write should accomplish its specific purpose and, at the same time, try to increase the reader's positive feeling toward your organization. Your letters should create an impression of a friendly organization that is interested in the people it serves.

Letters influence what people think about an organization. And what people think often determines where they buy. Consider each letter you write as an ambassador of goodwill—an opportunity to influence a person's attitude toward your organization, and possibly even an opportunity to make a sale. Even though you don't try to sell goods or services in every letter, you do try to sell ideas and the personality of the organization you represent.

Of course, no business or individual would intentionally destroy goodwill. But many letter writers do drive away old or potential new customers by conveying an attitude of indifference or by failing to make a conscious effort to build and maintain customer goodwill.

Promote Goodwill Through a Service Attitude

If you care about building goodwill, you will think of many ways to project a service attitude in your business correspondence. A service attitude is made up of sincere interest in the customer's welfare and the willingness to do a little more, to give a little extra. A service attitude, well expressed, will pay dividends both for your organization and for you. The rewards will often be monetary; both you and your firm may profit. In addition, of course, you will also have the personal satisfaction of doing a job well.

For instance, you can anticipate a question the customer has not asked—but might want to ask later—and give him or her the information now. You can include information that you know will be of particular interest, such as an article on a subject of concern to the reader or a brochure describing your product. Also, you can make it easy for the customer to do what your letter asks by enclosing an addressed, postpaid reply card or envelope. Gestures like these build *and* keep goodwill. People will notice and appreciate your thoughtfulness.

Let each of your letters remind the reader of your genuine desire to serve. Be sure to emphasize this desire rather than the profit motive and any selfish interests.

In letters that contain good news, building goodwill is fairly easy. But when organizational policy or other circumstances do not allow you to give customers the replies they would like to have, building goodwill is not easy. For instance, you may need to (1) answer "No" to a customer's request, (2) state that the customer has made an error, or (3) state that his or her criticism of the organization's products or service is unjustified. Such "problem" letters call for skill and tact—and imagination.

Let's look at a few ways to build goodwill even in these problem letters.

Begin With a "Goodwill Idea"

Open the letter with something the reader will be pleased to hear, whether the letter contains good news or bad news.

In a bad-news letter, rather than starting with an unpleasant idea and setting up a barrier between you and the reader, start with an idea the reader likes and agrees with. This way you have a chance to gain the reader's attention while you gradually introduce your point of view.

When you write a letter containing good news, however, don't be afraid to use an opening that gets immediately to the heart of the subject. Beginning with a goodwill idea does not mean making needless introductory remarks.

In Unit 6 we will discuss in detail how to get letters off to a good start.

Consider the Customer's Side

You can build and maintain goodwill by keeping the customer's point of view clearly in mind at all times. But how can you build goodwill when you must say "No" or "You are wrong—this is how it really is"?

The first step is to find out where the customer stands. In other words, try to assume the other person's attitude and to look at things the way he or she looks at them. You wouldn't, for example, try to sell Mr. Hyduke a suit by telling him how long it would wear or how much it was reduced if you knew he was a wealthy, fashion-conscious man interested only in how good he would look in it. If you wished to sell suits to men like Mr. Hyduke, you would try to find out *how* they felt about suit colors, fabrics, and designs and *why* they felt that way. Then you would know which selling points to stress.

Then, try to think how you would react if you were in the customer's place. Try to discover the benefits to the customer in a situation where few or none may be apparent. You may be able to use gentle persuasion by reminding the customer of likely benefits and the advantages of going along with you. Your letter should make it easy for the customer to agree with you. Above all, try to express the organization's point of view in such a way that the customer accepts it and is still friendly toward your firm.

Sell Your Organization's Viewpoint

In writing business letters dealing with problem situations, keep in mind that you do *not* build goodwill by losing your temper or showing annoyance, as the following excerpt reveals:

> You certainly are not entitled to the 2 percent discount you took, as you could clearly have seen if you had read the terms of our invoice.

The writer missed an opportunity to promote goodwill by taking a firm but courteous approach to the problem. To sell the organization's viewpoint, (1) explain the reasons behind the policy; (2) point out that this policy is fair to all customers, including the reader; and (3) if possible, show the customer how

this policy may benefit him or her in the long run. By doing these things, the writer could have handled the above situation diplomatically.

Dear Mr. Sandusky:

Thank you for your check for $1,372.84 in payment of our invoice 8970K for $1,400.86.

We notice that you have deducted from the invoice the 2 percent discount offered on payments made within ten days of the date of purchase. Your check is dated September 15, however, and our invoice is dated August 20. We assume that this was an oversight—that you intended to send your check within ten days.

Naturally, we wish we could allow a discount on payments made within thirty days. Payments made within ten days represent a saving to us, and we are glad to pass these savings on to our customers by giving them lower prices. But, as you can understand, payments made at a later date do not give us these savings to share with our customers.

May we have your check for $28.02?

Sincerely yours,

Notice that the writer doesn't *demand* payment but instead gets the reader's interest at the start by drawing attention to the difference in the payment amount and the invoice amount. Then the writer leads the customer gently to the organization's side of the fence. When the reader gets to the last paragraph of the message, he or she should be ready to answer "yes" to the question.

The following excerpt destroys goodwill by projecting a "Your business isn't significant to us" attitude toward the customer.

> You are mistaken in thinking that we would consider stocking Petite sizes in our Junior Department simply because it would be convenient for you.

Now read this letter which explains the organization's viewpoint but also maintains goodwill.

Dear Mrs. Figueiredo:

Your suggestion that we stock Petite sizes in our Junior Department is welcome—particularly since it comes from one of our good customers.

You may be interested to know that a selection of Petite styles was recently featured at our branch store in Raleigh. But these did not sell as well as had been expected, and the line was discontinued. As a result, The Toggery is somewhat reluctant to stock Petite sizes here in Somerville just now. We shall keep your suggestion in mind, however.

We understand that Michelle's, in the Beale Street Mall, carries a selection of Petite styles. You may be able to find what you need there. In the meantime, Mrs. Figueiredo, we look forward to continuing to help your family with other clothing needs.

Sincerely yours,

Shortsighted business people often act as if there were no competition—an unrealistic attitude, to say the least. Recommending another organization's source of supply for something you don't carry is evidence of a service attitude. Not only is it helpful, but it makes you look good in the customer's eyes—it's the little extra that you didn't really have to give. Nor does it cost you sales, as some people fear ("If the customer buys what I don't have from my competitor and likes my competitor, I may lose the customer's business to my competitor"). Remember that you are the "favored vendor." The customer came to you *first* and wanted to buy from you. You'll still have that in your favor after sending the customer elsewhere for something you don't have. If you are afraid the customer will like your competitor's products or service better than yours, maybe you should look for ways you can improve yours! And if you can't make improvements, at least you can build goodwill by following this suggestion.

These are only two examples of the "problem" letters that must be written every day in business. Each letter presents an opportunity to build goodwill or to tear it down. Before you begin to write such a letter, think the situation through carefully to decide exactly how you can best do the job and still keep the reader as a customer.

Use Letters as Goodwill Messengers

You can build goodwill only if you *care* how your letters sound. Try to visualize each letter as your organization's ambassador, as a salesperson meeting a customer. Ask yourself the same questions about your "letter salesperson" that you might ask about a real salesperson to determine whether he or she is doing a good job:

1. Does the salesperson choose correct, concise words and speak clearly? (You may review Units 1, 2, and 3 to be sure your "letter salesperson" talks well during the visit with the customer.)

2. Is the salesperson's tone friendly, courteous, and conversational, yet persuasive? (You may review Unit 4 to be sure your "letter salesperson" smiles and

holds the customer's attention and interest throughout the visit.)

3. Does the salesperson give the customer satisfaction? (Even if the customer cannot be given exactly what he or she asks for, the good salesperson tries to keep the customer's friendship.)

4. Does the salesperson answer all the customer's questions completely and promptly, giving all the facts needed to act or to make a decision?

5. Does the salesperson show interest in the customer's point of view as well as a genuine desire to be helpful?

You can supply positive answers to the last three questions about your "letter salesperson" if you follow the suggestions in this unit.

Answer All the Customer's Questions

A salesperson may be both personable and friendly but still not be successful. The salesperson leaves the customer dissatisfied if all of the customer's questions about the organization's products and services are not answered. In the same way, an incomplete letter leaves the customer dissatisfied and weakens the organization's chances of building goodwill. It may even lose a customer.

The friendliest and most tactful letter you can write does not build goodwill if it fails to satisfy the customer. When you do not know the answers to all the questions asked, you should supply the answers you know and tell the reader what you are doing about the others. Always check your reply with the inquiry to be sure you have not overlooked any of the customer's questions—actual or implied.

Suppose you are replying to a man about a reconditioned bicycle he is thinking of ordering for his daughter. In his letter, the customer asks about the cost of a 3-speed model, the guarantee, the condition of the tires, and the sizes in which the bicycle is available. In your reply, you stress the low price of $59.95, the one-year guarantee, and the fact that the tires are new and the paint job is fresh. You urge the customer to send his order promptly because you have only eight 3-speed bikes left in stock.

Your letter is friendly, courteous, and convincing. But it is not complete. What did you overlook? You did not answer the question about sizes. Naturally, the customer is annoyed. He hesitates to order a bicycle with a 24-inch wheel because he is afraid that the eight bargain bicycles left may not include this size. The customer wants the bicycle in time for his daughter's birthday, which is only two weeks away. He may decide to write again for the information. Or he may order from another supplier.

Failure to answer a customer's questions makes the customer suspicious. Why didn't you answer the question? What are you trying to hide? Is there some drawback to your product or service you don't want the customer to find out about? If so, what other dishonest thing may you try to do?

The customer assumes that you are out to do the best you can for yourself and your organization. Suspicion leads directly to distrust—perhaps not logically, but that's human nature. And distrust is unlikely to lead to sales.

Admitting you don't have an answer to a customer's question is not wrong. If this is the case, promise to get the answer and then follow through. If there is no answer, say so and explain why. Either course is preferable to ignoring a question you can't answer positively or at all.

And remember—a prompt response is an excellent beginning to building and maintaining goodwill.

Don't Make the Reader Guess

Often a reply to an inquiry—like the letter about the bicycle—is incomplete because the writer has overlooked a question asked in the inquiry, as you have just seen. You can answer all the questions, however, and still not say everything the customer needs to know. You may leave out an important detail just because you assume that the customer knows more than he or she does about the subject on which you are writing. But often the reader has to guess because you have assumed too much.

For example, in response to an inquiry, a writer may fail to answer a question because the question should be directed to someone in another department. Perhaps after answering the letter, the writer will turn the letter over to the appropriate person, who will then supply the missing answer. But does the reader know this? Even though the writer cannot handle part of the letter, for the customer's sake he or she should not ignore that part of the letter.

The writer cannot assume that the reader will know that the question will be answered by someone else. The reader will probably assume that the writer did not read the letter carefully enough to see the question or did not want to give a negative answer.

The writer could avoid making the reader guess simply by adding a short paragraph, such as this:

I am referring your question about subscribing to *Electronics* to Mr. Donald Valdez, Circulation Manager. You should hear from him in a few days.

Resell the Product and Your Organization

A major purpose of each letter you write should be to promote goodwill and resell the product and the business. "Reselling" means repeating the selling job that led to the purchase. The writer attempts to confirm the reader's faith in the writer's products, services, and organization. The purpose of reselling is to assure the customer that he or she made a wise choice in buying the product (even though it may not yet have been delivered) and to keep the customer from complaining or returning the goods.

Reselling your organization involves pointing out the services you render and the guarantees, policies, and procedures that will benefit your reader. Reselling is appropriate in a letter to a new customer, but it should also be included whenever you can tell a customer about a new service or benefit that your company provides.

When Jan O'Neill received the following letter, she probably felt that she had made a wise choice in subscribing to *The Executive's Guide to Communication and Motivation*, a monthly magazine of tips and case studies.

Dear Ms. O'Neill:

Your first issue of *The Executive's Guide to Communication and Motivation* will arrive in a few days. The feature article should be particularly interesting to you, Ms. O'Neill, because it discusses ways you can increase productivity and profits by improving interpersonal skills among your employees.

In the coming months, such noted communication experts as Anne Constantino and Paul Anderson will cover methods you can use to your advantage when communicating with either superiors or subordinates. For example, you will learn ingenious techniques that help get proposals approved and unique approaches that are usually successful in persuading others to go along with your ideas.

We know that you will enjoy reading every issue of *The Executive's Guide to Communication and Motivation* and that it will be as helpful to you as it has been to other executives in the past ten years.

Sincerely,

As you can see, the purpose of this letter is to promote goodwill and resell the product. Unit 15 will give you more "goodwill ideas" as you study special goodwill letters.

> **ASSIGNMENT:** *How successfully will you build and maintain goodwill for your organization? To find out, complete the Worksheet for Unit 5.*

Unit 5 Worksheet

BUILDING AND MAINTAINING GOODWILL

A *BUILDING GOODWILL IN PROBLEM SITUATIONS. Study the partial analyses of Problems 1 and 2. Then describe your problem solution in writing a goodwill-building letter. Also write an effective opening paragraph for each problem situation.*

1. In January Mrs. Terri Schultz returns several large cartons of Christmas decorations to Cloud Nine, where you are employed as a customer service representative. You must reply to the angry letter in which she insists that the cartons were delivered on the day before Christmas, too late for use in her home. You have obtained from the courier a delivery slip which was signed by Mrs. Schultz on December 16, the delivery date agreed upon at the time of purchase.

   Mrs. Schultz demands that the store accept the decorations, with a full refund to her.

   The company policy is that a full refund cannot be approved on this seasonal merchandise, since the Christmas buying season is over. The store will, however, charge Mrs. Schultz the January sale price, one-half off the regular price, and allow her to keep the decorations.

   a. *Your objective when you write to Mrs. Schultz:*

   _____

   _____

   _____

   _____

   _____

   _____

   _____

   _____

   b. *Opening paragraph:*

   _____

   _____

   _____

   _____

   _____

   _____

   _____

2. You work for the Portland (Oregon) Realty Company, whose manager agreed to hold up rental of a commercial studio for one week to give a client, Hugh Steele, time to make his decision. When the manager didn't hear from Mr. Steele within ten days, he leased the studio to another client. Soon afterward your company received a letter from Mr. Steele confirming his decision to lease the studio; the letter, correctly addressed and postmarked within the one-week limitation, had been mistakenly delivered to Portland, Maine.

   Mr. Steele has asserted his right to lease the studio.

   The company's position is that a lease between the company and the other client was entered into in good faith and is legally binding.

   a. *Your objective when you write to Mr. Steele:*

   _____

   _____

   _____

   _____

   _____

   _____

   _____

   _____

   b. *Opening paragraph:*

   _____

   _____

   _____

   _____

   _____

   _____

   _____

B IMPROVING POOR LETTERS. *Rewrite the following letters using positive language and showing a service attitude. Your goal is to build goodwill and to resell your products and your organization.*

3. I am sorry that you had to return a damaged copy of *Children's Classics* to us recently. It's too bad that several pages were so smeared. The enclosed copy is not damaged, as you can see. Now you and your children can read this great book.

   _____

   _____

   _____

   _____

   _____

   _____

   _____

   _____

   _____

_____
_____
_____
_____
_____
_____
_____
_____

4. We are very sorry that we failed to send the mirror for your new dresser. We are sending it today. Thank you for your order, and we look forward to serving you in the future.

_____
_____
_____
_____
_____
_____
_____
_____
_____
_____
_____
_____
_____
_____
_____
_____
_____
_____
_____
_____
_____
_____
_____
_____

5. Each month our billing department automatically sends invoices to all people to whom we have provided services during that month. Therefore, when we sent you a bill for service, we were merely following our routine billing procedure.

Of course, because your television is still under warranty, there is no charge for service. You should have told our service representative that the set is under warranty. Just disregard the bill for $35.

_____
_____
_____

_____

_____

_____

_____

_____

_____

_____

_____

_____

_____

_____

Unit 6
PLANNING AND PREPARING LETTERS

As you have discovered, writing effective business letters is a complex process. But having considered everything we have discussed so far, you are now ready to take another important step—planning the letter—and the most important step—actually writing it.

Planning the Letter

When a letter is written without proper planning, the writer may forget important details that are necessary if the letter is to do its job well. Then a second letter is usually required to complete the job.

The kind of plan you follow depends on the particular letter you are writing. But you should always start by considering the person who writes the letter (you), the person the letter is written to (the reader), and the background and purpose of the letter. Then decide upon the best approach and what you will say.

The Person Who Writes the Letter

As you begin your business career, you should learn all you can about the organization you will represent. You must prepare yourself to act on behalf of the organization and to treat your personal views as secondary.

You must make sure that your letters sincerely reflect the attitudes and policies of your organization. Occasionally you may feel that a policy is unfair; you may even suggest to your supervisors that it be changed. But until it is, you are bound by it. Never let a customer know that you disagree with your organization's policy. Nor should your letter seem to blame another person or department for an error or an unpopular decision. In writing business correspondence, you speak for the organization as a whole—not for yourself or for your department.

The organization, the group, speaks through you, the writer. It is your job to put what the organization has to say in terms that your reader can accept, to bring both sides to agreement. The good letter writer tries to represent the organization's point of view while showing the reader that it is a fair one.

The Person the Letter Is Written To

The most important factor to consider when you are planning a business letter is the person who will read it. The letter is successful only if the reader reads it, understands it, and reacts favorably to it.

Adapting to the reader means writing with the reader in mind, writing to fit the reader's capabilities and frame of mind. The more you know about how your reader thinks and feels, the better chance you have of getting the message across. If you know something about the reader's education, for example, you can adapt your vocabulary accordingly. If you know something about the reader's position and ambitions, you can choose a suitably challenging appeal.

To interest and influence the reader, you must be able to look at both your side of things and the reader's at the same time. By doing so you can learn what kind of help the reader expects to find in your letter. It takes practice, but you *can* do it. With the ability to see things from the reader's perspective as well as your own, you will soon be successful at persuasion.

If you have a letter to answer, you can learn much about your reader from the message he or she has written. Sometimes previous correspondence, call reports from sales representatives, and other records in the files will tell you more. If you have no letter to answer and no file records on which to draw, your general knowledge of human nature can help you plan an appropriate letter.

Consciously practice adapting to the reader as you write letters for the rest of this course, and you'll soon master the technique. Just remember to think through the situation, imagine your reader as best you can, and then write directly to him or her.

The Background and Purpose of the Letter

A business letter grows out of a *need to communicate*. To plan a letter efficiently, you must understand (1) *why the letter is needed* and (2) *the response it should bring*. For example, the credit manager of a store may write to customers whose bills are overdue and ask them to pay. Some customers may respond with checks; others, with letters explaining that they can't pay until later.

If you are answering a letter, use the background information contained in the letter itself. Always read the letter carefully to be sure you have learned all you can from it. If you need additional facts or if you have no letter to answer, check the files for previous correspondence and pertinent records. And of course, use common sense, as well as your general business knowledge and specialized knowledge of your organization, to decide what background facts are important and how they can best be used to make the letter successful.

As you think through the reasons for the letter and the background facts, you will find that the *purpose* of the letter becomes apparent. The purpose of a credit manager's writing a collection letter might be "to collect $125 from Travis Yates without losing him as a customer." And the purpose of Travis Yates's reply might be "to pay $50 on my account and promise the store the $75 balance in 30 days."

The Best Approach

As you continue to plan, your next job is to decide on the idea that will get the letter off to the right start. All the facts you have been thinking through will help you select an opening which will make a pleasant contact with your reader and which is appropriate to the situation and the purpose behind the letter. You will also be able to decide upon the most effective order to present the ideas in the letter.

Business letters can be grouped roughly into three categories:

1. Routine and "Yes" letters
2. "No" letters
3. Persuasive and sales letters

By far the largest part of business correspondence is the daily routine correspondence that requests or transmits information. If no problem is foreseen in getting the information requested or if the information supplied is routine and not displeasing to the reader, simple letters are written or form letters are used.

Routine and "Yes" letters can be written in a straightforward manner, since they tell the reader what he or she wants to hear or will be pleased to hear. This type of letter can get directly to the point; therefore, the way its parts are usually arranged is called the *direct approach*.

The problem letters in business are those that give the reader bad news or refuse the reader's request. These "No" letters have to be carefully prepared to avoid causing anger or loss of goodwill. This type of situation calls for an *indirect approach*.

The third group of business letters includes letters in which the reader must be persuaded to do as you ask, to be "sold" on an idea—for example, sales letters that attempt to obtain an order for a product or a service, or sales promotion letters that try to set up a sale in the future without pressing directly for an order. Letters of this type use the *persuasive approach*.

Let's look at these three approaches so that you can see how they work and learn to choose the right one for each situation you handle. As we discuss common business situations in later units and apply these three approaches to them, we will see how they can be varied to meet a wide range of writing problems.

The Direct Approach. When you can tell your reader "Yes" or transmit some good news, you have the easiest and most pleasant of writing tasks.

In these situations there is only one rule: *Start with the good news.* This will put the reader in a friendly, receptive frame of mind for anything else you may want to say.

Follow the "Yes" opening with the next most pleasant point for the reader, then the third most pleasant, and so on. The last paragraph of the letter, the ending, should refer to the good news in the opening, leaving the reader in a friendly frame of mind.

With a few exceptions, routine requests follow the direct approach, since such requests are a normal part of business. Examples are requests for appointments or reservations and requests for information about products and services. If there is no reason for the reader not to supply the information or if it is to the reader's advantage to do so, use the direct approach.

Routine replies to inquiries and requests should also follow the direct approach. Begin by giving the information the reader requested. However, if the information is obviously bad news for the reader or if it reflects negatively on another organization or person, consider using the indirect approach instead.

In summary, then, whenever you can say "Yes" or otherwise tell your reader something he or she wants to hear or will be pleased to hear, start your letter with that information. Here's an example.

The background: As credit manager for Beaumont Designer Eyewear, a wholesale dispensary for frames and sunglasses, write a letter extending credit to Ms. Rhonda Hamm, owner of Classic Eyewear.

The customer's request: Ms. Hamm has asked for credit by filling out one of your forms and supplying references, which you have checked.

Your organization's policy: Ms. Hamm's credit limit is $5,000. She will be billed on the 15th of each month for purchases made during the billing cycle. Payment is due by the 28th.

The letter's job: Welcome the customer, explain the credit terms, talk about Beaumont's service, and look forward to the customer's orders.

The approach: Since Beaumont is doing as Ms. Hamm has asked, you select the direct approach.

Dear Ms. Hamm:

Beaumont welcomes you as a credit customer. All you have to do to charge your purchases at our dispensary is give your account number, 409-1440-7, and sign the sales slip. The references you listed have given you a high credit rating.

You may charge purchases up to $5,000 a month. On the 15th of each month, you will receive a statement of your purchases made during that billing cycle. Your payment is due on or before the 28th.

When you order from our catalog, please include your account number on the order form so that we can process your order quickly. The merchandise you request will be shipped within 24 hours after we receive your order.

Sincerely,

The Indirect Approach. Having to give the reader bad news or to say "No" poses a problem in letter writing. If you blurt out the bad news in the first sentences of your letter, the reader will quickly become disappointed, angry, or both. Such feelings will color the reader's interpretation of everything else you say. If you start with the refusal, the reader isn't likely to accept your explanation, if he or she reads it at all! Why put the reader in a bad frame of mind at the start and destroy the effectiveness of the rest of the letter?

Instead, use the indirect approach. This often means simply using a "buffer paragraph." You try to place a "buffer" between the reader and the bad news, to avoid putting the bad news in the emphatic first-paragraph position.

The buffer paragraph is based on sound, practical psychology. People would rather hear good news than bad news. So if you have some bad news for them, tell them some good news first to help break the bad news as gently as possible.

Begin with something in the situation that you and the reader can agree on. It may only be that you agree the reader was right to come to you with the problem. If there are no facts you can agree on, pay the reader a compliment (but don't flatter), or say *something* friendly. You must not appear to be saying "Yes," however, because the reader will not forgive you for misleading him or her when later on in the letter you say "No." And your buffer paragraph must be on the subject of the letter; it should not be a time waster.

After the buffer paragraph, give the reasons for refusing or for giving the bad news. Begin with your best reason for refusal, go on to the next best, and so on. After you have given the explanation, use a middle paragraph for the actual refusal. What is important is that the reader get the message clearly, even though it may be subtly implied, and that he or she be in the most receptive frame of mind that you can manage under the circumstances.

By the end of the letter, you are over the rough parts. You can then offer a counterproposal to what the reader has asked or resell your point of view. This type of letter usually ends on a hopeful note.

Here's the technique in action.

The background: As advertising manager for an agricultural products manufacturer, answer a letter from Mr. Harold Beck, an independent dealer with an exclusive franchise to sell your products in his area.

The dealer's request: Each year you purchase an advertisement for him in his city's classified telephone directory. He also wants you to purchase advertisements in the two suburban editions of the telephone directory.

Your organization's policy: You purchase advertising only in classified telephone directories serving areas in which your dealers are located. Since this dealer is not located in the suburbs, but inside the city limits, you will continue to place advertising only in the city directory.

The letter's job: Refuse the dealer's request for company-paid advertising in the two suburban directories. Explain the policy behind your refusal: you have over 800 dealers; if you buy something for one, you must do it for all; the costs would be out of sight; requests would come in for you to purchase advertising in directories in neighboring counties and towns.

The approach: Since you will have to say "No" to the dealer, an indirect approach is called for: the buffer paragraph opening.

Dear Mr. Beck:

We agree that advertising in the Yellow Pages is important in calling the attention of prospective buyers to the availability of our products. We also agree that the more of it we do, the better.

Last year we considered the possibility of altering our policy on telephone-directory advertising. We calculated the cost of placing advertising for each of our 806 dealers in all the telephone directories within 125 miles of the dealer's location. It came to a staggering $965,000 a year! Even for just those directories in areas actually served by our dealers, the cost was over $650,000.

Since we would, of course, have to apply the same policy to each dealer, we regretfully set aside the question of increasing our telephone-directory advertising.

Any increase in one area of our advertising budget would have to be at the expense of other areas, and we know how reluctant you would be to see us cut out sponsorship of the State Fair exhibits, advertising in your state's farm magazines, or our successful outdoor billboard advertising.

Such activities, as well as telephone-directory advertising, are all part of the master marketing plan for Campbell Agricultural Products, and midyear changes tend to have a ''ripple-effect'' on the plan far beyond the actual changes themselves. Because the various telephone directories around the country are published at different times during the year (according to no particular pattern), the ''ripple-effect'' would be magnified.

In spite of recent negative publicity about agricultural chemicals, Campbell dealers have increased their share of the market, an achievement we are all proud of. We intend to continue to provide you with the best products on the market and to aggressively support you in your successful selling efforts.

Sincerely,

The Persuasive Approach. Letters that make special requests or try to sell the reader a product or service are persuasive or sales letters. Getting the reader to do what you want, to accept what you say, or to agree with you means using the persuasive approach.

If you want to write effective sales letters, you should take this advice from an advertising copywriter: "Don't use formulas. Rely on your knowledge of *why* people buy things." Successful copywriters are those who are able to make readers imagine themselves using the product or service. When you can get your reader to imagine himself or herself successfully using your product or service, you can close the sale.

Essentially, a good sales letter will be structured something like this.

First will come the opening paragraph in which some benefit or reward is promised or implied for the reader. This sets the tone of the letter, prepares the reader for what follows, and arouses the reader's interest so that he or she will read on.

Next, describe how the product or service would benefit the reader. In the description the "You" attitude is used to help the reader imagine himself or herself using the product or service.

After this come physical details of the product or service, such as dimensions and materials, and specifics about the guarantee, service, and so on. These details won't make the sale but will help clinch it.

CHOOSING THE BEST APPROACH

Anticipated Reader Reaction	Type of Message	Letter Approach*
Reader will be pleased.	Good-news	Direct
Reader will be displeased.	Bad-news	Indirect
Reader will be neither pleased nor displeased but will have at least some degree of interest.	Neutral or informational	Direct
Reader will have little initial interest.	Persuasive	Persuasive

*Refer to Psychological Organization for Business Letters, pages 56–57.

Finally, ask for the reader's response—or for the order, if appropriate. Of course, the request should make it as easy as possible for the reader to respond.

This is as much of a "formula" for a sales letter as you will need. No two products or services are alike, nor are any two groups of prospects. Each has to be treated individually if you are to be successful in getting the response you want.

Here is an example of the persuasive plan.

The background: As manager of the Life Insurance Department of Anchor Life Insurance Company, write a letter to Mr. Jason Talbert, a policyholder.

The letter's job: Persuade Mr. Talbert to purchase additional insurance with his accumulated dividends and arrange for future dividends to purchase more

LETTER PLANNING CHART

Procedure	Example
Step 1 Write down the main purpose of the letter in as few words as possible.	To provide cost estimates for printing
Step 2 List all secondary purposes concisely.	To convince the reader that we are dependable To confirm exact printing specifications
Step 3 Jot down all points to be covered in developing both primary and secondary purposes. Try to think of every detail you might need to include in the letter. Put these items down **as you think of them,** whether they are important or not. This process (called *brainstorming*) will stimulate both good and bad ideas that can be sorted out later.	Itemize paper, printing, collating, and shipping costs for 750, 1,000, and 1,250 copies Victory to supply binders Delivery within ten days Thank her for estimate request Confirm specifications in her letter Speedy delivery
Step 4 Cross out any of the listed items that can be omitted without sacrificing friendliness or completeness. Watch particularly for the repetition of ideas that brainstorming often produces.	Draw a line through "Speedy delivery." (You already listed "Delivery within ten days.")
Step 5 Check your plan for sequence, and then number the items. Select an item from your list that would make a pleasant contact with the reader—an item that either tells the reader what he or she wants to hear or puts the reader in a favorable mood to listen to something you want to way. **Number this item 1.** Arrange the other items on your list in the best order for emphasis and follow-through. Remember to keep the reader interested. Be sure the last item leaves the reader with a good impression of your organization and suggest any further action to be taken. **Number these items 2, 3, 4, and so on,** according to their places in the letter. You now have a complete outline from which you can quickly write the letter.	Then, when you have arranged the items in proper sequence, you will have: 1. Thank her for estimate request 2. Confirm specifications in her letter 3. Victory to supply binders 4. Itemize paper, printing, collating, and shipping costs for 750, 1,000, and 1,250 copies 5. Delivery within ten days 6. Call me with questions

insurance. You want him to fill out and return the enclosed form authorizing the conversions.

The approach: Get the reader's attention in the opening sentence by making a statement that makes the reader stop and think, then continue reading.

Dear Mr. Talbert:

Did you know that your Anchor Life policy No. 275330 has accumulated dividends amounting to $1,431.63? As you know, the interest earned on the dividends is reportable as income each year.

Here is a suggestion: Take your present dividends and buy $2,366.10 in additional paid-up insurance and arrange for future dividends to also buy paid-up insurance.

This would be a wise move, in my opinion, because:

1. You will no longer have interest to report as income.

2. The paid-up insurance will increase the death benefit to your wife.

3. The cash value of the additional paid-up insurance is guaranteed never to be less than the dividends declared.

4. The purchase is made at net cost—there is no charge to purchase these dividends. As you can see, at present each $1 in dividends will buy about $1.65 of additional paid-up insurance.

If you would like to take advantage of this arrangement, please sign the enclosed form and return it to me in the enclosed postpaid envelope.

                    Cordially,

You will study more techniques for writing persuasive letters in Unit 16.

You can choose the best approach for each letter by anticipating the reader's reaction and considering the type of message you are creating, as illustrated in the "Choosing the Best Approach" on page 54.

Developing a Plan

So far you have been *thinking* about your plans for writing a letter. Often when you just think, your ideas are not very clear. Now that you are ready to plan the content and organization of the message,

---

PSYCHOLOGICAL ORGANIZATION FOR BUSINESS LETTERS

THE DIRECT APPROACH	DIRECT PLAN
For Inquiries and Requests	
Opening: Inquiry or request	_____ Main idea
	_____
	_____
Middle: Details, explanation or questions that will help the reader give a specific answer	_____ Details or
	_____ Explanation
	_____
	_____
Closing: Specific request for action tied with appreciation	_____ Appreciation
	_____ for Desired
	_____ Action
For Good News and "Yes" Letters	
Opening: Good news or "Yes"	_____ Positive
	_____ Statement
	_____
Middle: Details or explanation of good news	_____ Explanation
	_____ or
	_____ Development

PSYCHOLOGICAL ORGANIZATION FOR BUSINESS LETTERS (continued)

THE DIRECT APPROACH	DIRECT PLAN
Closing: Brief reference to good news; appropriate goodwill remarks; or resale on organization and/or product	Goodwill or Resale

THE INDIRECT APPROACH	INDIRECT PLAN

For Negative News

Opening: Pleasant, neutral—but relevant— statement	Buffer
Middle: Reasons, explanation, or facts about the negative news—tell the reader *why*. Make the explanation reader-oriented. Negative news is ideally subordinated or clearly implied through positive explanation— *what you can or will do instead of what you can't or won't do*	Main Reason — Supporting Reasons or Explanation — Refusal— Stated or Implied
Closing: Pleasant, relevant comment to end on a positive note	Buffer

THE PERSUASIVE APPROACH	PERSUASIVE PLAN

For Sales Letters and Special Requests

Opening: Relevant idea that will make the reader keep reading	Attention
Middle: Explanation and description that expands opening idea and leads the reader to desire or conviction. Reader benefits should stand out. Also, mention warranties, guarantees, and enclosures. Subordinate cost and other possible negatives	Interest — Desire or Conviction
Closing: Request for action that is courteous and specific, and makes it easy for the reader to say "Yes"	Action

you can make your ideas more concrete by writing them down.

Besides clarifying your thoughts, a written plan helps to ensure that you won't forget any important details and makes the actual writing of the letter faster and easier. A written plan is especially helpful when you are first learning to write business letters. After you have had more practice, you may find that you need to write out your plans for only the most complicated and the most important messages you prepare.

Keep your written plan as brief and simple as you can. Don't put into it everything you will say in your letter. Just jot down a few words that will suggest the points you are thinking through and the things you want to say. Write the plan on scratch paper or in the margin of the letter you are answering. To save time, write in shorthand or abbreviated longhand—just be sure that what you jot down will be readable later.

Many beginning letter writers have found it helpful to use the planning procedures outlined in the "Letter Planning Chart" on page 55. You will be wise to follow these steps exactly in planning your first letters. Later, as you gain experience, you may eliminate some of the steps and adapt the procedures to your own work habits.

Then study the chart on pages 56 and 57, "Psychological Organization for Business Letters." The suggestions will guide you as you learn to develop your outlines into rough drafts.

Writing a Rough Draft

After studying all the facts related to the letter, you have made notes on what you should say and decided on the best order for saying it. Now, as you develop the outline into a letter, keep in mind two of the factors that have influenced your planning: (1) the person to whom you are writing and (2) your reason for writing.

You know that if a letter is to accomplish its purpose, its content must be correct and appropriate, its style clear and natural. Remember also that you should build goodwill in every letter you write. You can do this by (1) emphasizing the things the reader wants to hear, (2) avoiding or subordinating negatives and other ideas unpleasant to the reader, and (3) using friendly words and reflecting a sincere desire to serve.

Because there are so many things to keep in mind while writing the letter, you will probably do a better job faster if you prepare a rough draft. In composing the first draft, concentrate on content alone. Afterward you can review the draft—with particular attention to correct mechanics, style, and tone—before you prepare the letter in good form for mailing.

Later, when you have had practice in business letter writing, you should find that correct and effective expression of your ideas becomes a habit. Then you can dictate or keyboard many of your letters directly from an outline.

In actual business practice, most letters are written without a detailed outline. But for long, complex letters and for "problem" letters, most people do jot down an outline and make a rough draft. You may compose your rough draft at the computer. Or you may dictate your ideas and instruct your assistant to "rough them out" on the typewriter or enter them into the word processor and print a copy so that you can mark changes on the draft.

Develop your rough draft directly from the outline. Write the first draft as quickly as you can. Use abbreviations and any other helpful shortcuts you know. Don't waste time checking spelling of words or points of grammar or referring to principles in your text—yet. While looking up a point, you might forget what you started to say. Or you might write a letter that sounds jerky because it is composed of disconnected sentences or paragraphs instead of being written as one complete message. You can probably finish the letter-writing job faster if you write the first draft without stopping and then do all the correcting as you edit.

Leave plenty of space in the margins and between the lines of your first draft for revisions. If you are composing on the computer or on the typewriter, use double spacing. If you are writing in longhand on lined paper, write on every other line.

Write the message in your own words. Remember that the words you use in everyday conversation are the words that will sound natural and friendly to the reader. Try to imagine that the reader is across the desk from you or at the other end of the telephone. Perhaps then you can write what you want to say as naturally as you would say it.

Study the rough draft on page 59. It was developed from the example in the "Letter Planning Chart" and entered on the word processor.

```
                      ROUGH DRAFT

        We want to thank you for asking us to estimate the cost

    of printing of your new company manual, "Quality Control Pro-

    cedures."  We are delighted to be of service.  In your letter

    it specified that the new manual will be 207 pages long.  It

    will be printed on 8 1/2 x 11," 20 lb. white paper and all

    pages will be 3 hole punched, collated, inserted into your

    lose leaf binders which Victory Industries will be providing.

    As you requested and based on these specs we have itemized

    the costs of paper, printing, collating, and shipping for

    quantities of 750, 1000, and 1250 copies.

                750 Copies   1000 Copies  1250 Copies

    Paper         $336.75      $449.00      $561.25
    Printing       123.75       151.00       176.25
    Collating       29 25        39.00        48.75
    Shipping        23.25        31.00        38.75
      TOTAL       $513.00      $670.00      $825.00

    If you wishto discuss these estimates, please call me.  As soon

    as you select the quantity and deliver you typed pages and

    loose leaf binders.  We will process your order and deliver

    the manuals to your office within ten days.
```

This first draft was written rapidly. It contains abbreviations, shortcuts, and errors, which will be edited.

ASSIGNMENT: *The Worksheet for this unit will help you to develop your skill in planning, organizing, and preparing written messages.*

Unit 6 Worksheet

PLANNING AND PREPARING LETTERS

A *CHOOSING THE BEST APPROACH. For each of the following situations, tell which writing approach you would take: direct, indirect, or persuasive.*

1. To confirm a reservation.

2. To refuse a request for credit.

3. To send a requested brochure.

4. To ask for an opportunity to demonstrate your new energy-saving device.

5. To decline a speaking invitation.

6. To thank a customer for placing a large order.

7. To interest a potential customer in advertising in your magazine.

8. To replace a defective product.

9. To reject a job applicant.

10. To ask for more information about a product advertised on TV.

11. To compromise on an adjustment.

12. To collect an overdue account.

13. To congratulate a former classmate on a promotion.

14. To reactivate business.

15. To notify club members of an upcoming meeting.

1. _____

2. _____

3. _____

4. _____

5. _____

6. _____

7. _____

8. _____

9. _____

10. _____

11. _____

12. _____

13. _____

14. _____

15. _____

B *OUTLINING AND PREPARING A ROUGH DRAFT. As assistant sales manager for Brasel Professionals, a placement service for office temporaries, you must answer a request from Mr. Jason Byrd for "more information about Brasel's services." Mr. Byrd is office manager of Independent Researchers Inc., 121 Ashlea Drive, Fort Worth, TX 76129.*

Your letter should have two purposes: (1) to impress upon Mr. Byrd that he should think of Brasel whenever he needs temporary office help and (2) to smooth the way for a representative to call on him.

Here are the outline notes you have made:

Monica Randolph will call
Established 1966
Professional help when *you* need it
Clients include Fortune 500 (example)
Clients include small firms (example)
Well-trained secretaries
Clerical help (filing clerks)
Others (typists, receptionists)
Also accounts receivable help
Word Processing help
Telephone survey specialists
Page 4 of brochure (research services)
Wide range—help for one day or one year
Sales rep—appointment
Staff is experienced
In business for many years
Research specialists (brochure, p. 4)
Thank you

16. Revise your outline notes, crossing out items that are unnecessary or repetitious and joining items that should be combined. Number the items in the order in which you decide they should be presented in the letter. Then, in the space provided, rewrite your notes in the sequence in which you have numbered them.

_____
_____
_____
_____
_____
_____
_____
_____
_____
_____
_____
_____

17. Prepare a draft of the message outlined in Problem 16.

_____
_____
_____
_____
_____
_____
_____
_____
_____
_____
_____
_____
_____

Unit 7

DICTATING, EDITING, AND PROOFREADING

The ability to communicate well through writing means being able to produce communications that are error-free and that represent the highest professional standards. Office professionals and support personnel must all develop the necessary skills to produce such communications.

Dictating, editing, and proofreading skills have always been important, but advances in office technology have made them a qualification for, or at least a performance element of, many jobs. Word processing equipment and computers have sped up the production process and have made office professionals' and support personnel's jobs easier. But automation will never replace the tasks of dictating, editing, and proofreading. These skills are essential ones—and sharpening them can give your career a boost.

Dictating the Message

Although longhand is the most frequently used method of originating correspondence (75 percent of the input into word processing centers is in longhand), it is very time-consuming and costly. Executives should be doing the jobs for which they are paid.

Why do business executives dictate written communications? Dictating to a secretary or to a machine has the advantages of speed and convenience. Dictating allows business executives to hand over a very time-consuming part of communication, the mechanical act of producing correspondence, to someone else—the secretary or transcriptionist. In addition to saving time, dictation also frequently results in a more conversational style, avoiding the formality that often creeps into business writing.

Many executives prefer to dictate to a secretary because they resent the impersonal aspects of machine dictation. They depend on their secretaries' professional skills in producing superior-quality correspondence.

Portable dictating machines are gaining in popularity because they allow executives to dictate in automobiles, trains, hotel rooms, and airports. Users can also take the machines home to catch up on dictation at night and on weekends.

Dictation may look easy—but it's not. To orally compose a concise, unified message requires a good deal of practice and a working knowledge of the principles of effective communication. The person who can dictate a fluent, well-organized message to a secretary or a machine has worked very hard to develop that skill.

Whether you dictate directly to a secretary or use dictating equipment, the following guidelines will help you to form good dictation habits.

Preparing to Dictate

1. Know how to compose good business messages—with appropriate style, tone, psychological organization, and degree of persuasion.

2. Plan your dictation time by selecting a quiet location and avoiding interruptions. Twenty minutes of concentrated dictation is likely to be more productive than an hour of interrupted dictation.

3. Gather all the data you will need, the correspondence to be answered (underline the points to be covered), and the enclosures. If you are writing a reply, reread the communication you are answering.

4. Clearly define the purpose of the communication to be dictated. Determine precisely the reaction you want from the reader, and keep that desired reaction uppermost in your mind.

5. Visualize your reader. A communication is always more effective if written with its specific audience in mind.

6. Prepare an outline, decide on the plan, and determine the order in which your facts and ideas should be presented.

7. Plan to dictate a rough draft if you are an inexperienced dictator or if the communication is an especially long or difficult one. If a key phrase or the right way of saying something pops into mind as you plan your dictation, jot it down right then.

8. Before dictating to a machine, read the operating instructions. Then practice using the machine for a few minutes to be sure that your voice is clear and neither too loud nor too soft. In most instances, it is advisable to hold the microphone 2 or 3 inches from your mouth.

Actual Dictation

1. Relax and speak clearly and distinctly. Speak in your natural voice at a fairly constant speed, a little slower than your normal rate.

2. Use voice inflection, and vary the tone of your voice. You will then avoid a monotone and help the transcriber recognize where punctuation goes, as well as where the instructions leave off and the message itself begins.

3. When dictating to a secretary, ask the secretary to let you know whether you are speaking too rapidly.

4. If you are dictating to a machine, start by giving your name and department.

5. If the material is confidential, say so at the beginning of the dictation.

6. State what the item is—letter, memo, and so on—and whether you want a rough draft or a final copy, and when you need it. Until you've mastered dictation techniques, it's a good idea to ask for a rough draft first.

7. Indicate how long the document should be stored (that is, if it is to be typed on a memory typewriter, word processor, or computer).

8. Indicate the type of stationery (letterhead, memo form, plain paper, or second sheets); special envelope size, if required; and mailing service to be used.

9. Specify the letter style and punctuation style, if you have a preference.

10. List the enclosures. Indicate the number of carbon copies or photocopies to be made, to whom they are to be sent, and the recipients' locations or addresses.

11. Spell the title and address of the addressee (this step may be omitted in face-to-face dictation if the secretary is given copies of incoming correspondence or has access to the correspondence files).

12. Dictate complete phrases or thoughts, and pause at natural points.

13. Indicate punctuation marks, paragraph breaks, and the placement of tabulations or lists.

14. Spell proper names, technical terms, and similar-sounding words.

15. Clarify long figures. For example, say, "Gross revenue for 19— totaled two hundred million, three hundred ninety-four thousand, eight hundred sixty-seven. That's two-zero-zero comma three-nine-four comma eight-six-seven."

16. Give corrections clearly and as soon as you are aware of the error. You will make errors or change your mind as you are dictating. Say, for example, "Correction. Substitute this sentence. . . ." Or, "Correction. Change that to forty-eight dollars and fifty cents."

17. Specify the complimentary close you prefer and your title, if you want it typed in the signature lines.

After Dictation

It is the support person's job to transcribe dictated communications into final form, but the final draft is the ultimate responsibility of the executive. That the dictator has made a slip does not excuse the transcriber's making the same error; however, the impression the communication makes will be attributed to the signer. Editing and proofreading, the next two segments of this unit, will help you check communications closely to determine when an unacceptable draft should be retyped.

Editing the Message

Written messages containing incorrect facts, figures, dates, and even more serious errors are sent and received every day by business people and customers. Avoiding these and other errors in written communications is a matter of knowing the rules of language usage and developing editing and proofreading skills.

Proofreading means checking the final draft to make sure it is free from errors.

Editing means revising a communication that is often still in rough draft. It involves correcting spelling, grammar, punctuation, and similar errors but also encompasses much more. Editing requires looking at a written communication critically to see if revising it will improve it.

Editing requires two readings.

Read for Meaning

Careful reading and attention to details are essential. When reading is done without concentration and without attention to meaning, errors may not be detected and corrected. Many errors go undetected because the executive or the typist or both have merely "eyeballed" the message for typing accuracy but have not read it for meaning and sense. Consult your notes, dictionary, thesaurus, or English handbook if any word, phrase, or sentence doesn't look or sound quite right.

You want your business messages to give you the image of an intelligent, professional writer. Try to look at the rough draft through the eyes of the reader. The reader *will* notice a polished message, but he or she will pay even more (negative) attention to one that contains errors.

You may find that because of a slip in dictating or a careless typing error, the letter says something you did not intend to say—even something that may irritate or offend the reader. Very few people appear to be indifferent to flaws in the business communications they receive; the vast majority react to sloppy communications with either irritation or amusement. Mistakes in meaning often occur because the typist misreads shorthand or longhand notes, misunderstands dictation on the tape, is annoyed by interruptions, or is thinking about something else. Concentrate on ideas instead of meaningless words. Be sure each sentence makes sense.

Now is the time to give the message an overall check for content, style, and tone. Ask yourself these questions:

1. Does the message contain words that are used incorrectly, words that are too general, or words that can be eliminated?

2. Does it contain sentences that are incomplete, choppy, too long, wordy, or awkward?

3. Are the paragraphs choppy, too long, or poorly organized and connected?

4. Is the meaning so clear throughout that it cannot be misread or misunderstood?

5. Does the message follow the best approach—the one most likely to achieve your purpose?

6. Does it reflect the "you" attitude?

7. Does it sound positive, natural, and sincere?

8. Will it keep the reader's friendship and interest?

The answer to these questions will tell you whether you need to rewrite one or two paragraphs or the whole message.

Read for Mechanical Accuracy

Check the message word by word to be sure it is appropriate and correct in every detail. Ask yourself these questions.

1. Are capitalization, number usage, and the use of abbreviations, apostrophes, hyphens, and so on, appropriate?

2. Are any words misspelled? Review the list of "Words Frequently Misspelled in Business Communications" on page 254 in the Reference Section.

3. Should any punctuation marks be changed, inserted, or omitted to make the message clear and easy to read?

In revising the draft copy, mark changes or corrections in a standard way, so that all typists and business writers can understand them. Take a moment to look at the chart "Revision Symbols" on page 255 in the Reference Section. These symbols provide an easy system for marking corrections.

Now look at the edited rough draft given below, which illustrates the use of revision symbols (also called proofreader's marks). The rough draft was entered on a word processor and printed. Changes and corrections were penciled in, and then only the changes and corrections had to be keyboarded on the word processor to produce the final draft shown on page 67.

Proofreading the Message

After the letter has been corrected and typed or printed, it should be proofread against the original edited version to be sure *all* revisions have been made and no *new* errors have been made. You have now progressed to the final step in the letter-writing process: determining whether the finished product is mailable.

The right time to proofread a typed letter is just before it is removed from the typewriter. As you know, corrections are more easily made while the letter is still in the machine. It is hard to line up the typing exactly if you must reinsert the paper.

If you are using a word processor or computer, proofread screen by screen, before you print the final draft. Or, if you have printed a rough draft, you may refer to it as you enter corrections before printing the final draft.

The right way to proofread is to scrutinize every detail of every part of the letter, starting with the date. You would be surprised how many business letters are mailed without dates and signatures because of carelessness. Also, check for errors in numbers; an error in keying the street address or ZIP Code may delay a letter several days.

The following frequent errors need special attention when you proofread a letter:

1. Confusion of similar words—*to, too, two; quite, quiet; its, it's; led, lead; hear, here; by, buy; there, their.*

2. Transposition of letters within a word—*makrs* for *marks; from* for *form; instructoin* for *instruction.*

3. Transposition and repetition of words—*it if is* for *if it is; will let let you know* for *will let you know.*

4. Omission of one or more letters of a word, especially in words with double or recurring letters—*adress* for *address; excelent* for *excellent; Febuary* for *February; libary* for *library; determing* for *determining.*

5. Omission of words, of phrases, of spaces between words, and of one of a pair of commas, dashes, quotation marks, or parentheses.

```
                    ROUGH DRAFT


     We want to thank you for asking us to estimate the cost

of printing of your new company manual, "Quality Control Pro-

cedures."  We are delighted to be of service. ¶ In your letter
                                                          and
it specified that the new manual will be 207 pages long\  It
                              inch
will be printed on 8 1/2=×  11=" ⨯ 20=(1b) white paper, and all
                                                       and
pages will be (3) hole punched, collated, inserted into your
                                                         c
lo se=leaf binders, which Victory Industries will be providing.

¶ As you requested, and based on these (specs) we have itemized

the costs of paper, printing, collating, and shipping for

quantities of 750, 1000, and 1250 copies.

            750 Copies   1000 Copies   1250 Copies
Paper        $336.75      $449.00       $561.25
Printing      123.75       151.00        176.25
Collating      29.25        39.00         48.75
Shipping       23.25        31.00         38.75
 TOTAL       $513.00      $670.00       $825.00
                 #
If you wish to discuss these estimates, please call me.  As soon
                                              r
as you select the quantity and deliver you typed pages and

loose=leaf binders\  We will process your order and deliver

the manuals to your office within ten days.
```

A rough draft must be edited.

Read the letter on page 68. What do you think Mrs. Bishop's reaction is likely to be?

Unless a letter has good form, it will not make the best possible impression on the reader. As you proofread, skim the letter for errors in format and style. Go over the general appearance of the letter; it should not detract from the message. Attractive arrangement and balanced placement are important to the appearance of the letter. In addition, the letter will make a better impression if you pay careful attention to typing quality, neatness of corrections, and envelopes.

Unit 10, "Letter Format and Letter Styles," will give you more information about specific letter parts, their placement, arrangement styles, formats, and envelopes.

Here are the steps the typist followed in preparing the finished letter on page 67; they will also help you type the letters you write in good form before you mail them or hand them in to your instructor.

1. Select the appropriate stationery, letter style, format, and side margins for the letter. Unit 10 will help you with these details before you type your first completed letter to hand in to your instructor.

2. Type the heading, inside address, salutation, body (the edited message), complimentary closing, signature, and any special notations.

3. Proofread and correct the letter word by word, sentence by sentence, and as a whole *before you take it*

Presto Print

560 Peachtree Boulevard, Atlanta, Georgia 30312
TEL. 404-568-2000

August 1, 19--

Mr. Watson M. Villines
Manager, Purchasing Department
Victory Industries
6900 Carlisle Avenue, S.E.
Atlanta, GA 30303

Dear Mr. Villines:

Thank you for asking us to estimate the cost of printing your new company manual, <u>Quality Control Procedures</u>. We are delighted to be of service.

Your letter specified that the new manual will be 207 pages long and will be printed on 8 1/2- by 11-inch, 20-pound white paper. All pages will be three-hole punched, collated, and inserted into your loose-leaf binders, which Victory Industries will provide.

As you requested, based on these specifications we have itemized the cost of paper, printing, collating, and shipping for quantities of 750, 1,000, and 1,250 copies.

	750 Copies	1,000 Copies	1,250 Copies
Paper	$336.75	$449.00	$561.25
Printing	123.75	151.00	176.25
Collating	29.25	39.00	48.75
Shipping	23.25	31.00	38.75
TOTAL	$513.00	$670.00	$825.00

If you wish to discuss these estimates, please call me. As soon as you select the quantity and deliver your typed pages and loose-leaf binders, we will process your order and deliver the manuals to your office within ten days.

Sincerely yours,

Amanda Starling

Amanda Starling
Manager

kdv

The final draft must be proofread carefully.

from the typewriter or, if you are using a computer or word processor, *before you print the final draft.* Give spelling, punctuation, and grammar a final check even though you have typed carefully and consulted your dictionary or reference manual as you keyboarded the copy. If your computer has a spell-check function, now is the time to take advantage of it.

"The Most Common Errors in Written Business Communications," shown on page 69, is designed to build your awareness of the types of errors observed most frequently in written business messages. How many items on the list do *you* have difficulty with? Turn to the Reference Section to review those trouble spots and to learn how to correct errors as you edit and proofread written communications.

Before you give final approval to any written message, ask yourself the following questions:

Is it courteous?

Is it clear?

Is it complete?

Is it concise?

Is it correct?

If you can identify weaknesses in these areas and correct them, you can give written communications the final touch that ensures they are as close to perfect as possible.

BRONCO AIRLINES

711 Gamblers Boulevard
Denver, Colorado 41215
Tel. 1-800-Cockpit

February 10, 19--

Mrs. Vonnie Bishop
3315 Keats Road
Spokane, WA 98406

Dear Mrs. Bishop:

Good news! Bronco Airlines will begin service to
Spokan on March 1. And we would like to introduce
you to our Frequent Flyer Program, your passport to
a world of fee or discounted travel.

You'll like Bronco Airlines because ot our low fares,
convient air schedules, and exellent personnel service. When your seated in our Business Section.
Your copy of "The Wall Street Journal" will be waiting for you.

Take our Early Bird fright to Seattle for only $39
or to to Portland for only $1099. Save money-save
the day-thats the Bronco sprit!

See the enclosed Bronco world route map and the
brocure describing our fully automated Frequent
Flyer Program. Then call your Bonco agent to make
your first reservation and accumulate your first
bonus pints!

Sincerely,

Will McGoof

Will McGoof

err

2 Enclosures

This letter made a very poor impression on the reader because the dictator and the secretary who produced it failed to proofread. How many careless errors can you find in the letter?

The Most Common Errors in Written Business Communications

1. Comma usage
2. Run-on sentences and sentence fragments
3. Subject-verb agreement
4. Spelling
5. Typographical errors—omissions, transpositions, repetitions
6. Verb tense
7. Word usage—homonyms, pseudohomonyms, synonyms
8. Improper style and format
9. Paragraphing
10. Redundancies
11. Parallel structure
12. Shift from active voice to passive voice (and vice versa)
13. Misplaced and dangling modifiers
14. Plurals and possessives
15. Capitalization
16. Contractions
17. Double negatives
18. Pronoun usage
19. Adverbs, adjectives, and articles
20. Prepositions and conjunctions
21. One word, two words, or a hyphenated word
22. Number usage
23. Word division
24. Abbreviations
25. Quotation marks with other punctuation

ASSIGNMENT: For dictating, editing, and proofreading practice, complete the Worksheet.

Unit 7 Worksheet

DICTATING, EDITING, AND PROOFREADING

 A PROOFREADING SENTENCES. *Locate any spelling, typing, and mechanical errors. Use the revision symbols on page 255 to indicate changes.*

1. The new laser printer will be installed in in our word processing center next week.

2. Renew you subscription to ''Contemporary Living'' by filling out and returning the enclosed card today.

3. The restaurant will close at ten p.m. on New Years eve.

4. We hope you will be among the crows visiting our store during our Jaunary White Sale.

5. I recieved a memo form the accounting dept. outlining the firms' travel and entertainment policies.

6. Micro computers saves a great deal of time in recordkeeping for our department.

7. Both managers' were transfered out of state.

8. The sale ended last week therefore the memory telephone is now available at the regular price of $59.95.

9. Please refer back to page 29 to the discussion of redundancies and unecessary words.

10. The new word processer should reduct stationary cost by approximately 25%.

B *DICTATING, EDITING, AND PROOFREADING PRACTICE*

11. Practice dictating the following letter on a dictating machine, if available, or to a classmate. Pause at the end of each line.

Operator, this is (your name) of the Athletic Department.

My telephone extension is 2030.

I have one letter. I need a rough draft, double-spaced on plain paper.
Enter it on the word processor to be run on Athletic Department letterhead
and merged with the alumni and fans mailing list, after the final draft has
been approved.
Use today's date.
Leave room for the inside address.
Dear blank:
The Ramada Inn, 160 Union Avenue
parenthesis across from the Peabody Hotel
close parenthesis
has been designated as the official
Alumni-Razorback Fans Headquarters

in Memphis for the Liberty Bowl Game. paragraph
An information booth will be set up
in the lobby of the hotel at 1 p.m.
Wednesday, December 26. paragraph
So that all alumni and fans can gather
and vent their enthusiasm before the game,
the Alumni Association will sponsor a reception
in the East Conference Room
on the Second Floor
from 3 p.m. until 5 p.m.
on Thursday, December 27.
A pep rally will be held at 4:30 p.m.
paragraph
Since the game has been sold out,
we look forward to a tremendous turnout
from Arkansas alumni and fans.
Make your reservations now at the Ramada.
The phone number is 901-526-5261.
Sincerely,

12. Dictate from this finished letter, remembering to give the same instructions you did in Problem 11.
After dictating, listen to your dictated letter and compare it with the script for Problem 11. Did you include all the information and instructions?

Current Date

Dear   :

The Ramada Inn, 160 Union Avenue (across from the Peabody
Hotel) has been designated as the official Alumni-Razorback
Fans Headquarters in Memphis for the Liberty Bowl Game.

An information booth will be set up in the lobby of the hotel
at 1 p.m. Wednesday, December 26.

So that all alumni and fans can gather and vent their enthusiasm before the game, the Alumni Association will sponsor a
reception in the East Conference Room on the Second Floor
from 3 p.m. until 5 p.m. on Thursday, December 27. A pep
rally will be held at 4:30 p.m.

Since the game has been sold out, we look forward to a
tremendous turnout from Arkansas alumni and fans. Make your
reservations now at the Ramada. The phone number is
901-526-5261.

Sincerely,

Your Name

sab

13. From this outline, dictate a letter giving the same message as the letter in problems 11 and 12. Then compare your dictation with the script in Problem 11.

Paragraph 1
Liberty Bowl headquarters: Ramada Inn
160 Union

Paragraph 2
info booth Wed. 26th at 1 in lobby

Paragraph 3
Alumni Assn. reception Thurs. 27th 3-5
East Conf. Rm. 2nd Fl.
Pep rally at 4:30

Paragraph 4
reservations—Ramada ph. no. 901-526-5261
expect great Arkansas turnout

14. Edit the rough draft you prepared in Unit 6, Problem 17. Be sure to use the appropriate revision symbols.

15. Proofread the Bronco Airlines letter on page 68. Can you find 18 careless spelling, typing, and mechanical errors? Rewrite the body of the letter in the space below or retype it on a separate sheet of paper, correcting the errors.

Part 2

WRITING EFFECTIVE MEMORANDUMS AND REPORTS

As the modern business world becomes even more sophisticated and complex, the flow of accurate, reliable information and ideas through effective internal communications—memorandums—becomes essential to efficient operations.

Routine memorandums and memorandum reports are written to communicate facts, ideas, statistics, and trends within an organization. They travel upward (to top executives), laterally (between people of equal rank), and downward (to subordinates). Top executives, managers, and supervisors rely heavily on all types of information they receive through memos and memo reports as the basis for sound decision making.

The volume of routine memos passing through the in-house communications network many times surpasses that of letters that are written to people outside the organization. In Unit 8 you will learn to format and write routine memorandums.

Most of the reports written in business are prepared in memo form. They range from brief memos to longer, detailed reports based on research. Unit 9 focuses on memorandum reports and meeting correspondence—notices, agendas, and minutes.

Your objective for Part 2 is to learn to compose and transmit courteous, clear, complete, concise, and correct memorandums, memorandum reports, and meeting correspondence.

Unit 8

FORMATTING AND WRITING ROUTINE MEMORANDUMS

Written communications within a business organization are called *internal memorandums,* or *memos.* In many organizations, particularly large ones, memos exchanged internally far outnumber the letters that are exchanged with people outside the organization. In all organizations, the memos sent in-house are vital to efficient operations. And every memo is important because it has a job to do, whether it's a simple reminder or a persuasive request.

The memo is a valuable tool for internal communications. It carries a special informality and gets a friendly reception because both writer and reader are part of the same organization. It provides a written record, whereas a phone call does not. It is delivered instantly if done by electronic mail: an electronic scanner connected by telephone lines can transmit a facsimile (copy) of a memo quickly from one branch office to another. (If the same memo were hand-delivered, it could take from 1 hour to 24 hours to get from one floor or building to another.)

The main reason for using memos as interoffice correspondence is to save time. They are not typed on letterhead stationery, nor do they require the formality of an inside address, salutation, or complimentary closing. Among the advantages of using interoffice memorandums, then, is the simple form which permits the writer and the typist to concentrate on the content.

Writing Routine Memorandums

Routine memorandums serve the same purpose *within* an organization that letters serve outside it. Memos are used to:

1. Transmit
2. Instruct
3. Announce
4. Congratulate
5. Express appreciation
6. Inform
7. Direct
8. Request
9. Reply
10. Confirm
11. Recommend
12. Persuade

Often, as discussed in Unit 9, memos are used to make informal reports.

Many organizations tell their employees to put in writing all important information that crosses their desks, to clarify responsibility for the information, to be sure that the right people see the information, and to keep written records. Even a file copy of a simple transmittal memo is valuable in case of loss, because it lists the documents that were attached and tells when they were sent.

The following guidelines for writing routine memorandums will help you learn to communicate effectively within your organization.

Tone

The tone of a memo may differ from that of a letter or a report written to someone outside the organization, because the writer of the memo is often more interested in presenting facts and letting the reader form his or her own opinions. Although the memo writer does not forget about tact, courtesy, and friendliness, he or she assumes that the reader—a coworker—will work with the writer to serve the needs of the organization.

In most organizations, the trend is toward informality. The tone depends on the rank of the writer in relation to the rank of the reader. Generally, memos addressed to top executives or to those above the writer's rank are more formal than memos addressed to the writer's peers or subordinates.

Other considerations include the personalities of the reader and the writer, the reader's background knowledge of the subject, and the subject matter itself. For instance, a memo announcing the recreation schedule for the annual picnic would obviously differ in tone from a memo justifying costs that have run over budget.

The effective memorandum writer will weigh all these factors before writing the memo and will read the message for the final time from the reader's viewpoint.

Organization

Good organization of the message appeals to the reader because arranging the material in a logical order allows it to be reviewed and read quickly and easily. A poorly organized memo will confuse the reader and may necessitate a second or even a third reading.

The organization of the memo is closely tied to the three approaches for writing effective business letters discussed in Unit 6.

Most memos follow the *direct approach,* presenting the main idea in the opening statement, then giving supporting details or facts, and concluding with a statement of future action or a request for further guidance.

Occasionally, however, you may decide that the *indirect approach* would be a better plan; for instance, if you are presenting conclusions and recommendations which you know the reader will be opposed to, you may be wise to first give the details and facts leading up to them. Don't waste words, but do lead the reader to come to your conclusion by first explaining and building a strong case.

A memo requesting a special favor should follow the *persuasive approach.* Remember to first get attention and interest by showing a benefit to the reader, if possible. Then encourage the reader to say "Yes" by presenting your logic before making the request.

Purpose

Be sure to clarify the purpose of the memo. You may refer to a previous memo, to a meeting, to a phone conversation, and so on. The information that follows will be valid and pertinent if you first identify your reason for writing. The purpose of the memo may be stated in one of the following ways:

1. Here is the information you asked for last week explaining the nature of the entertainment expense I submitted on my September 27 travel and entertainment report.

2. At the June meeting of the Property Owners' Association, I was asked to recommend a method for collecting delinquent dues. I submit the following ideas for your consideration prior to our next meeting on Tuesday, August 4.

3. During my recent visit to the Philadelphia office, I observed several ticket-process-

ing procedures that I believe would result in greater efficiency in our office. I would like to share these ideas with you.

Message

The most important rule for writing effective memos is to write from your reader's point of view. Too often the "you" attitude and benefits to the reader disappear as writers allow a dictatorial tone to creep into their memos. *Will you please* is a better statement beginning than *You will.* Reader benefits are an important part of persuasive strategy in memos and letters.

The opening paragraph, in particular, should be reader-oriented. You must get attention in the all-important first sentence, which often determines whether the rest of the memo is read or tossed into the wastebasket.

Get to your main point in the first sentence unless you have some negative news; if you do, lead up to the main point by first giving some facts, reasons, or explanations. Write in a convincing, positive tone; remember that positive words are more effective than negative words.

Provide adequate information. Be sure to cover all points your reader will need or want covered. For example, the reader will want to know the causes if you bring up a problem and the reasons for your suggested solution.

If you are writing a directive, employees will want to know *why* as well as *how.* Therefore you must provide enough information to enable them to understand new procedures and follow directions; and you must also give realistic and logical explanations. Memos that offer insufficient information not only cause confusion; they cast doubt on the administrative or management abilities of the writer as well.

Conclusions

The ending usually consists of conclusions or suggestions for future action. These must be tied strongly to the statement of purpose or the recommendation made in the opening. Begin a new paragraph here, to separate your comments from the facts you have presented in the middle of the memo.

The first part of the ending might, for example, summarize the important points you have listed or summarize the implications of a table you have just presented. A suggestion for future action is made in the last sentence.

Most routine memos will shape up nicely, if you orient your writing to your reader and follow the suggestions in this unit. Edit each memo for clarity, logic, and psychological effect. Then proofread carefully to add the final touch. Composing and transmitting an informative, useful message should be the goal of every memorandum writer.

Formatting Memorandums

Memos are designed to be efficient and to save the typist's time. Memo format is much simpler than letter format, as you can see in the illustration at the bottom of the page.

The headings *To:, From:, Date:,* and *Subject:* are usually printed on 8½- by 11-inch paper. Most organizations prefer to use this size so that all correspondence in the files will be the same size; however, some do use half sheets (8½ by 5½ inches). Some organizations do not use printed forms; the headings are merely typed on a blank sheet of paper.

If the organization has several divisions or has offices in more than one location, the memo forms may also include the headings *Division:* or *Department:* and *Location:* or *Floor:,* to facilitate transmittal between various branches of the firm. (These sections need not be filled in when writer and addressee work in the same department.) In addition, such forms may include the heading *Phone or Ext.:.* The examples in this unit and the next show that the headings may be tailored to fit each organization and also that they may be arranged in different patterns.

Notice that the Crye-Leike memo-letter on page 79 lists the branch offices, making it very easy for the writer to give his or her return address and phone number by merely checking the appropriate box. Also notice that there is room in the space beside and below the heading *To:* for several names—up to six, if

the first names are changed to initials to leave room for two names on each line. Or the extra lines could be used to specify the addressees' locations, especially if copies are to be mailed to other branches.

The Pilot Speed Letter illustrated on page 80 provides space for both the writer's message and the addressee's reply. This two-way memo-letter is gaining in popularity among organizations with representatives in the field who do not always have support personnel available to type their correspondence. The memo-letter is very quick to use and quick and easy to reply to; the snap-out form is a preassembled carbon pack that provides an original for the recipient, a carbon copy to be returned to the writer, a file copy for the writer, and an extra carbon copy for a third person, if needed.

The Addressee

Interoffice memorandums may be addressed to an individual, to several individuals, to a division or department, or to all personnel.

If the memo is being sent to more than one person, it may be possible to fit two or more names in the space following *To:.* If it is not possible to fit the names of the addressees in the heading of the memo, type *Distribution* after *To:.* Then on the third line below the reference initials, enclosure notation, or copy notation (whichever comes last), type *Distribution:.* Double-space and list the names of the recipients, arranged either by rank or in alphabetical order. If space is tight, arrange the names in two or more columns.

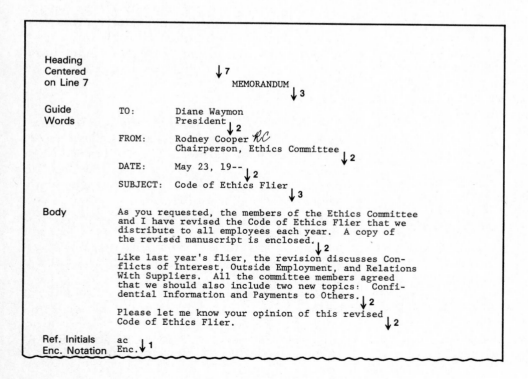

The various parts of an interoffice memorandum typed on plain paper are illustrated here.

CRYE-LEIKE Realtors

☐ **GERMANTOWN**
1727 KIRBY PARKWAY
MEMPHIS, TN 38138
(901) 756-8900

☐ **BARTLETT**
2963 ELMORE PARK
BARTLETT, TN 38134
(901) 372-3690

☐ **RALEIGH**
4339 STAGE ROAD
MEMPHIS, TN 38128
(901) 388-8320

☐ **HICKORY RIDGE**
5804 WINCHESTER
MEMPHIS, TN 38115
(901) 794-9925

☐ **COMMERCIAL-INVESTMENT DIVISION**
1727 KIRBY PARKWAY
MEMPHIS, TN 38138
(901) 756-8900

☐ **RELOCATION DIVISION**
1727 KIRBY PARKWAY
MEMPHIS, TN 38138
(901) 756-8900

MEMO~LETTER

TO Gary Garland, Commercial Division

Elaine Smoak, Relocation Division

DATE November 11, 19--

SUBJECT Teamwork Effort to Capture Relocation Business

Please meet in my office on Friday, November 15, at 2:30 p.m. to discuss a team-work approach which I believe will translate into profitability for your divisions.

Because mobility in staffing contributes to corporate growth and profitability, corporations are relocating some 400,000 employees a year. However, they are encountering increased resistance from employees, primarily because of the high costs of relocation. Statistics show that 72 percent of the Fortune 500 companies now use an outside real estate firm for relocation services.

I believe that the timing is right and that we are ready to take over a sizable share of the relocation business. I have some ideas to present that will help your divisions work together to contact the major corporate accounts in Memphis. Please be prepared to present your own ideas as well, and let's develop a plan.

Harold Crye HC

This memo form is used by realtors to transmit information quickly between branch offices. It is often handwritten and it provides a carbon copy for the sender. (Courtesy of Crye-Leike Realtors)

When the memo is finished and copies have been made, place a check mark on each copy beside the name of the person who is to receive it. The memo on pages 82 and 83 shows the copy of a memo intended for L. Valdez.

Courtesy titles (Mrs., Ms., Miss, Mr., and so on) are generally omitted. Business titles (Vice President, Sales Manager, and so on) may be used when:

1. The addressee has several titles, and this particular memo pertains to the responsibilities associated with only one of them.

2. The name of the addressee is the same as, or could easily be confused with, that of another employee.

3. The writer wishes to show deference to a superior.

4. The writer wishes to assure prompt and accurate delivery of the memo.

The Writer

The writer does not use a courtesy title but may include a business title, department, location, and/or phone number, for identification purposes and to facilitate a response.

The Date

Just as in letters, the date should be written in full and not abbreviated or expressed in figures. The complete date is as necessary to a memo as it is to a letter, to prevent oversights and miscommunications, and for future reference.

The Subject Line

The subject line should be a brief statement that accurately and specifically describes the content; it is not a

Pilot Life
Insurance Company
P O Box 20727
Greensboro, N C 27420
Telephone 919 299 4720

PILOT SPEED LETTER

MAIL TO (Use Mail Codes when applicable)
Chris Campbell, Jr.
Greensboro 210

From (Show Mail code, if any; otherwise, show complete address)
C. L. McComas, CLU
Memphis 048

Pilot Life

Subject   Change of Beneficiary on
Message   Policy No. AB9022

Mr. Gary Cooper, owner of Policy No. AB9022, has requested that the

beneficiary of this policy be changed. The appropriate change form,

signed by the owner, is attached.

Please expedite this change and return the company-endorsed change copy

to me, for delivery to the insured.

Signed *Bill McComas*   Date 12/29/--

Reply

The new tax law requires that the Social Security number or Tax Identi-

fication number of the owner be obtained for all policies issued or

changed after January 1, 1986. Please furnish us with Mr. Cooper's

Social Security number, since we do not have it on file.

Company-endorsed change of beneficiary is enclosed for delivery to the

owner. Please attach it securely to the policy.

Signed *Chris Campbell, Jr.*   Date 1/4/--
B-2108E   COPY FOR PERSON ADDRESSED

This memo-letter is used by insurance agents to communicate with each other as well as to facilitate quick replies from policyholders. The snap-out form provides three carbon copies. (Courtesy of Pilot Life Insurance Company)

complete sentence but rather a concise phrase that prepares the reader for the message and aids in filing the memo for future reference.

When Typing a Memo on Plain Paper

1. Set the left and right margins for a 6-inch line (or approximately 1½ inches).

2. Center and type the heading *MEMORANDUM* in all capital letters on line 7 (leaving a 1-inch top margin).

3. Start typing the guide words on the third line below the heading *MEMORANDUM.* The easiest and fastest way is to double-space and block the headings at the left margin. Use all capital letters, and type a colon after each guide word.

4. Set a tab two spaces after the colon following the longest guide word; then align and type all entries.

5. Begin typing the message at the left margin on the third line below the last guide word.

6. Use single spacing, with double spacing between paragraphs.

7. The paragraphs are usually blocked, to save typing time; however, it is permissible to indent them.

8. Some writers prefer to have their names or initials typed at the bottom of their memos. Type the name or initials on the second line below the last line of the body, beginning at the center point. Type the writer's title (if desired) on the following line, beginning at the center point; or, if the headings are in a two-column format, start typing these lines at the second tab stop you set.

9. Some writers prefer to initial or sign their memos. The memo may be initialed after the writer's name in the heading *From:*. Another method is to type the writer's name or initials on the fourth line below the last line of the body of the memo, beginning at the center point.

10. Type the reference initials in lowercase letters on the second line below the last line of the body or the writer's name, initials, or title—whichever is last. Block the reference initials at the left margin.

11. Type an enclosure notation, if needed, on the line below the reference initials, blocked at the left.

12. Type a copy notation, if needed, on the line below the enclosure notation or the reference initials—whichever is last—blocked at the left margin. (If you do not want the addressee to know you are sending a copy of the memo to one or more other persons, use a *blind carbon copy* notation. See page 108 for the proper way to handle such notations.)

13. If the memo continues beyond the first page, type a heading in the format shown on page 83 on plain paper for the second and succeeding pages. Continue typing the message on the third line below the heading.

When Typing on a Printed Memo Form

1. Set the left margin two spaces after the longest guide word in the heading (or in the left half of the heading, if the headings are arranged in a two-column format).

2. Set a tab stop two spaces after the longest guide word in the right half of the heading (if the headings are arranged in a two-column format).

3. Set the right margin approximately the same number of spaces or inches from the right edge of the paper as the left margin is from the left edge.

4. Type in the appropriate information after each printed guide word, using capital and lowercase letters.

Now follow guidelines 5–13 in the section "When Typing a Memo on Plain Paper."

Proper format for a printed memo form is illustrated on page 82. Notice that the second-page heading is typed on plain paper, just as it is when no form is provided.

ASSIGNMENT: To test your ability to format memorandums, proofread and correct the errors in Section A of the Worksheet. Then plan and prepare (preferably type) the routine memorandums in Section B.

INTEROFFICE MEMORANDUM

To:	Distribution	**From:**	James S. Brown
Dept.:		**Dept.:**	Administration
Floor:		**Floor and Ext.:**	2/905
Subject:	Part-time Employment and Early Retirement for Nonprofessional Staff	**Date:**	August 14, 19--

I need your suggestions about ways to encourage part-time employment or early retirement for approximately 700 of our full-time nonprofessional staff. Our professional staff is adequate; but the number of nonprofessional employees in relation to occupancy rates is very high and costly to operations.

Let me summarize the key points brought out in the executive staff meeting last Friday:

1. Methodist is experiencing declining occupancy rates in its three facilities, as are other hospitals in San Antonio and throughout the nation.

2. Year-to-date through July, Methodist Central had a 78.8 percent occupancy rate; Methodist North, 76.8; and Methodist South, 68.6 percent.

3. These rates were in the 80th percentile in years past and are projected to decrease even further by the end of the fiscal year.

4. Changes in Medicare reimbursement policies, increasing trends toward insurance copayments, wellness, and outpatient clinics are some of the major factors contributing to fewer hospital admissions and shorter stays.

With hopes of avoiding layoffs next year, Methodist is urging employees to go to part-time status or to take early retirement. Currently, 11 percent of our 4700-member work force is classified as part-time, and we need to double that figure. Another 200 workers are eligible for early retirement options.

This request memo illustrates proper format for a two-page memorandum, using a printed memo form.

Distribution   2   August 14, 19--

Please give me your immediate feedback as to how we can achieve these
necessary goals through attrition instead of layoffs.

James S. Brown
James S. Brown
Administrator

dwm

Distribution:

O. Link
J. Nutter
H. Sitz
J. Stewart
L. Valdez

Unit 8 Worksheet

FORMATTING AND WRITING ROUTINE MEMORANDUMS

A *PROOFREADING FOR FORMAT ERRORS IN MEMOS. Mark the four format errors in each of the following memos. Then in the space provided on page 86, explain how you would correct the errors.*

```
                    MEMORANDUM

        TO:      All Employees

        FROM:    Ken Kessinger

        DATE:    December 6, 19--
        Subject: December Publishing Schedule


        The East Lansing Shoppers News will not be published
        Christmas week or the week following.  Our sales
        record for this two-week period during the past three
        years indicates that there is insufficient interest
        in classified advertising during the holidays to
        make publishing our weekly flier profitable.

        This time is to be used by full-time employees as
        additional vacation with pay and by part-time em-
        ployees as time off without pay.

        The last working day of this month will be Friday,
        December 18, when the December 19 edition rolls off
        the press.

        Have a happy holiday season, and come back on Mon-
        day, January 4, ready to prepare the first edition
        of the Shoppers News for 19--.


        KEN KESSINGER
        Editor

        bas
```

1.

a. _____

b. _____

c. _____

d. _____

_____

MEMORANDUM

TO: Milford Friedrich

FROM: Bill Miles *BM*

DATE: February 2, 19--

SUBJECT: LOCATION FOR JUNE STAFF MEETING

      I recommend that our June staff meeting be held
at the Diamondhead Executive Conference Center on
Paradise Isle.

Paradise Isle is located in the rolling hills of
Arkansas, overlooking a crystal-clear 30,000-acre
lake. The recreational attractions include a
championship 18-hole golf course, clay tennis courts,
sailing, and guided fishing and float trips.

To conclude the meeting and reward the staff for
an excellent first half, we could hold the banquet
at the 4-Star Paradise Isle Inn.

Please look over the enclosed brochure and let me
know your thoughts.

Enclosure
vb

2.

a. _____

b. _____

c. _____

d. _____

B WRITING ROUTINE MEMORANDUMS. *Using separate sheets of paper, plan and prepare (preferably type) clear, concise memorandums for Problems 3–6. Organize the information given, plus any other information you wish to assume, into effective interoffice memos.*

3. As training director of Camtro Industries, prepare a memo to all support personnel announcing a word processing seminar to be held a week from Saturday, from 8:30 to 12 noon. Send carbon copies to Joanna Starr (personnel director) and Mitchell Augustine (payroll and benefits director). Overtime will be paid (1½ times the regular hourly rate). The seminar will be conducted by Miss Faith Wilson, word processing coordinator for the Computer Educational Center. This intermediate course is open to all who completed the beginners' course last month. Ask those attending to bring their training packets from the first course. The seminar will be held in Conference Room C on the third floor.

4. As manager of Tempo Records and Tapes, prepare a memo to Hugh Sitz, your employer, suggesting that the daily sales reports you now prepare be condensed into a weekly report. The seven reports, though prepared daily, are now submitted each Monday for the preceding week.
   Some of your reasons are:
   a. One report would reduce paperwork for you and save on paper and copying costs.
   b. It would take less of your employer's time to read one condensed report than it does at present to go over the seven daily reports.
   c. Seeing a full week's sales information on one sheet would provide a more meaningful picture than do seven individual reports.
   Outline your suggestion, reasons, and recommendation in the memorandum to Mr. Sitz. Also, advise him that you have attached a draft of your proposed weekly sales report to the memo. (You need not prepare such a form.)

5. On a recent flight, you read a magazine called *The Executive's Guide to Communication and Motivation,* which you found very interesting. You think the magazine would be valuable to other people in your office too. Prepare a memo to your office administrator, Clarice Schroeder, asking her to subscribe to the magazine in your organization's name. It is a monthly publication. The yearly subscription rate is $24.

6. Prepare a congratulatory memo your regional manager, Howard Byers, Jr., can send to all sales personnel. A wire to Mr. Byers has just arrived from the New York office announcing that the Southern Region exceeded its goals for the fiscal year—gross sales came in at 148 percent of last year's sales. Your message, though short, should project jubilance.

Unit 9

MEMORANDUM REPORTS AND MEETINGS CORRESPONDENCE

The flow of correct and usable information within an organization is vital to effective decision making. The reports you write often serve as a basis for decisions that top executives, managers, and supervisors must make and also as a basis for evaluating your ideas and thinking. The development of report writing skills, therefore, is very important to your success in business.

Memorandum Reports

As you begin your business career, you will probably be more directly concerned with memorandums than with any other type of report, because the memo report is the most popular form for routine communications within an organization.

Memorandums are reports if they are written to answer a request for information, to report progress, to make recommendations, or merely to state facts.

Memorandum reports are written to communicate facts, ideas, statistics, and trends within an organization. The timely flow of internal communications is essential, since business executives rely heavily on the written information that is reported to them as the basis for making decisions.

A memorandum report is usually informal, giving facts and opinions in the first person ("I suggest . . . ") and written in conversational language and style. The trend is definitely away from the stiff, formal writing style that characterized business reports of several years ago.

A formal business report demands thoroughly documented, objective, and detailed preparation. It is longer than a memo report and usually includes the following parts: title page, letter of transmittal, table of contents, summary or synopsis, introduction, text, conclusions, recommendations, appendix, and bibliography. The formal report is appropriate for reports that are sent outside the organization; it is used inter-

nally when the importance or length makes the memo report inappropriate.

Some internal communications are simply progress or status reports, written on fill-in forms and sent each day, week, month, and so on, to those who need the information. Others are fairly brief narrative reports—they may be responses to requests for information, ideas, explanations, or simple recommendations. Longer, more involved memo reports may contain recommendations supported by financial data or operating results.

Many business reports are routine and are prepared at regular time intervals—daily, weekly, monthly, quarterly, or annually. Sales reports and financial reports are among the most common periodic reports prepared in business organizations. A monthly sales report is illustrated on page 90.

When a memo report contains statistical material, it should be displayed in tabulated form for easier reading. Be sure to precede displayed material with an appropriate introductory statement, as in the memo on page 90.

Periodic reports are often prepared on printed forms. The use of printed forms reduces the likelihood that essential information will be omitted and also reduces the time required to prepare the report, by providing blank spaces in which information is recorded.

Reports may also be prepared according to standardized outlines to ensure uniformity. Sales reports, credit reports, audit reports, and many legal reports are prepared in such standardized format.

Most of the reports written in business are simple, straightforward factual presentations, and they should be worded as such. Their purpose is to communicate information—facts, ideas, statistics, or trends—in a direct manner. For an informational report, you will gather, organize, and present facts and figures; and you may be asked to make recommendations as well.

MEMORANDUM

To: Dan Salvemini   From: Lucy Good

Subject: Season Ticket Sales   Date: November 1, 19--
         for October

October season ticket sales increased 6.9 percent
over last year's figures. We sold 8666 season
tickets, as compared with last October's 8109.

As a result of our advertising efforts and the
upcoming season opener, soccer fever continued to
build during this last month of the campaign.
October sales continued the upward trend we saw in
July, August, and September.

A final tabulation is being prepared and will be
released next week.

kik

A periodic report is one of the most common types of business reports.

MEMORANDUM

To: Dan Salvemini   From: Lucy Good

Subject: 19-- Season Ticket Sales Totals   Date: November 10, 19--

Season ticket sales for 19-- increased 15.1 percent over 19--.
This year we sold 18,366 season tickets, as compared with
last year's total of 15,960. This represents a healthy increase of 2,406, which will certainly boost our operating
budget as we begin the season.

Here are the season ticket sales results, as they were reported monthly, for both years:

Month	19--	19--	Increase	Percent of Increase
July	1,134	845	289	34.2
August	2,456	1,255	1,201	95.7
September	6,110	5,751	359	6.2
October	8,666	8,109	557	6.9
Totals	18,366	15,960	2,406	15.1

The combination of our league championship and second-place
finish in last year's playoffs had a dramatic impact on pre-
season ticket sales. Virtually all season ticket holders
renewed, and non-season ticket holders bought early to ensure
good seats for this season.

The season ticket sales campaign has officially ended. I
hope you are as proud of the results as we are in the
Marketing Department.

kik

The statistical material in this memorandum report is displayed in tabulated form for easier reading.

The accessibility of data retrieved from a computer's memory will help you prepare informational reports quickly. In most cases, the computer will provide the data requested; the rest—your interpretation of the data, for example—you must create. You have the responsibility of evaluating results, reaching conclusions, and recommending possible solutions to the problem. You may be able to save retyping the data by (1) printing statistical information directly from the computer and using a simple memo transmittal form or (2) copying the data to create a new document, then building the memorandum format and your remarks around the data.

Your memo report should contain enough facts to inform your reader fully, but if you have a mass of material, consider putting most or all of it in a supplement to your memo. This method allows the reader to scan the supplement for supporting evidence or documentation, and it allows you to focus on the facts you think are essential to the body of the memo. Don't overwhelm the reader with a barrage of data or statistics within your memo.

If you have been asked to make a recommendation, make it the main point of your memo. Also, consider whether you should mention alternatives to your recommendation, and check to see whether you should explain more specifically how to carry out your proposal. Including this information will make your memo report complete—by telling the reader what he or she has asked for and by offering your ideas and suggestions.

Gathering Information

Because the office memo type of report is often needed quickly, gathering the information for it is frequently more casual and less scientific than for the longer, more professional report that is sent outside the organization. If you are asked to collect data for an informal memorandum report, make the process as thorough and the results as factual as your limited time allows.

Now suppose you receive from your employer the memorandum shown on page 92. How will you go about gathering data for the report?

First, you read the request carefully to make sure you know exactly what information Mr. Dunn is asking you for. Since his memorandum is clearly written and you understand what you are to do, you need not telephone him for further explanation.

You decide to start with Aspenwood Apartments Inc., by finding out the yearly costs of salaries, benefits, maintenance, equipment, and supplies.

Next, you look in the Yellow Pages and begin phoning property management firms. They give you general information about their services and an estimate of the fee which would be charged for managing the apartment complex. After studying this informa-

tion, you narrow the choices to four firms which are well-known for dependability and which give you comparable estimates.

You set up appointments with representatives from the four firms to meet with you to look at Aspenwood, discuss contract terms, and negotiate an annual fee.

Your next step is to visit two of the complexes managed by each of the four firms to get a firsthand look at the buildings and grounds and at the interior of a few of the units, to form an opinion of the condition of the properties. While you are visiting, you talk with some of the tenants at each complex to determine whether they are pleased with the management.

After you have analyzed these data and compared cost and service, you are ready to select the firm you believe will provide the best management at the lowest cost. To confirm your decision, you visit two more complexes managed by the firm you have selected.

Mr. Dunn has requested a recommendation and given you a short time in which to prepare it. You feel, therefore, that the research you have done and the comparisons you have made support your conclusions and recommendation.

Now you are ready to organize the information you have gathered into a memorandum report to Mr. Dunn.

Writing the Report

One of the most common and effective techniques of memo organization is to itemize the information. A report that contains complex facts and ideas will be easier to read if items are separated into paragraphs and either enumerated or preceded by side headings. This technique will also help you to write concisely and to organize carefully, as you can see by reviewing the memo shown on pages 94 and 95.

No rigid rules govern the content and organization of interoffice memorandums that function as reports. The memo report should follow the form best suited to its particular function.

Now you must determine the best way to present your findings to Mr. Dunn. Remember that he expects your report to be factual and reliable. You will, of course, present the facts with absolute fairness and accuracy. You must also be careful not to mix your opinions with the facts you report. Reserve your comments for your conclusions and recommendations.

The results of your work are transmitted in the memorandum report illustrated on pages 94 and 95. It is well done from two points of view: (1) The information is presented in an orderly, easy-to-read fashion; (2) The report represents something extra because you not only make the recommendation Mr. Dunn has asked for but also take the time to pres-

```
              MEMORANDUM

      TO:      Greg Renault

      FROM:    Ed Dunn

      DATE:    December 15, 19--

      SUBJECT: Property Management Study

      Because of the increasing costs of salaries, benefits,
      maintenance, equipment, and supplies, I am wondering
      whether contracting with a commercial property man-
      agement firm would be a wiser choice for Aspenwood
      Apartments Inc.

      Will you please investigate the major property man-
      agement firms in the Boston area and compare their
      fees with our current operational expenses.

      I suggest also that you (1) take a firsthand look
      at several complexes managed by these firms to
      observe the interior and exterior conditions and
      (2) survey the tenants to see if they are satisfied
      with the quality of management.

      If you find that by contracting with one of these
      firms we can realize substantial savings while
      maintaining our high standards of management, please
      present your recommendation to me as soon as you
      have gathered and analyzed this information.

      aks
```

This request memo will launch an informal study and generate a response in the form of a memorandum report.

and show him a concise but complete comparison. In writing reports, as in other phases of a job, remember to do a little more than is required. You and those around you will benefit from your extra effort to produce a comprehensive, well-written report.

Meeting Correspondence

Face-to-face oral communication among groups of people is essential to certain phases of business. Meetings represent an important segment of business communications, because they often achieve results that would be difficult to generate by phone or letter.

Meetings range from very informal to formal. Formal meetings follow strict parliamentary procedure, which is a set of rules for conducting meetings. An

excellent reference book for parliamentary procedure is *Robert's Rules of Order*, revised edition.

Meetings may be called on short notice, depending on the urgency and the number of people involved and their accessibility; or they may be set well in advance, to stimulate attendance and to allow preparation time.

Meeting Notices

People who are to attend a meeting may be notified in advance of the meeting by a written notice. In especially important meetings, a notice may be followed by a reminder a few days before the meeting.

The meeting notice and reminder should contain: (1) the day and date of the meeting, (2) the time, (3) the place, (4) the purpose of the meeting or an agenda, and (5) any other applicable information, such as materials to bring. Notices and reminders may be in the form of an announcement, a letter, a memo, or a postcard. A reply card or a reservation slip may be enclosed.

Here is a sample meeting notice.

TO: All Relocation Division and
           Commercial—Investment Division
           Personnel

FROM: Ann Faught

DATE: November 18, 19—

SUBJECT: Teamwork Effort to Capture
           Relocation Business

A joint meeting of the Relocation Division and the Commercial—Investment Division will be held on Friday, November 22, at 3 p.m., in Conference Room C on the fifth floor.

The purpose of the meeting is to discuss a teamwork approach that will capture a sizable share of the relocation market in the St. Louis area.

Please review the enclosed list of major corporate accounts to be contacted following this meeting, and be prepared to share your ideas for developing this business.

rah
Enc.

Meeting Agenda

An *agenda* is a program, or a list of the items in the order they are to be discussed at a meeting. A typical agenda includes some or all of the following:

1. Call to order
2. Roll call
3. Approval of minutes
4. Reading of correspondence
5. Treasurer's report
6. Officers' reports
7. Committee reports
8. Old business
9. New business
10. Program
11. Announcements
12. Adjournment

Preparing an agenda will help make a meeting more productive, especially if the agenda is sent out in advance. Specific items of business may be designated, to give the attendees time to prepare for the discussion. The secretary of an organization is usually responsible for preparing the agenda after consulting with the chairperson.

Minutes of Meetings

Minutes are an official written record of the business that is conducted at a meeting. Minutes are important, even for an informal meeting, to prevent any misunderstanding of what took place.

Minutes are a type of report and should be a summary of the meeting rather than a verbatim report. They should be written objectively, concisely, and in past tense.

It is important for the recorder or secretary to listen for key ideas and take good notes during the meeting. The minutes should be prepared as soon after the meeting as possible, while the proceedings are still fresh in the recorder's mind. It may be the organization's custom to mail the minutes prior to the next meeting, distribute them at the next meeting, and/or read them at the next meeting.

The top of the first page should give the *who, what, when, where, how,* and *why.* This information should be followed by a summary of each item on the agenda in chronological order. Put each item of business in a separate paragraph. Marginal headings, side headings, or paragraph headings help to locate items quickly in the minutes.

Be sure to include the specifics of each motion made, including any amendments; the names of both the person who made the motion and the person who seconded it; and whether the motion passed, failed, or was tabled.

When it is necessary to make a correction on minutes that have already been distributed or read, draw a line through the error, usually with a red pen, and write the correction above it. If several lines need to be corrected, draw a line through each incorrect line, make the note "See page—," and type the correction on a separate sheet with the appropriate page number. The entire set of minutes should never be retyped, because of the danger of making additional errors in the process of retyping.

Minutes of a meeting and the agenda that was mailed prior to the meeting are shown in the illustrations on pages 96 and 97.

ASSIGNMENT: Complete Section A of the Worksheet to test your ability to write effective memorandum reports. Section B will exercise your skills in preparing meeting correspondence.

```
                    MEMORANDUM


        TO:     Ed Dunn

        FROM:   Greg Renault  GR

        DATE:   December 29, 19--

        SUBJECT:  Property Management Study


        As you requested, I have investigated the feasibility of engaging the
        services of a property management firm to provide total management ser-
        vices for Aspenwood Apartments Inc.


        Recommendation

        To save Aspenwood Apartments Inc. approximately $7000 a year in
        property management expenses, I recommend that we contract with AMPCO
        Management Inc. on a year-to-year basis.


        Findings

        1.  According to the College Bureau of Economic Research, AMPCO
            Management Inc. manages more commercial and residential space than
            does any other property management firm in the Boston area.

        2.  The large volume of business which AMPCO has built during the
            past 12 years enables it to execute management contracts at lower
            rates than its competitors.  AMPCO bid 7 percent of gross rental
            revenues, while the other three property management firms con-
            sidered bid 8 percent.

        3.  The 7 percent rate is guaranteed for a minimum of two years.  We
            would maintain the right to renew or terminate the contract at the
            end of the first year.  If we renewed the contract, the rate
            could be renegotiated at the end of the second year.

        4.  A survey of four AMPCO-managed apartment complexes showed three
            to be in excellent interior and exterior condition and to have
            generally satisfied tenants.  One, due primarily to the economic
            area in which it is located, had less satisfied tenants but was
            in good condition.
```

Note the content and organization of this report, which was written in response to the request on page 92.

Ed Dunn   2   December 29, 19--

5. AMPCO would provide the following:

    a. Salaries and benefits for a resident manager and two assistant
       resident managers.

    b. Rental expense on the resident manager's furnished apartment.

    c. All maintenance--interior, exterior, and landscaping--through
       its service contracts.

    d. All equipment and supplies.

Cost Breakdown

The following is a comparison of the present cost of managing Aspenwood
with the estimated cost of contracting with AMPCO to provide this
service.

Annual salary, furnished apartment, and other benefits for resident manager	$14,524
Annual salaries for two assistant resident managers	4,800
Annual salary and benefits for one maintenance employee	11,261
Contracted repair work	3,722
Maintenance equipment and supplies	3,216
Miscellaneous costs	1,212
19-- EXPENSES	$38,735
PROJECTED EXPENSES FOR 19--	$39,897
ESTIMATED ANNUAL COST OF CONTRACTING SERVICES OF AMPCO MANAGEMENT INC.	$32,800
SAVINGS EFFECTED	$ 7,097

Ed Dunn   3   December 29, 19--

Conclusions

1. Total responsibility for property management--including payroll
   records, hiring and firing, and purchasing equipment and supplies--
   would rest with AMPCO.

2. This year's expenditures total $38,735. Anticipating a 3 percent
   increase in total expenses for next year, the estimated annual
   operating expense is $39,897. AMPCO's bid is 7 percent of gross
   rental revenues, or an estimated $32,800 for next year. Contracting
   with AMPCO would save about $7,097 next year, while maintaining
   high quality of management.

rms

```
                    AGENDA
          GERMANTOWN ZONING COMMISSION
                MONTHLY MEETING
            Tuesday, September 17, 19--

     1.  Call to Order
     2.  Secretary's Report
     3.  Committee Reports
     4.  Old Business
     5.  New Business
     6.  Announcements
     7.  Adjournments
```

*Preparing an agenda such as this will help make a
meeting more productive.*

```
                        GERMANTOWN ZONING COMMISSION

                        MINUTES OF THE MONTHLY MEETING

                         Tuesday, September 17, 19--


Presiding:        Donna Golightly

Present:          Jack Andrews          John Nash
                  Barbara Brogdon       Pam Raymond
                  Glen Doris            Brian Thompson
                  Lynda May             Carol Williams

Absent:           Randall Matthews


Call to Order     The regular meeting of the Germantown Zoning Commission was
                  called to order by Donna Golightly, Chairperson, at 7:30 p.m.

Secretary's       The minutes of the August 15, 19--, meeting were approved
Report            as read.

Committee         Pam Raymond, Chairperson of the Mayor's Advisory Review
                  Committee, reported that she had conveyed to the mayor the
                  wishes of the Zoning Commission that a traffic signal be
                  placed at the intersection of Poplar Avenue and Kirby Parkway.

Old Business      Etto Corporation submitted a request for final approval of the
                  building plans for a 15-unit townhouse project at 1722 Riverdale
                  Road.  Lynda May questioned whether the Germantown Design
                  Review Committee had approved the landscaping plans and was
                  advised affirmatively by Donna Golightly.  Steve Woodyard, the
                  developer, presented blueprints and reviewed the completed plans.
                  After some discussion, John Nash moved for final approval.
                  Carol Williams seconded.  The motion was approved unanimously.

New Business      Alworth Development Company submitted an application for
                  rezoning of 22 acres on the southwest corner of Mt. Moriah
                  Extended and Ridgeway Boulevard from RTH (Townhouse) to
                  GO (General Office).  At the request of Barbara Brogdon,
                  this application was tabled until the next regular meeting,
                  to allow the members time to study the proposal.

Announcements     The next meeting will be October 16, 19--, at 7:30 p.m.

Adjournment       The meeting was adjourned at 9 p.m.

                                        Respectfully submitted,

                                        Rick Esposito

                                        Rick Esposito, Secretary
                                        City of Germantown
```

*Minutes serve as written record of the business conducted
at a meeting.*

Unit 9 Worksheet

MEMORANDUM REPORTS AND MEETING CORRESPONDENCE

A   *WRITING MEMORANDUM REPORTS. For the following problems, much of the information needed has been gathered for you. You are to organize the information into a meaningful memorandum report. As you do so, make up and add any details that will help make your report complete and effective. Organize and outline each report; then prepare (preferably type) each one.*

1. You are the Assistant Sales Manager for Worldwide Films Corporation, a movie distribution company. Three months ago, you suggested to your boss, Jacqueline Durham, that Worldwide would probably do very well to rerelease some of its older films because of the "nostalgia" fever among so many people. You suggested testing the idea by rereleasing only three movies in selected markets: New York, Boston, and Atlanta.

   The results of the test proved that you were right: In the past two months, one movie, *The Last Roundup*, grossed $1.2 million in New York, 1.34 million in Boston, and 1.10 million in Atlanta. The second movie, *Inside City Hall*, grossed $1.43 million in New York, $1.62 million in Boston, and $1.54 million in Atlanta. The third movie, *The Witness*, grossed $850,000 in New York, $945,000 in Boston, and $1.25 million in Atlanta. Because you are confident that these results prove that Worldwide's other older films can be rereleased very profitably, you decide to prepare a memo in which you will (1) summarize the results of rereleasing these films and (2) suggest other films that could be just as successful.

   (Hint: In your memo to Ms. Durham prepare a table showing the gross sales for each film by city. Use the discussion of the success of these three films to convince your boss that she should approve the rerelease of other films. Also include another chart of estimated sales for the other films you suggest for rerelease. Make up the names of films and the estimated gross receipts for each.)

   Memorandum report plan:

   _____

   _____

   _____

   _____

   _____

   _____

   _____

   _____

   _____

   _____

   _____

_____

_____

_____

_____

_____

2. You are Assistant Warehouse Manager for Durable Plastics Inc., a middle-sized manufacturer of miscellaneous plastic products. The main office and the warehouse for this company are located in Los Angeles, California. About two years ago, Durable opened its first branch office, a sales office in New York, where four full-time sales representatives sell Durable products on the East Coast. These four men and women have developed annual sales on the East Coast of approximately $3.56 million—a growth of about $3 million in only two years! In the same period, Durable's West Coast business has grown from about $12.2 million to $17.6 million. To meet the tremendous increase in the demand for its products, Durable expanded its manufacturing facilities last year, but its warehouse space has remained the same.

Everyone in the company (including you and your boss, Tom Chang, warehouse manager) is aware of the obvious need for more warehouse space. In addition, everyone agrees that Durable should lease a new warehouse (rather than expand its present warehouse or build a new warehouse)—but where? Most people in the company have assumed that Durable should lease another warehouse in the Los Angeles area, but you are convinced that this is not the best solution.

Having studied the problem carefully, you are ready to recommend that Durable should lease a warehouse in New Jersey, not in Los Angeles. Among your reasons are the following: The Los Angeles warehouse is spacious enough to handle all of Durable's West Coast business for many years. Although business has grown in recent years, company analysts agree that sales on the West Coast are now at about the maximum level; they do not expect West Coast sales to increase substantially in the next ten years. Everyone agrees that future growth will come from New York, Pennsylvania, Massachusetts, and Connecticut. A warehouse in the New Jersey area would be able to handle orders for these states faster than a Los Angeles warehouse; in addition, shipping would be cheaper from a New Jersey warehouse. The space available in the present Los Angeles warehouse would be sufficient to take care of all West Coast business; and the New Jersey warehouse could then take care of all East Coast business.

Through a real estate broker, you have found three suitable sites in New Jersey, in Trenton, Somerville, and Secaucus. Each site has more than 200,000 square feet of space available, and each is available for long-term leasing at reasonable rents. You plan to enclose with your memo to Mr. Chang a description of the three warehouses that the real estate broker supplied.

After preparing a report plan in the space provided, write your memorandum report to Tom Chang on a separate sheet of paper.

Memorandum report plan:

_____

_____

_____

_____

_____

_____

_____

_____

_____

_____

_____

_____

_____

_____

B PREPARING MEETING CORRESPONDENCE. *Using separate sheets of paper, plan and prepare (preferably type) clear, concise solutions. Use page 102 to plan and organize Problems 3, 4, and 5.*

3. As employee benefits coordinator for your firm, prepare (preferably type) a memo to the Management Bargaining Team scheduling a meeting two weeks from today at 4 p.m. in the East Conference Room. Representatives from three insurance companies will present proposals. Ask each team member to bring the salary and fringe benefit surveys distributed at the last meeting.

4. Prepare (preferably type) an agenda for the meeting described in Problem 5 that might have been prepared and mailed to the members prior to the meeting.

5. Organize the notes below and prepare (preferably type) the minutes of the meeting described below.

BACKGROUND: You are secretary of the Administrative Board for the local Boy Scout Council. The purpose of this board is to oversee the council's programs, make recommendations for activities and equipment purchases, and serve as a public relations group for the council. There are nine members on the board, which meets four times a year. The following notes were made during the January 8 meeting.

NOTES: Minutes from last meeting (October 9) approved as read. Chairperson, Andrew Juliano, called to order at 12:30 p.m. in Board Room at council office with following members present: Michael Truax, Don Norenburg, Gary Thor, Phil Smith, Angela Garcia, Rose DeMayo, Van Burnett, Ed Brock (and you). Meeting adjourned 1:30 p.m.

Phil Smith suggested awarding perfect attendance certificates to scouts at end of each quarter rather than once a year. Several members felt this was a good idea and would be an excellent motivational technique to help scouts develop the habit of being dependable.

Van Burnett gave an update on annual Scout-O-Rama. Since the last meeting, he has received survey cards from 25 Cub and Boy Scout units expressing an interest in participating. Angela Garcia suggested date be changed from last Wednesday in February to last Wednesday in March because of past problems with bad weather in February which reduced attendance. A vote was taken and the motion passed. After a lengthy discussion of pros and cons, the change was presented as a motion by Ed Brock and seconded by Gary Thor.

Next meeting will be April 3 at 1 p.m.

Gary Thor, chairperson of Advancement Committee, reported that he felt the council should recruit more volunteer specialists to assist units with advancement in the more difficult areas. Gary distributed a list of areas needing advancement assistance and some statistics showing the need. After discussion a motion was made by Michael Truax and seconded by Rose DeMayo to adopt this recommendation and forward it to the council executive for implementation. A vote was taken and the motion passed.

The treasurer's report, by Rose DeMayo, was placed on file for audit. She indicated there is $2,770 current cash on hand.

Part 3

WRITING EFFECTIVE BUSINESS LETTERS

Now it is time to apply the techniques and principles you have learned to writing various types of business letters. Many of the examples you will read in Part 3 are real-life business letters—some good and some bad. Analyze each to determine what makes it good or bad and why. After studying the examples, you will begin to write, first routine letters, then more complex ones. Remember to look at each example—and your own writing, too—from the reader's viewpoint. Before you begin to study and write these letters, you should have a checklist of the ideal contents of a business letter. The "Checklist for an Effective Business Letter" on page 104 will help you analyze the letters that you are about to read and the ones you will compose.

As you write the letters for the Worksheets for Units 10–19, remember that:

1. Every letter is a unique blend of writer, reader, circumstances, and purpose.

2. A good letter reflects your sincerity and interest in the welfare of the reader.

3. The circumstances surrounding a particular letter must be considered.

4. To be successful, the letter must achieve its purpose.

As you come to understand the principles of effective letter writing and develop your skill in writing through practicing these principles, you will find yourself writing more quickly and more confidently. Your first letters may not be sparkling, but they will do their job efficiently and build goodwill . . . which is really what modern business correspondence is all about.

Checklist for an Effective Business Letter

A Good Letter is Unmistakably Clear

Unless a letter is easily read and its meaning immediately clear, it is a barrier rather than an aid to communication. As you analyze good and bad letters, begin by asking yourself:

1. Is this letter easy to understand?
2. Is its message simple, concise, and economical?

A Good Letter Does Its Specific Job Well

A business letter is written to accomplish a definite purpose. Usually it plays a specific part in a business transaction. The letter should do what it has set out to do; it should help push the transaction to a successful outcome. A letter which, for example, is well written and friendly and builds goodwill but fails to answer the customer's request does not fulfill its purpose or satisfy the customer.

Continue to build your concept of a good letter by asking yourself:

1. Of what business transaction is this letter a part?
2. What is the letter's specific job in carrying out the transaction?
3. Does the letter accomplish its task?
4. Does the letter tell the reader clearly what he or she is expected to do and how to do it?

A Good Letter Has a Pleasing Personality

Just as your own personality is made up of many distinctive traits, so is the personality of each letter you write. In determining what traits in a letter will please the reader, ask yourself:

1. *Is its appearance attractive?* A letter, like a person, should make a good first impression.
2. *Is its expression correct, active, and natural?* A letter, like a person, is judged by "the way it talks."

3. *Is its tone friendly?* A letter, like a person, attracts friends by being friendly. And letters can smile!
4. *Does it reflect a sincere and helpful attitude?* A letter, like a person, influences others if it convinces them that the writer's thoughtfulness and desire to serve are more than merely pleasant words and polite manners.
5. *Does it stress a "you" viewpoint?* A letter, like a person, pleases if it focuses on the reader and emphasizes that the reader's interests are important to the writer and the writer's organization.
6. *Are negative elements positioned carefully and explained or minimized?* A letter, like a person, should emphasize the positive aspects.

A Good Letter Is Interesting to the Reader

A business letter need not be clever and entertaining, but it should attract and hold the reader's attention so that he or she reads the message through and then acts on it—or at least reacts to it. To determine whether a letter is interesting, ask yourself:

1. Does the opening sentence say something of interest to the reader? Will it capture the reader's attention?
2. Do the friendly tone and "you" viewpoint make the reader want to go on reading?
3. Do the clear, natural style of writing and the logical development of ideas make the letter easy to read and understand?
4. Does the letter continue to keep the reader involved?
5. Does the ending drive the point "home"?
6. Does the letter's sincere and helpful attitude make the reader feel that the writer actually *wanted* to write the letter and is genuinely interested? Or does it sound as though its writer is tired and bored?

Unit 10

LETTER FORMAT AND LETTER STYLES

The appearance of your letter is the first impression your reader has of you and the organization you represent. You want that impression to be a positive one, so it is important to format your letter correctly and use a correct letter style. The *format* of a business letter refers to the horizontal positioning of the parts of a business letter—heading, opening, body, and closing. *Style* is the arrangement of these four parts into a block or modified-block letter style.

How your letter is placed on the page will make an impression on the reader. Your letter will look balanced and the impact of its message on the reader will be heightened if the left and right margins are equal as well as the top and bottom margins.

Format of a Business Letter

The parts of a business letter must be arranged in a horizontal sequence that makes the letter meaningful.

The Heading

Return Address. A heading is needed when you write your letter on plain paper. Start about 2 inches from the top of the paper with your street address as the first line and your city, state, and ZIP Code as the second line. Never put your name or that of your organization in the heading.

Another way to include your return address is to type it below the writer's typed name:

Sincerely,

Larry Allison

Larry Allison
304 East 11th Street
Tifton, GA 31794

Putting the address after the signature is becoming popular because it seems so logical; however, it doesn't look as formal.

Dateline. Type the date immediately below the city, state, and ZIP Code as follows:

4083 Robinson Street
Abilene, TX 79601
September 10, 19—

When you use a company or organization letterhead, the dateline is the only part of the heading you need. The street address, city, state, ZIP Code, and phone number are already printed on the letterhead. The dateline should be at least two lines below the letterhead and at least four lines above the inside address.

Always spell out the month and year; for example, *May 4, 19—*. Using all digits can lead to misinterpretation. For example *7/9/89* may mean *July 9, 1989* to you, but to a military person or a European it means *September 7, 1989*. European or military datelines are written with the day preceding the month (for example: *4 May 19—*) and no comma.

The Opening

The purpose of the opening is to direct the letter to its destination and to greet the reader. It may include an inside address, an attention line, and a salutation.

Inside Address. When writing the inside address, include the name and courtesy title of the addressee; the name of the addressee's company (when available); the street address; and the city, state, and ZIP Code. You can avoid errors if you follow these guidelines:

Write the addressee's name exactly as he or she writes it, and spell it correctly.

If you know the correct courtesy title (*Mr., Mrs., Miss, Ms.*), use it with the name. If you are unsure of the addressee's sex (*Terry, Chris, Gerry*), omit the courtesy title. If you are writing to a woman and are unsure of her marital status and her preference for a courtesy title, omit the courtesy title rather than offend her. Surveys show that many women do not like the title *Ms.*

When addressing a letter to a doctor, use the abbreviation *Dr.* for the courtesy title, and avoid using double titles as in *Dr. Sara E. Briggs, M.D.* (*Dr.* and *M.D.* mean the same thing.) Either of these forms is correct; both use a salutation of *Dear Dr. Briggs.*

Dr. Sara E. Briggs
Sara E. Briggs, M.D.

Use the addressee's job title (*Personnel Manager, Sales Manager, Maintenance Superintendent*) when you know it. This title can be located in one of three places: (1) after the addressee's name, (2) on the second line of the inside address by itself, or (3) on the second line of the inside address in front of the organization name. You should choose the location that will make the lines of your inside address most nearly the same length. Let's look at an example of the position title in all three locations:

Mrs. Anita Cook, Personnel Manager
Continental Shale & Coal Company

Dr. Ellsworth A. Cunningham
Manager, Creative Designs

Mrs. Carol Ghibaudy
Owner and Manager
Harold's Star Market

House numbers and building numbers are expressed in figures, except for "one" (*One Carriage Lane*, not *1 Carriage Lane*), and are written without a prefix (*520 Dawn Street*, not *#520 Dawn Street* or *No. 520 Dawn Street*).

In street names write out *North, South, East, West, Southeast, Northwest*, and the like, to avoid misreading.

If the street name is a number, spell out numbers up to and including ten: *7430 Seventh Street.* Use figures for numbers over ten: *606 14th Avenue.* Omit the ordinal endings *st, d*, and *th* when a word like *North* or *South* separates the two numbers: *324 South 57 Street.*

Write *street, avenue*, and similar designations in full.

Type abbreviations for sections of a city this way: *3535 North Vermilion, NW* or *3535 North Vermilion, N.W.* When you have a section designation, it is important that you include it as part of the street address.

A post office box number may be used in place of the street address:

Mr. Randy Felgenhauer
P.O. Box 852
Albion, MI 49224

If both a street address and a post office box number are provided, the box number should be typed just above the city, state, and ZIP Code. This almost always means your letter will reach the addressee quicker.

The city, state, and ZIP Code should always be on one line. Do not abbreviate the name of the city unless it is customarily abbreviated. For example, *St. Louis* and *St. Paul* should be written with the word *Saint* abbreviated. Use the two-letter state abbreviations (both capital letters with no periods and with no space between them) recommended by the U.S. Postal Service, or write the name of the state in full. A list of the states and Canadian provinces and their corresponding two-letter abbreviations is provided in the Reference Section. Leave one space (use no punctuation) between the state and ZIP Code.

Attention Line. Use an attention line to speed up the handling of a letter when it is addressed to an organization rather than to a named addressee. There are several accepted forms. You may include the person's name and courtesy title. If you do not know the name of the person, refer to him or her by title or use the name of a particular department.

Leave a double space between the inside address and the attention line and also between the attention line and the following salutation. The attention line may be typed in all capital letters, or typed in initial caps and underscored. Use a colon after the word *Attention.*

Attention: Miss Julia Malivuk
ATTENTION: CUSTOMER SERVICE MANAGER

When an attention line is used, the salutation should be *Ladies and Gentlemen:* or *Ladies:* or *Gentlemen:*.

Salutation. The salutation is the greeting to the reader and helps set the tone of the letter. When typing salutations for business letters, leave a double space above and below the salutation. Abbreviate the titles *Mr., Mrs., Ms.*, and *Dr.* but spell out titles such as *Major, Professor*, and *Reverend.* Capitalize the first word and any noun or title in a salutation: *My dear Miss Marsh, Dear Father Tedrick, Dear Senator Taylor.*

With the increased emphasis on avoiding sexist language, salutation problems arise. Following are some solutions to salutation problems. The salutation must agree with the first line of the inside address. If the first line of the inside address is to:

1. An individual, such as Mr. Jeff Winland, the salutation should be *Dear Mr. Winland.* If you are friendly with Mr. Winland, use *Dear Jeff.*

2. An organization or a box number that you might find in a blind ad in the newspaper, the salutation should be *Ladies and Gentlemen* or the more conventional *Gentlemen.* If the group is composed entirely of women, use the salutation *Ladies*. You should never put *Dear* in front of these salutations.

3. A person's title, use *Dear Sales Manager* or *Dear Personnel Manager*.

When you are sending a form letter, use an appropriate nonsexist salutation such as *Dear Customer, Dear Friend, Dear Parents*.

The use of the sexist *Dear Sir* and *Dear Madam* is rapidly declining in business correspondence.

Unusual salutations—sometimes referred to as "dearless" salutations—which start letters in a friendly, conversational way are growing in popularity. These have been used for some time in sales promotion letters but are now being used in other informal business letters. Among the unusual salutations are the greetings *Good morning, Mr. Wilson; Hello, Mrs. Tabels; Merry Christmas, Ms. Skoog*. A letter may also start right out with the message. The reader's name is then inserted in the first sentence.

Miss Margaret D. Ryan
One South 42 Street
Adrian, MI 49221

Thank you, Miss Ryan, for your suggestions, which will help us to serve you more efficiently.

The Body

The body of the letter is where the writer's thoughts are presented to the reader. It consists of the message and, optionally, a subject line.

Subject Line. A subject line precedes the message to tell the reader in one glance what the letter is about. It is typed a double space above the message and a double space below the salutation.

The subject line may be typed in all capital letters, or typed in initial capitals and underscored, as you can see in the examples below. It may be centered, begun at the left margin, or indented, depending on the letter style that you are using.

Dear Mr. Butcher:

Subject: Revision of City Sales Tax

Dear Mrs. Manning:

SERVICE CALLS ON WEEKENDS

Message. When typing the message, single space each paragraph and double space between paragraphs. You may either block or indent the first line of each paragraph five spaces if you are using a modified block style letter.

Paragraphs that are too long are not easy or inviting to read. A good rule to follow is that your first and last paragraphs should be no more than four lines long and all other paragraphs should be no more than eight lines long.

The Closing

The closing in a business letter typically includes a complimentary closing phrase, the writer's name and title, and reference initials. It may also include the typed name of the organization, an enclosure notation, a mailing notation, a copy notation, and a postscript.

Complimentary Closing. The complimentary closing is a parting phrase that indicates the message has ended. It is typed on the second line below the last line of the message. Only the first word is capitalized. The complimentary closing is followed by a comma unless you are using open punctuation.

The tone of the complimentary closing should match that of the salutation. If you have greeted your reader with *Dear Marcy*, you will probably close with *Sincerely*. Here are some typical closings:

Formal	Personal
Yours truly,	Sincerely yours,
Respectfully yours,	Cordially yours,
Yours very truly,	Sincerely,
Very truly yours,	Cordially,
	Best wishes,

Organization Name. Some business organizations include their name to indicate that the organization—not the writer—is legally responsible for the message. If used, the organization name should be typed in all capitals on the second line below the complimentary closing (see the illustration following the next paragraph).

Writer's Name and Title. Leave three blank lines for the handwritten signature, and type the writer's name. The writer's title or department can go on either the same line with the writer's name or a separate line, depending on which location will make your lines most nearly the same length.

Sincerely yours,
TROGLIA CONCRETE CO.

Art Troglia

Art Troglia, President

Cordially yours,

Eleanor E. Turner

Eleanor E. Turner
Reservations Manager

A man does not use a courtesy title (*Mr.*) before either his handwritten or his typed signature unless his name could also be a woman's name. A woman who is sensitive about her courtesy title (*Miss, Mrs.,* or *Ms.*) should include the courtesy title in the signature. It may be added to either the handwritten or the typewritten signature.

Several correct forms of a writer's signature along with the appropriate courtesy title are shown in the five illustrations that follow:

Sincerely,

Alice Wernigk

Ms. Alice Wernigk

Sincerely,

Elizabeth L. Weaver

Elizabeth L. Weaver, Ph.D.

Sincerely,

(Miss) Grace Stevenson

Grace Stevenson

Sincerely,

Catherine Smith

Mrs. Catherine Smith

Sincerely,

Lynn Winkle

Mr. Lynn Winkle

Reference Initials. The initials of the dictator and the transcriber are usually typed at the left margin. They should be placed a double space below the last line in the signature section. The dictator's initials may be omitted in situations where the dictator is the signer of the letter.

Some popular reference-initial styles are:

SME:PRG	MVL/ef
GCBrown:sn	owc (typist's initials only)

Enclosure Notation. An enclosure is anything included in the envelope with the letter. The enclosure notation is positioned at the left margin below the reference initials. The notation helps both writer and reader to confirm that the enclosures to be included are there when the letter is sent and received. If there is more than one enclosure, the number is indicated.

Enclosure	Check enclosed
2 Enc.	Enclosures:
	1. Catalog
Enclosures 2	2. Reply card

Copy Notation. If you wish the addressee of the letter to know you are sending a copy to someone, type a copy notation one line below the enclosure notation (if used) or below the reference initials. With the increased use of photocopy machines, *pc* (photocopy) is being used in place of *cc* (carbon copy). Here are some accepted styles:

JCC:dh	JCR:al
Enclosure	PC: Slayton & Sisk
cc Mrs. Opal Sheetinger	
PCN/rl	RWP:jeh
CC James Broderick	Enc. 4
	pc: James Busch
	Geneva Byerly

If you do not want the addressee to know you are sending a carbon to one or more other persons, type the notation *bcc* or *bpc (blind copy)* in the upper left corner of the file copy and any other copy on which the notation is to appear. The original letter should be removed from the typewriter before typing the blind copy notation to keep any impression of the letters off the original. Any of the forms used for a regular copy notation may be used for a blind copy notation.

Postscript. A postscript can be used to give strong emphasis to an important idea that has been deliberately withheld from the body of the letter.

Postscripts should be limited to occasions when you wish to take advantage of their attention-getting qualities. Using a postscript to express an afterthought may be viewed as poor planning and organization.

A postscript is typed on the second line below whatever was typed last. Type *PS.* or *PS:* and leave two spaces before the first word of the postscript, or omit the abbreviation *PS.*

The following are accepted postscript styles:

mls
Enclosure

PS. Mail the card today!

EEB:dm

    For your complimentary copy, just call collect (903) 644-4289.

Styles of a Business Letter

When selecting a letter style, consider the design of your organization's letterhead as well as the image you want to convey. The two most popular letter styles today are *modified-block* and *block*.

Modified-Block Style

The letter style that is used most often is known as the *modified-block style;* its features are explained in the illustration shown below.

Block Style

Another appropriate letter style used in business offices is *block style,* which is illustrated and explained on page 110.

Punctuation Style

The two punctuation styles commonly used today are *standard* (or *mixed*) *punctuation* and *open punctuation.* Standard punctuation calls for a colon after the salutation and a comma after the complimentary closing. Open punctuation requires no punctuation after the salutation and the complimentary closing.

Continuation Pages

If a letter is more than one page in length, each page after the letterhead should be typed on plain paper that matches the quality of the letterhead. Each continuation-page heading begins on the seventh line from the top of the page and consists of (1) the name of the addressee, (2) the page number, and (3) the

The Quaker Oats Company, Merchandise Mart Plaza, Chicago, Illinois 60654

April 9, 19--

Mrs. Heather Michaels
Berbaum Corporation
43 Brickyard Road
Fredricksburg, VA 22401

Dear Mrs. Michaels:

The modified block style is the most frequently used letter style in business today.

The format for this letter style has the date line, complimentary closing, company name, and writer's signature and title beginning at the horizontal center. All other lines begin at the left margin (unless you wish to indent the paragraphs). Enclosed is a sample letter showing indented paragraphs.

The modified block style usually uses standard or mixed punctuation. This means that a colon is typed after the salutation and a comma after the complimentary closing, as illustrated in this letter.

Please return the enclosed reply card if you would like to receive one of our Training Department's booklets on letter formats.

The enclosure notation below shows an acceptable style for specifying the items that are enclosed.

Sincerely yours,

QUAKER OATS COMPANY

Dennis R. Hillard

Dennis R. Hillard

DRH/ism
Enclosures
1. Letter
2. Reply Card

Modified-block style letter
(Courtesy of the Quaker Oats Company)

Kansas City Royals

P.O. BOX 1969
KANSAS CITY
MISSOURI 64141
(816) 921-2200

February 15, 19--

Mr. Larry Irons
Hutton, Irons & Hesser
Attorneys at Law
102 Ray Court
Hillsboro, TX 76645

Dear Mr. Irons

Subject: Block Letter Style

All lines begin at the left margin with a block style letter,
as shown here. The primary appeal is that it is faster to
keyboard than the modified block style.

This letter also illustrates the open style of punctuation,
which means that punctuation is omitted after the salutation
and complimentary closing.

When a subject line is used, it may be typed as shown here.
The word Subject may be omitted, or the entire line may be
typed in capital letters. Since the subject line is considered part of the body, it should be typed a double space
above the body and a double space below the salutation. On
a block style letter the subject line begins at the left
margin.

This style has a neat, streamlined appearance, as you can see,
and looks very modern. It eliminates many extra keyboarding
strokes and motions and, therefore, helps to increase letter
production rates.

The "cc" notation below shows an acceptable style for indicating that copies of this letter are being sent to two
persons.

Sincerely

Mary L. Carr

Mary L. Carr
Public Relations Director

lk
cc Ralph Lawrence
   Jim Barnes

Block style letter (Courtesy
of Kansas City Royals)

date. Leave two blank lines below the last line of the
continuation-page heading. The following are two
acceptable styles:

Mr. Edward Orr
Page 2
August 28, 19—

Mrs. Erna Averstreet   2   May 3, 19—

In typing continuation pages, follow these guidelines:

1. Carry at least two lines of the body of the letter to
the second page; do not type only the closing lines of
the letter on the second page.

2. If a paragraph is divided at the end of a page, leave
at least two lines at the bottom of the first page, and

carry at least two lines to the top of the second page.
Do not divide a paragraph containing fewer than four
lines.

3. Never divide the last word on a page.

Addressing Envelopes

The minimum size for envelopes allowed by the U.S.
Postal Service is 3½ by 5 inches, and the maximum
size (without paying a surcharge) is 6⅛ by 11½
inches.

Most business letters are mailed in No. 10 envelopes (4⅛ by 9½ inches); some correspondence is
mailed in No. 6¾ envelopes (3⅝ by 6½ inches). A
correctly addressed No. 10 envelope is illustrated on
page 111.

CARGILL

1283 North Conant Street
P.O. Box 179
Maumee, Ohio 43537

Postage

```
NAME OF RECIPIENT
INFORMATION/ATTENTION LINE
DELIVERY ADDRESS
POST OFFICE STATE ZIP CODE
```

Correctly addressed No. 10 envelope. The notations "Certified" and "Registered"
are each typed on the ninth line from the top edge of the envelope and about five
spaces in from the right-side edge. (Courtesy of Cargill, Inc.)

When addressing a No. 10 envelope, such as the one illustrated above, follow these guidelines.

1. Single space the address regardless of the number of lines.

2. Address should be on the lower half of the envelope and all lines start at the center.

3. The mailing address may be typed in all capital letters with no punctuation.

4. Always write the city, state, and ZIP Code on one line and use the same rules as for inside addresses on page 105. Since the advent of automated mail sorting by the postal service, you should never type anything below the city, state, and ZIP Code on the envelope. Using the ZIP Plus Four allows automatic sorting in the order the mail is delivered on the route.

5. Write special mailing notations (AIRMAIL, CERTIFIED OR REGISTERED) in all capital letters below the stamp or postage meter insignia.

6. Recipient notations PERSONAL, HOLD FOR ARRIVAL or CONFIDENTIAL should be written on the third line below the return address.

7. Attention lines may be written as the second line of the mailing address or on the third line below the return address.

Folding Letters

When folding a letter for a No. 10 envelope, fold the bottom third of the letter up, then fold the top third down, and insert the last crease into the envelope first. When folding a letter for a No. 6¾ envelope, bring the bottom half up to within ⅜ inch of the top and crease. Next fold the right third toward the left and crease, fold the left third toward right and crease, and insert the last crease into the envelope first.

The illustration given below shows the correct way to fold letters for both large and small envelopes.

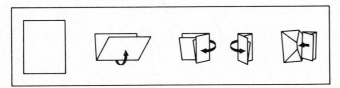

FOLDING A LETTER FOR A No. 6¾ (SMALL) ENVELOPE

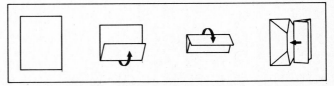

FOLDING A LETTER FOR A No. 10 (LARGE) ENVELOPE

ASSIGNMENT: Complete Sections A, B, C, D, and E of the Worksheet to apply the principles you learned in Unit 10 about letter format and letter style.

Unit 10 Worksheet

LETTER FORMAT AND LETTER STYLES

A *Identify the letter style and punctuation style illustrated in each of the stick letters below. Incorrect examples should be identified as such.*

1. Letter style: _____

Punctuation style: _____

2. Letter style: _____

Punctuation Style: _____

3. Letter style: _____

Punctuation style: _____

4. Letter style: _____

Punctuation style: _____

B *ARRANGING LETTER PARTS. Each of the letter parts below is correct in itself, but the order of the lines in each part is incorrect. Arrange the lines in correct order using the blank lines provided in the answer column.*

5. The heading:
  a. Greeley, CO 80631

  July 19, 19—

  111 Cronkhite Lane

a. _____

_____

_____

b. February 16, 19—

    P.O. Box 2383

    Akron, OH 44304

b. _____

   _____

   _____

c. University, AL 35468

    785 Dawn Avenue

    October 24, 19—

c. _____

   _____

   _____

6. The opening:

  a. ATTENTION: MR. LEE INGRAM

    112 East Walnut Street

    Ladies and Gentlemen

    Jean's Added Touch

    San Angelo, TX 76901

a. _____

   _____

   _____

   _____

   _____

  b. Burlington, NC 27215

    24637 North 62 Street

    Miss Claudia Notar

    Subject: Homecoming

    Dear Claudia:

b. _____

   _____

   _____

   _____

   _____

  c. Manager, Sales Department

    Gilbert Auto Supply

    433 North Gilbert Street

    Fairbanks, AK 99701

    Mr. Ken Christie

    Dear Mr. Christie:

c. _____

   _____

   _____

   _____

   _____

7. The closing:

  a. Sincerely yours,

    Director of Marketing

    Ernest B. Baker

    Enclosures 3

    ERB:ms

a. _____

   _____

   _____

   _____

   _____

  b. BERKOWITZ MUSIC CO.

    Cordially,

    TS/jw

    Mrs. Terry Swaim, Manager

    cc Mr. Dale Beyers

b. _____

   _____

   _____

   _____

8. The heading:
   a. No. 735 West 8th Street
      Montgomery, Ala, 36109
      Dec. 6th, 19—

      a. _____

   b. 830 No. Clay St.
      New Haven, Conn. 06511
      July 2nd, 19—

      b. _____

9. The opening:
   a. Personnel Manager
      Williams Travel Firm
      Fourteen 7th Street, N.W.
      Washington, 20003 DC
      Dear sir,

      a. _____

   b. Fairchild Real Estate
      #207 Fairchild Street
      Fairbanks, Alaska, 99701
      ATTENTION: MS. SALLY LIN
      Dear Ms. Lin,

      b. _____

10. The closing:
   a. Sincerely Yours,
      Word Processing Digest
      Miss Marcy Sanders
      es, MS
      CC to Mr. David Sheehan,
         Mr. Shawn Young

      a. _____

   b. Cordially,
      FINLEY ELECTRONICS
      Mr. Kyle Fioch, Sales mgr,
      KF/oy
      Enclos. 3

      b. _____

D · MAKING A FINAL COPY FROM AN EDITED ROUGH DRAFT

11. Write (preferably type) the final copy from the rough draft you edited in Unit 7, Problem 1. Proof the final copy carefully.

E · ADDRESSING ENVELOPES AND FOLDING LETTERS

12. Use a No. 10 envelope or cut a piece of paper the size of a No. 10 envelope (4⅛ x 9½ inches) and type or print the following information in the correct place: (a) Certified; (b) Confidential; (c) Mr. William Fields, 246 North 16 Street, Elizabeth City, NC 27909 0402; and (d) your return address.

13. **a.** A letter folded properly for a No. 6¾ envelope has _____ folds.
b. A letter folded properly for a No. 10 envelope has _____ folds.

Unit 11

WRITING ROUTINE CORRESPONDENCE

An office employee with the ability to scan, underline, annotate, and then respond to routine incoming mail can heighten office productivity.

Your ability to write routine letters and memos is an important asset for promotion. Many people in management positions today have found that their ability to organize, set priorities, and write effectively has contributed to their career advancement.

Routine letters and memos that office support personnel may be asked to write include:

1. Requests for information.
2. Answers to routine inquiries.
3. Acknowledgments.
4. Referrals.
5. Transmittals.
6. Travel-related communications (reservations and appointments).
7. Invitations and replies to invitations.
8. Follow-up letters.
9. Meeting notices.
10. Instructions to other office personnel.
11. Messages of appreciation, congratulation, or sympathy.

Use the basic outline for good news and neutral news letters on page 55 when composing these routine messages.

Signing the Letter

When writing a routine letter or memo, you must decide whether to send it over your own signature or your employer's.

1. *Letters and memos that you sign* should reflect your writing style. For instance, your employer should be referred to in the third person—"Ms. Parker suggested" or "Mr. Paxton requested." Type your name and title below the complimentary closing, as illustrated below.

2. *When you write over your employer's signature*, try to adopt your employer's writing style, making the message sound like one he or she would have written. Use the first person ("I" or "we") instead of "Ms. Parker" or "Mr. Paxton." Add your own initials when you sign the executive's name.

Sincerely,

Janice Cole

Janice Cole
Assistant to Larry Paxton

Sincerely,

Larry Paxton
JC

Larry Paxton
Sales Manager

Accepting Correspondence Responsibilities

You will find many ways to improve your correspondence skills, whether the employer is in the office or traveling. Increase your ability to handle routine correspondence by accepting these five basic responsibilities.

1. *Check incoming letters for discrepancies in dates, facts, and figures.* Suppose you receive a letter that mentions the date of a monthly meeting as Tuesday, May 6. Automatically consult the calendar to verify that Tuesday is the 6th. Should you find that Tuesday is the 7th, you must check further and write for clarification. You may determine that these meetings are regularly held on Monday rather than Tuesday. In your response you then might tactfully ask, "Am I correct in putting this meeting on the calendar for Monday, May 6?"

2. *Note in your tickler file all promises of further correspondence made in outgoing letters.* For example, when you write a letter in which you mention that your employer will write the addressee again in a few weeks to arrange a meeting, immediately enter a follow-up reminder in the tickler file. Then, at the appropriate time, call your employer's attention to the need to firm up arrangements for the desired meeting.

3. *Confirm (in writing) appointments, invitations, and similar telephone and in-person conversations.* Embarrassing and costly mixups often occur when the time, place, and other details arranged orally are not confirmed in writing.

4. *Recognize the importance of writing letters of appreciation and congratulation and other goodwill messages promptly.* You can fulfill this responsibility by regularly checking newspapers and trade journals for items that suggest occasions for goodwill messages from your employer.

5. *Proofread carefully the letters and memos you write, sign, and mail for your employer.* Errors in typing, spelling, and word usage that you fail to detect reflect unfavorably on you, your employer, and the organization you both represent.

Preparing Routine Communications

Typical examples of correspondence written on your own initiative or at your employer's request follow.

Information Letters

You may often find it appropriate to prepare letters giving routine information. The following exchange between office support personnel with Commonwealth Edison (Washington, D.C.) and the Alpena (Michigan) Chamber of Commerce illustrates such correspondence.

Dear Alpena Chamber of Commerce:

Will you please send me the opening and closing dates of your Springfest this year. A group of our managers would like to include a

---

day at your famous festival during a conference trip to Alpena.

Sincerely yours,

Mrs. Martha Pentecost

Martha Pentecost
Assistant to Tom Bracewell

Dear Mrs. Pentecost:

Our Springfest this year opens on Thursday, May 2, and ends on Saturday, May 11.

We have added your name to our mailing list to receive all special announcements concerning the daily parades, shows, concerts, and other attractions. We believe your representatives will find our Springfest an enjoyable part of their trip.

Sincerely yours,

Dennis Hart

Dennis Hart
Assistant to Kelly J. Moore

Units 12 and 13 will give you additional principles for writing clear, concise inquiries, requests, and replies.

Acknowledgments

One kind of routine letter that you frequently write for your employer is the acknowledgment of a communication received when your employer is away from the office. Some typical acknowledgments are:

1. Letters. When you receive a letter that must be held for your employer's attention, business courtesy requires that you send a stopgap letter. It is a short, direct acknowledgment that explains (1) why an answer will be delayed and (2) when it may be expected. Be careful not to obligate your employer or to give out confidential information about why he or she is absent. An acknowledgment letter might read like this:

Dear Mr. Melecosky:

Thank you for your May 14 letter asking Mrs. Langas to speak at your meeting on July 10.

Mrs. Langas is out of the office this week. As soon as she returns, I shall bring your invitation to her attention.

Sincerely yours,

Jeanene Lowery

Jeanene Lowery
Assistant to Mrs. Langas

Another example of a stopgap letter is one written to explain that more time is needed to prepare a complete answer. Often a person writing for information does not realize that it might take several days and communication with several departments to get the facts together for a reply. When this is the case, send a short note—usually over your employer's signature—to explain the delay. For example:

Dear Mr. Ingersoll:

You can expect the information you asked for in your March 21 letter in a few days. In order for my report to be helpful to you, I must get data from both the sales and the advertising departments.

I am glad to cooperate with you on this project and expect to send a complete answer by the end of the week.

Cordially yours,

Frank Larsen
pg

Frank Larsen
District Manager

When a delayed reply is a common occurrence, a form letter or postal card may be sent. With a word processor, you can easily make a form letter appear to be an individually written letter. If you were employed in an office that handled numerous property loss claims, for example, you would build goodwill by acknowledging each claim on the day it was received with a brief message such as:

Dear Mrs. Brown:

Your recent notice of loss has arrived, and it is receiving our prompt attention. You will receive a complete reply as soon as the property loss you described is evaluated.

---

2. Information or Material. You should write acknowledgments when packages, requested information, and other messages or materials are received. These acknowledgments should be direct, concise, and courteous. They should thank the reader and include the details needed to identify the items received, since they become a record for the files. A form message may be useful for many similar acknowledgments.

The principles of good writing are illustrated in the following example of a routine acknowledgment of signed contracts.

Dear Mrs. Sennhenn:

The signed contracts relating to the Kestell case arrived this morning. Thank you for sending them so promptly.

Sincerely,

George Byron

George Byron
Assistant to Diane Turner

---

3. Gifts and Favors. Simple and sincere thank-you acknowledgments should be written for gifts and favors as well as for congratulatory and other goodwill letters received from clients and friends.

Dear Miss Fabrizio:

You were most generous to send copies of your interesting booklet *Dictation for Productivity* for all the members of our office staff.

Your commonsense discussion of dictating—with checklists and clever illustrations—will certainly help our dictators and the office support personnel in our Word Processing Department.

Sincerely yours,

Jennifer Kerner

Jennifer Kerner
Assistant to Mrs. Rice

---

4. Remittances. Remittances by check are often not acknowledged. The sender's canceled check serves as notice that the payment has been received. However, some managers believe that the goodwill gained by a written acknowledgment outweighs the time and expense of writing the letter.

A letter acknowledging a remittance should (1) be brief, (2) express appreciation, (3) give the amount and form of remittance, (4) tell what the remittance is for, and (5) build goodwill through a warm, friendly tone. Two occasions on which you should always send a letter acknowledging a remittance are: (1) when a customer pays his or her first invoice and (2) when the remittance is an unusually large one.

Dear Mr. Fitzgerald:

Your Check 482 for $350 arrived today and has been credited to your account.

We do appreciate your prompt payment, which reduces your account balance to $150.

    Cordially,

Mark Adams
        ms

    Mark Adams
    Credit Manager

The acknowledgment of orders is discussed in Unit 14.

Referral Letters

Letters received in an office can sometimes be answered better by someone elsewhere in the organization. If the person you refer the letter to is not in the same office, or, for any other reason, cannot reply immediately, you should send a referral letter to the writer. A copy of this letter, along with a request to reply, is then sent to the person to whom it is being referred. Here is a short, courteous referral letter.

Dear Terry Campbell:

Your question about service on your telephone answering machine can be answered best by our distributor.

I am therefore referring your letter to Mr. Adam Passavage, manager of the Service Department at Columbia Private Telephone Inc.

    Cordially yours,

Lynn Swanson
        rr

    Mr. Lynn Swanson

cc: Mr. Adam Passavage

Transmittal Letters

Transmittal letters are cover letters sent to accompany information or articles. Cover letters are discussed in detail in the section "Writing Cover Letters" in Unit 13. The transmittal (or cover) letters you might write may be as simple as this one to a dealer.

Dear Mrs. DeBarba:

Here are the advertising mats you requested.

Your interest in promoting the Schwinn bicycle in Milwaukee's newspapers is appreciated.

    Sincerely,

Melinda Kelly

    Melinda Kelly
    Assistant to Brian Carpenter

Invitations and Replies to Invitations

There are two types of invitations that you may be called upon to handle:

1. Formal. Formal invitations follow an established pattern and are usually printed with each line centered. To prepare a formal invitation or write a reply to one, you should refer to an up-to-date book of etiquette (one of the "must" reference books in the office) for correct wording and arrangement. Even when an invitation is printed, you should check the copy for accuracy of dates, time, place, spelling, and other details.

Invitations that include an R.S.V.P. (which means "please reply") require an answer. Replies to formal invitations should be handwritten on folded notepaper. Write in the third person and follow the style and wording of the invitation. If accepting, express pleasure; refuse with regret and give a reason.

A formal invitation with corresponding acceptance and refusal are illustrated on page 122.

2. Informal. Informal invitations are written in letter format and are more casual than formal invitations. In addition to "inviting," they should specify the day, date, time, place, type of function, reason for the function, who is included in the invitation, dress requirements (if any), and a request for a reply. Here is an informal invitation.

Dear Mr. Hoggatt:

Mr. Allen is inviting the members of the Restoration Committee for the Southern Aire Opera

House to meet with him for lunch on Friday, June 8, at The Rusty Nail at 12 noon. He would like very much for you to come.

Mr. Allen would like the committee to discuss specific suggestions for the fund-raiser to be held in October.

Will you please let us know by Monday morning whether you will be able to attend the luncheon and meeting?

Sincerely yours,

Lucy Monroe

Lucy Monroe
Assistant to Mr. Allen

When responding to an invitation, express pleasure at being asked, confirm all the details, and make it clear exactly who will be attending. If the invitation must be refused, express regret.

An acceptance of an informal invitation might look like this:

Dear Mrs. Gilbreath:

Thank you for asking me to speak at the annual meeting of the National Association of Physical Therapists in San Diego on Friday, November 9. I shall be delighted to do so.

As you suggested, I have made a reservation for Friday night at the Travelodge on Toronto Road. Since my plane (TWA Flight 526) is scheduled to arrive in San Diego at 4:10 p.m., I should have plenty of time to check into the hotel before the 7 p.m. meeting begins.

I look forward to seeing you on November 9.

Very truly yours,

Rhonda Lappen
sk

Rhonda Lappen, Manager
Physical Therapy Department

Follow-Up Letters

You may be expected to follow up on (1) information or articles that were requested or promised and not received promptly or (2) enclosures that were omitted from correspondence. Use a tone of reminding rather than of criticizing. Be brief, but include enough information for the recipient to recall the earlier letter or discussion. Identify the promised item(s), and clarify what you want the recipient to do.

Dear Mr. Natho:

We have not received the committee report on proposed changes in insurance coverage which was promised for last Friday, April 3.

Mrs. Johnson must have it by April 10. She plans to use it as a basis for preparing for a meeting with the insurance company on the 13th.

Sincerely yours,

Beth Sullivan

Beth Sullivan
Assistant to Mrs. Johnson

Dear Ms. Sutton:

Your letter of March 24 mentioned as an enclosure the Treasurer's Report for the American Chemical Society. However, the report was not in the envelope when the letter reached us.

Will you please send us another copy today?

Sincerely,

Tom Barnett

Tom Barnett
Assistant to Dr. Engle

Meeting Notices

Sending notices about meetings is another type of routine correspondence that you will be called upon to handle. Meeting notices, along with agendas and minutes, are discussed in Unit 9.

Internal Communications

You frequently will be asked to write notes or memos to other people in your organization. Tone is important in these informal messages. Even though you write and sign internal communications, the recipients will react to them as if they were personally written by your employer. The memo on page 123 is an example of a concise internal communication that you might write.

Messages of Appreciation, Congratulation, or Sympathy

There will be occasions when your employer will want you to write a letter to a friend who has been promoted or has received an award, or to acknowl-

FORMAL INVITATION TO DINNER

Mr. and Mrs. John Sleevar
request the pleasure of
Mr. and Mrs. Eric Nelson's
company at dinner
on Friday, the twenty-first of May
at seven o'clock
Thirty-six Daisy Lane

R.S.V.P.   Black Tie

Formal invitation to dinner.

REFUSAL OF FORMAL INVITATION TO DINNER

Mr. and Mrs. Eric Nelson
regret that a previous engagement
prevents their accepting
the kind invitation of
Mr. and Mrs. John Sleevar
on Friday, the twenty-first of May
at seven o'clock
Thirty-six Daisy Lane

Refusal of invitation to dinner.

ACCEPTANCE OF FORMAL INVITATION TO DINNER

Mr. and Mrs. Eric Nelson
accept with pleasure
the kind invitation of
Mr. and Mrs. John Sleevar
to be present at dinner
on Friday, the twenty-first of May
at seven o'clock
Thirty-six Daisy Lane

Acceptance of formal invitation to dinner.

Snow Cream Castle

```
TO:        All Staff Members

FROM:      Carol Craig

DATE:      December 12, 19--

SUBJECT:   Reception for Marilyn Hunter


This is just a reminder that the reception for
Marilyn Hunter is next Friday, December 16, from
3 to 5 p.m. in the Hospitality Room.

Because of your generous contributions, we shall
present Marilyn with a gold pendant in appreciation
of her valuable contribution to our organization
during the past 30 years.

cc
```

edge a marriage or anniversary, or a similar happy event. You may also be asked to write a letter to offer sympathy for a death or personal misfortune. These goodwill letters are discussed in Unit 15.

Evaluating Your Writing

Business communications, no matter how simple or informal, require careful planning, preparation, and review. As you reread a message you have composed, answer these questions:

1. Does it look attractive?

2. Is it accurate with respect to language, grammar, punctuation, spelling, and typing?

3. Is it concise while including enough information to make the message clear?

4. Will the reader know exactly what to do and when to do it, without further communication?

5. Is the tone positive rather than negative?

6. Have you used the "you" attitude by talking about your reader rather than yourself or your organization?

7. Does your message present a favorable image of you, your employer, and your organization?

If you can answer "Yes" to these questions, congratulations! You have written an effective business message!

ASSIGNMENT: *The Worksheet problems will give you an opportunity to plan and prepare the routine correspondence discussed in Unit 11.*

Unit 11 Worksheet

WRITING ROUTINE CORRESPONDENCE

A *PREPARING ROUTINE COMMUNICATIONS—EXECUTIVE OUT OF THE OFFICE. Using separate sheets of paper, plan and prepare (preferably type) letters and memos to fit the situations described in the following problems.*

Background for Problems 1–5: You are an assistant to Mrs. Fern Lockhart, a vice president of Procter & Gamble. Mrs. Lockhart is also a member of the executive board of the Colorado Historical Society. Her office address is 403 S. Forrest Avenue, Littleton, CO 80120. Today is Wednesday, February 10. Mrs. Lockhart left last Friday for a two-week vacation and you are to handle the correspondence while she is away.

1. You receive a letter from Robert Payne, Public Relations Director, Eastman Kodak, 942 Warrington, Yuma, AZ 85364, asking the dates of the Old Pioneer Days Festival that your company cosponsors each year. Prepare a reply to this request for information. The festival begins with a 10 a.m. parade, June 2, and closes with 10 p.m. fireworks, June 5. Procter & Gamble has cosponsored the event since 1956. Profits are to go to needy people in the community. Food is available, and life in the days of the covered wagon will be demonstrated. Sign your own name.

2. Dr. Charles Evans, President of Austin College, 1700 La Costa Boulevard, Sherman, TX 75090, has written Mrs. Lockhart, an honor graduate of Austin College, inviting her to present the commencement address at this year's graduation which will be held at 2 p.m. on Friday, June 15. Prepare an acknowledgment of this invitation, and sign your own name.

3. About a month ago, Mrs. Lockhart wrote a letter to Miss Lois Holmes, Customer Service Manager, Anderson-Gordon Design Inc., 3715 Illini Street, Auburn, ME 04210, asking for 100 copies of the pamphlet *Packaging With Pizzazz*, which she plans to distribute to each sales manager attending Procter & Gamble's national sales meeting (March 5–11). The pamphlets arrived today. Prepare the letter acknowledging receipt of the pamphlets, and sign Mrs. Lockhart's name.

4. You receive a check (Check 306 for $17.25) from Jim Cintella in your Legal Department for the book *Our Colorada Heritage*, recently published by the Colorado Historical Society, which Mrs. Lockhart sent him on approval. Write the memo acknowledging receipt of the check, including the appropriate information for the *To:*, *From:*, *Date:*, and *Subject:* lines. Put your name in the *From:* line.

5. In today's mail is a letter from Larry Rife, Manager of Rife's Market, 723 Oak Street, Bacone, OK 74420, asking for information about stocking Procter & Gamble products in his store. Refer Mr. Rife's request for information to Tony Johnson, Marketing Manager. Write the referral letter, and sign Mrs. Lockhart's name.

B PREPARING ROUTINE COMMUNICATION—EXECUTIVE IN THE OFFICE. *Using separate sheets of paper, plan and prepare (preferably type) letters and memos to fit the situations described in the following problems.*

Background for Problems 6–10: You are an assistant to Mr. Freemont Ireland, Marketing Director, Lakeview Medical Center, Berea, OH 44017. In addition to his responsibilities at the Medical Center, Mr. Ireland has had a leadership role in the Berea United Way for several years and last year served as general chairman of the fund drive.

6. Mr. Ireland asks you to get a copy of last year's Lakeview Medical Center Annual Report and send it to the administrator of Children's Research Hospital, 800 Harmon, St. Petersburg, FL 33733. Mr. Ireland met the administrator, Mr. F. M. Hoskins, on a recent business trip and promised to send him an annual report. Prepare this transmittal letter, and sign your name.

7. Write a letter for Mr. Ireland's signature to welcome Donald L. Glines, a new member of the board of Lakeview Medical Center. Invite him to lunch next Wednesday at the Rivercrest Country Club at noon for the purpose of discussing matters concerning the Medical Center. Ask Mr. Glines to confirm by telephone whether he can accept the invitation.

8. Your follow-up file indicates that you should have received facilities-utilization statistics (occupancy rate of hospital beds) for the past six months from the Accounting Department yesterday for a marketing report Mr. Ireland is preparing. Prepare a follow-up memo from you to Rita Calvert in Accounting. The complete report is due one week from today.

9. Write a letter for Mr. Ireland's signature accepting an invitation that arrived today for him to speak about the United Way Fund Drive on Tuesday, October 1, at the Lions Club noon meeting to be held at the Ramada Inn. Explain in your acceptance that the United Way gives assistance to local people and that you hope his talk will prompt Lions Club members to "dig deep" for contributions. The invitation came from the program chairperson, Don Baldwin, 1237 Perrysville Road, Berea, OH 44017.

10. Write a transmittal memo to Mary Brant, Payroll Department Manager, sending her a copy of an article, "Advantages of Direct Deposit," from the last issue of *Newsweek*. When you had coffee with her a couple of days ago, she mentioned that she would be interested in investigating direct payroll deposit for your organization.

Unit 12

WRITING INQUIRIES AND REQUESTS

People write *inquiry* letters—letters that ask for information—when they want to know more about a product or service. People write *request* letters when they want a specific action taken. Inquiry and request letters can be grouped into four types.

1. *Appointment and reservation requests.* These letters set up meetings or reserve overnight accommodations.

2. *Buying inquiries.* These letters ask for information about products or services the writer is interested in purchasing.

3. *General requests.* These are requests for information, without any intention on the part of the writer to buy or sell. They ask for details and facts the reader can give with a minimum amount of time, effort, and expense.

4. *Persuasive requests.* These are requests for cooperation, gifts, or favors, without any intention to buy or sell. They attempt to persuade the reader to spend time or money, or to go to some trouble to help the writer—usually without benefit to the reader.

The first three types use the direct approach (see page 57), while the fourth uses the persuasive plan (see page 57). Let's look at each of these four types of inquiries and requests. Notice the change in approach between the letters that will benefit the reader and the ones that will benefit the writer.

Appointment and Reservation Requests

Business people often write letters making or changing appointments and reservations. These letters are short and businesslike, but the writer must be certain to include exact dates and all other necessary details to prevent any misunderstandings.

Use the direct plan (see page 57), and follow these suggestions for appointment and reservation requests.

1. *Make sure the facts are accurate.* Think of the problems one error in the date could cause for the reader and for you. You can prevent such errors by always giving the day of the week with the date. Also, develop the habit of checking the day and date with your calendar every time—don't trust your memory!

2. *Give all necessary details.* Remember, simple requests should be concise and specific. (See the paragraphs that follow and the letters illustrating them.)

3. *Keep the tone courteous and friendly.* Write in the attitude of "please" rather than in a demanding tone that will leave a bad impression of you.

4. *Close by expressing appreciation, indicating possible action, or looking forward to the event.*

Requests for Appointments

Details to include are day and date, time, place, and purpose of the appointment or meeting. It may save some correspondence if you offer alternate dates and times. If you must change the time or date of an appointment, do it as soon as you know and give a satisfactory reason. The other person deserves better than a last-minute excuse.

This sample letter asks for a change in the date of an appointment, states the reason for the change, and then gives the reader the opportunity to set the date for the next appointment.

Dear Mr. Farrar:

Will it be convenient for me to demonstrate our new Mirror XL Copier to you next Thursday instead of next Tuesday? Can we reschedule our meeting for July 23 at 3 p.m.?

We are exhibiting at a business and office products show in Milwaukee on July 21 and 22, and I have been assigned to work that exhibit.

If Thursday, July 23, is not convenient for you, would you suggest a later date? I'm looking forward to meeting with you.

Sincerely,

Requests for Reservations

Reservations for overnight accommodations should include the following details: number of adults and number of children, number of rooms, number and size of beds per room, number of nights, arrival and departure days and dates, and the name of the convention or group meeting you are attending (if applicable). Be sure to request a corporate rate when you make the reservation if you are traveling for your organization. If you will arrive after 6 p.m., you should either (1) ask that the room be held for late arrival, (2) guarantee the reservation, or (3) send a deposit. Ask the hotel to send you a written confirmation of the reservation including the details above as well as the rate. This way there will be no surprises.

Here is a sample reservation letter:

Marriott Hotel
5161 River Road
Washington, DC 20016

Attention: Reservations Department

Ladies and Gentlemen:

Please reserve a moderately priced room with one double bed for one adult for six nights—Sunday, April 7, through Friday, April 12. I will be attending the National Information Systems Convention.

I would appreciate receiving a written confirmation before April 1.

Sincerely,

Buying Inquiries and General Requests

When you write a buying inquiry or a general request, you are asking for information. Use the direct plan (page 57), and follow these suggestions.

1. **Begin With Your Questions.** Get to the point immediately and tell the reader exactly what you need to know.

2. **Word Each Question Carefully.** Ask for specific information so as to avoid ambiguous questions.

Use questions rather than statements. Notice that the question below is shorter than the statement. And the question mark immediately tells the reader that an answer is expected.

POOR: I would like to know the colors in which Doubleday Mills sculptured shag carpet is available.

BETTER: What colors are available in Doubleday Mills sculptured shag carpet?

Make the question specific—not general. A general question usually brings a general answer, which often repeats what you already know instead of giving you the details you want.

POOR: What can you tell me about your computer?

BETTER: How does your computer compare with the Satellite II computer in price, features, memory size, and portability?

Be careful of the question that can be answered "Yes" or "No" and still not tell you what you really want to know. A "Yes" answer would be satisfactory for a question such as "Do you have it in stock?" But what about a "Yes" answer to "Is it available in any other color?"

POOR: Is the guarantee on the Westminster grandfather clock a good one?

BETTER: What is the length of the guarantee on the Westminster grandfather clock, and what does it cover?

3. **Briefly Explain Why You Are Asking.** Include all facts—such as the use you plan to make of the information requested—that will help the reader answer you. This is especially important if you are requesting general information with no intention of buying products or services.

4. **Omit Details Not Helpful to the Reader.** Incidental comments clutter up a letter and make it harder for the reader to determine the exact information you want. However, if you are writing in response to an advertisement you've seen, you should mention the name, date, and page number of the publication.

5. **Stop When You Are Finished.** Too many beginning writers tend to repeat in the closing sentences things they have already said, just because they do not know how to stop. A good way to end is by saying you *are looking forward to* or *will certainly appreciate* receiving the information.

If you are going to ask several questions in one letter, put each question in a separate paragraph. A letter that groups several questions in a single paragraph is hard to answer. The reader must make a special effort to identify each question and may easily overlook one.

You can make your questions stand out by numbering them, as in the inquiry below. You may include explanations at the beginning, at the end, or in the paragraph with the question (see question 3), whichever is most appropriate.

Ladies and Gentlemen:

Please send me answers to the following questions about the Centurion Computer advertised on page 59 of your current COMPUTER CATALOG.

1. Will the CRT screen remain sharp and clear after continuous use for several months?

2. How should I clean the CRT screen?

3. Will prolonged use of the CRT screen cause eyestrain and headaches? I would like to purchase a computer to use on my job, but I hesitate to because I have heard that looking at a CRT screen can cause permanent damage to the eyes.

I shall appreciate receiving this information within two weeks, since I am planning to purchase a computer soon.

Sincerely,

As you begin to *answer* inquiries and requests in Unit 13, you will see the importance of *writing* inquiries that follow these suggestions.

Persuasive Requests

When you read the persuasive letter at the top of the next page which was sent to alumni of Arkansas State University, you will see how effectively it captures the interest and secures the cooperation of the reader with its approach and its use of the "you" attitude. When you write a persuasive request, follow the persuasive plan on page 57 and follow these suggestions:

1. Begin With Something That Will Interest the Reader. You already know a great deal about the opening paragraphs of persuasive letters from the discussion under "The Best Approach," which was included in Unit 6.

The approach for persuasive requests is entirely different from the approach for direct inquiries. When you ask someone about a product or service he or she is trying to sell, the reader becomes interested because the inquiry is an opportunity to sell. But when you ask for a gift or favor, you must point out

the advantage to and stimulate the interest of the reader. If the request is made bluntly or selfishly, the reaction is likely to be "Why bother?" Since you want a favorable response, avoid starting with the request. Get the reader interested in your story before asking for an answer.

Successful persuasive approaches often stress the following themes:

Altruistic appeal, with emphasis on benefits to others, as illustrated in this opening paragraph of a letter from the Easter Seal Society:

Nobody works harder than crippled children to overcome their handicap. But they need help . . . your help and ours.

Reader-benefit appeal, as illustrated in the following excerpt from a sales manager's plea to salespersons to improve their personal appearance:

How often do you take time for a second look at your appearance? Your customers do every day.

Your appearance is a preview of the way you might handle your customers' affairs. When you take pride in yourself, your customers feel that you also take pride in what you do for them.

Individual-responsibility appeal, as illustrated in the approach an editor used in a request for information from readers:

You are part of a carefully selected sample of candy industry executives receiving this letter. Over the last 5 years, your experience and leadership as an experienced candy industry executive have played a major role in improving the CANDY KING CATALOG.

Your answers to the enclosed questionnaire are extremely important in providing your industry with *the* most useful CANDY KING CATALOG possible.

Personal-experience appeal, as illustrated in the recall of childhood memories in this excerpt from a letter trying to persuade the reader to donate money to help build a zoo:

Remember the kick you got out of going to the zoo when you were a youngster? Seeing the strange animals and birds was quite a thrill, wasn't it? And the excitement of feeding time! Won't you agree that such experiences are long remembered by youngsters lucky enough to visit a zoo—and that they should be a part of every child's growing up and every grownup's reminiscing?

2. After You Select the Strongest Theme for Your Approach, Follow Through with a "You" Attitude Explanation of the Reason for the Request. Effective explanations often contain two popular features:

a. *Emphasis on an advantage to someone other than this writer*—to the reader or the reader's organization—as illustrated in this paragraph from a letter asking

ARKANSAS STATE UNIVERSITY

OFFICE OF THE DEAN
COLLEGE OF BUSINESS
P.O. BOX 970
STATE UNIVERSITY, ARKANSAS 72467
TELEPHONE 501/972-3035 JONESBORO

October 8, 1986

Dear Alumni:

The College of Business is conducting a survey of our alumni in an attempt to obtain information which will assist in improving the quality of our academic programs and thereby benefit our current and future students. The information received from you will aid us in identifying the kinds of activities in which our graduates are involved and the progress they have made in their professions, including salary attainment.

In addition, our Academic Program Review Committee can benefit from information from former students regarding the strengths and weaknesses of our programs as well as suggestions for improving them.

The individual information collected will be held in confidence and only released in the form of college and department summary statistics. My staff and I eagerly await your reply. Please return the survey in the enclosed envelope by November 20.

Sincerely,

L. E. Talbert

L. E. Talbert, Dean
College of Business

ss
Enclosure

This letter persuades by emphasizing the benefits its request will bring to the reader's university. (Courtesy of Arkansas State University)

wholesale clothing buyers to complete a questionnaire for a fashion merchandising organization.

> Your cooperation in this project will be of definite help to the garment industry, as you can readily see. But it will be of even more benefit to you as buyers, because the results of the survey will be used by our members to develop better merchandising methods and to give better service to individual buyers.

b. *Complimentary reference to the reader,* as illustrated in this sentence from a letter asking a business executive to address the high school FBLA Club:

> We know that any pointers you can give us on management techniques will be stimulating and helpful to our students.

3. State the Request in Definite and Specific Terms after you have prepared the way for it. Be sure the reader knows exactly what you want and how and when he or she is to respond. Notice how explicitly this writer requests the cooperation of a club member.

> Specifically, Jane, these are the things I am asking you to do:
>
> 1. Attend the monthly meetings.
>
> 2. Chair the Club Carnival Committee. You are to form the committee and send a list of the members to the Secretary by March 1. Submit a plan for this year's Club Carnival to the Secretary by April 15. Your annual committee report will be due on July 30.
>
> 3. Serve as adviser to the Recreation Committee. Your experience should be especially valuable to this

committee, and I have asked its chairperson to contact you directly.

4. Write a cover letter for the attached questionnaire, which will be sent to all members.

4. Stimulate Action with Closing Remarks Suggesting That Compliance Will be Easy and Satisfying.
Doesn't this closing paragraph make viewers feel that supplying the information requested by a TV station will be simple yet worthwhile?

Our questions are easy to answer. We will not use your name—no one will try to sell you anything. We have stamped the ballot—so no postage is necessary. But we *do need* your vote—so please fill in the few blanks on the enclosed ballot, fold it, seal it, and drop it in the mail.

5. Reflect Appreciation of and Confidence in the Reader's Favorable Response. Sincere belief in peo-

ple and an optimistic outlook shine through every paragraph of most successful persuasive letters.

Notice the positive tone in the following excerpt from a persuasive request.

This will be the most important vote you will cast between now and November 2. And this vote will count more, because you are one of 1500 AMS members but just one of 50 million voters in the presidential election.

Here is another excerpt using the positive tone.

For many of us, our Beta Xi Foundation experience has been a spark which has helped light our lives. Your financial support of the Foundation today can create a living endowment to light many more lives yet to come.

More complex persuasive requests will be discussed in Unit 16, "Writing Persuasive Letters."

ASSIGNMENT: Complete Section A of the Worksheet for practice in improving poorly worded inquiries. Then try your hand at planning, composing, and writing (preferably typing) inquiries and requests in Section B.

Name _____

Date _____

Unit 12 Worksheet

WRITING INQUIRIES AND REQUESTS

A *REVISING POOR INQUIRIES*

1. The following inquiries are unsatisfactory because they are poorly worded, incomplete, wordy, or ambiguous. In the space provided, rewrite each question, making sure that your revision is concise and that it asks for the exact information needed. Make up any information you need to correct a fault.

   a. How much does a coat cost?

   _____

   _____

   b. Could you give me information about renting a camera?

   _____

   _____

   _____

   _____

   c. What can you tell me about the cruise you advertised in the paper the other day?

   _____

   _____

   _____

   d. May I take my electric hair dryer with me and use it in Germany?

   _____

   _____

   e. How much should I expect to pay for a hotel close to Disney World?

   _____

   _____

   _____

2. This wordy and rambling letter needs tightening up. The six jumbled questions should be presented as a list for easy identification. Rewrite the letter in the space provided.

Ladies and Gentlemen:

While visiting a friend last week, I saw his electronic typewriter, which is a Type-Master 400, and I liked it. So I decided I might like to have one of my own. However, since my
friend's typewriter was a gift, he didn't know anything about
the cost, etc. I'm wondering if you could answer some of the
questions that my friend couldn't answer.

I would like to know the cost of the typewriter if I ordered
it from you and whether the shipping charges would be extra.
My friend's typewriter is red, but I wonder if it comes in
other colors. Also I'd like to know if it comes with a carrying case and if proportional spacing is available. Could you
tell me whether the typewriter has a guarantee?

If you will please answer all these questions, then I can decide whether to buy or not to buy a Type-Master.

B *PLANNING AND COMPOSING INQUIRIES AND REQUESTS. Make
a plan for each message in Problems 3–8. Use the space after each problem
for your plan. Follow the suggestions in the "Letter Planning Chart,"
Unit 6, pages 55 and 56. On separate sheets of paper, write a rough draft
from each plan, edit each rough draft, and then prepare (preferably type)
each letter in correct format. Make up or assume any information you need
to be specific in each inquiry.*

3. *Appointment Letter.* Write a letter to Mr. Collins to set up an appointment the first Wednesday of next month to
review the requirements for this year's Interstate Industries annual report.

Richard Collins
Manager

Sun Graphics Inc.

148 Industrial Parkway
Parsons, Kansas 67357
Phone: (316) 421-6200

Letter Plan:

_____

_____

_____

_____

_____

_____

_____

4. *Reservation Letter.* Make reservations for you and three other executives at the Holiday Hotel, 51 South Gilbert Street, Albuquerque, NM 87120. You want separate rooms for the nights of April 7 and 8. You will be arriving around 10 p.m.; you need to know the checkout time. Enclose a list giving the names and addresses of the other three executives.

Letter Plan:

_____

_____

_____

_____

_____

5. *General Request Letter.* Write a letter to Pitney Bowes asking for 10 copies of the free booklet *How to Address Your Mail for More Efficient Processing in the Electronic Age*, which was advertised in this month's issue of *The Secretary*. You plan to distribute the copies to the administrative assistants in your organization. Also, ask for some literature about a postage meter suitable for an office mailing fewer than 200 pieces a day.

Letter Plan:

_____

_____

_____

_____

_____

6. *Persuasive Request Letter.* Write a persuasive request as a representative of Toys for Tots, an association that tries to make sure that every child in the community receives a toy at Christmas. Address the request to the Rotary Club in your town and ask that the group "adopt" a child for Christmas. The club may select its child from descriptive (though anonymous) lists prepared by Toys for Tots, who will distribute the gifts donated.

Letter Plan:

_____

_____

_____

_____

7. *Buying Inquiry Letter.* You are an assistant at Food Pack Inc., 500 North Atlantic Avenue, Lorman, MS 39096. Fred Miller, the General Manager, gives you the note shown below.

Compose the inquiry letter for Fred Miller, after preparing a letter plan in the space provided. Assume the calendar shown here is the calendar for the current year.

> **From the desk of Fred Miller**
>
> Please write a letter to the Sheraton Inn in Lorman to inquire about arrangements for our annual Spring Banquet (May 20) for our 20 department managers and their spouses. Plan for a minimum of 25 and a maximum of 40 to attend.
>
> Ask for sample menus and prices for the dinner.
>
> The dinner is to be served at 6:30 p.m., but we will want the use of the private banquet room until 10:30 p.m.

MAY

SUN	MON	TUE	WED	THU	FRI	SAT
○ FM 5	● LQ 12	1	2	3	4	5
6	7	8	9	10	11	12
13	14	15	16	17	18	19
20	21	22	23	24	25	26
27	28	29	30	31	● NM 19	● FQ 27

Letter Plan:

_____

_____

_____

_____

_____

8. *Persuasive Request Letter.* As president of the Student Advisory Council of your school, write a persuasive request to Don Newcombe (104 Harvey, Philippi, WV 26416), a noted lecturer. Ask Mr. Newcombe to address an assembly to be held on the first Friday of next month at 2 p.m. in the Conference Center on the topic "Drugs and Alcohol." You can pay travel, meals, and hotel expenses but no fee.

Letter Plan:

_____

_____

_____

_____

_____

Unit 13

WRITING REPLIES TO INQUIRIES AND REQUESTS

When you receive an inquiry or a request letter about your organization's products or services, you have a prospective customer. Answer the inquiry that very day, while the sender's interest is highest. It takes no more time to answer the letter today than it does to answer it next week, and the results will be better. If you cannot answer the inquirer immediately, write and explain the reason for the delay and also give a time when you can send an answer. Many organizations spend thousands of dollars on advertising to attract inquiries and then throw away the results of that advertising by the haphazard way they handle the inquiries. A prompt answer improves your chances of turning an inquirer into a customer.

Answering "Yes" to Inquiries and Requests

Use the direct plan (see page 57) when you say "Yes" to an inquiry or request, and be sure to do the following in your reply:

1. Give the Exact Information Requested. Say in the first sentence that you are granting the request or answering the inquiry. A common error in answering inquiries is the failure to answer some of the questions asked. Prevent this common error by developing the habit of marking on the letter of inquiry the points or questions to be addressed. Before your reply is typed, double-check with the original letter to see that each point or question has been adequately covered. When answering "Yes" to a request for an appointment or reservation, repeat in your letter all the details such as date, time, and place.

2. Express Appreciation for the Inquiry. Tell the customer, either directly or by implication, that you are glad he or she has written to you about one of your organization's products or services. Write in the spirit of service and goodwill. The tone of your reply should express your appreciation.

3. Sell Your Organization or Product. Put "sell" into every letter you write. An inquiry tells you the customer was interested when he or she wrote, but what guarantee do you have that the interest is still "hot"? Stress the benefit of converting interest into action.

4. End With a Positive Closing. Offer to give further assistance, and end with a goodwill closing.

When inquiries are clear, concise, and specific, they are easy to answer. Here's a good example.

Ladies and Gentlemen:

Please send me some information about the paper you make that is used for letterhead stationery.

I've been asked to do some research and write a proposal to recommend the paper and the layout for new letterhead stationery for my organization.

Specifically, I'd like to know:

1. What weight of paper you would recommend for letterhead.

2. What percent of cotton fiber content the paper should have.

3. Whether it is proper to use colored paper for letterhead.

4. What information should be included in the letterhead.

Could you please reply by July 7, since my proposal is due a few days after that?

Sincerely,

Immediately after this request was received, the following reply was written and sent. Since all the customer's questions could be answered positively, the writer used the direct approach.

Dear Mr. Warfield:

Enclosed are samples of the paper we recommend for letterhead stationery. We are happy to answer the questions in your June 15 letter because the content and design of your organization's letterhead create a first impression of your organization.

1. Letterhead is printed on 16-, 20-, or 24-pound paper. The weight is figured as the weight of four reams of 8½- by 11-inch paper.

2. Paper for letterheads should have a minimum of 25 percent cotton fiber content. Paper to be used for documents that need to be kept over 10 years should contain 100 percent cotton fiber content. The higher the weight and the higher the cotton fiber content, the higher the quality (and the price) of the paper.

3. Although white is the predominant color of paper used for letterheads, colors like beige, ivory, pale blue, and pale green are gaining popularity today.

4. A good letterhead should answer the questions Who? (name of your organization), What? (the nature of your business), and Where? (mailing address). Be sure to include a phone number in addition to your address. Many organizations also include a logo or trademark.

I've enclosed a booklet called The Letterhead Analyzer, which will give you an analysis of the psychological effect of different colors used for letterheads. The booklet also contains several sample letterheads that won awards for outstanding design and layout last year.

I would suggest you consider hiring a professional artist to help you with the design of your letterhead. If you have additional questions, please write again or call me at (109) 823-3312.

Sincerely,

When you reply to a letter containing several questions, be sure to answer every question completely. Put each answer in a separate paragraph. If the questions are numbered in the inquiry, number your answer to correspond, as the writer of the preceding letter did.

If you have a positive answer for every question, numbering the answers is easy to do. But if you don't have a positive answer for every question, start with your most positive answer and work your way down to your weakest answer. This sequence will prevent you from starting your letter with a negative answer! Reread the inquiry on page 129; then read the following reply to that inquiry. Could this reply have been strengthened by putting the answers in a different order?

Dear Judy Cooper:

Thank you for your interest in our Centurion Computer. Your letter of October 2 asks some very intelligent questions, which we are happy to answer for you.

1. The CRT screen should remain sharp and clear for years, not just a few months.

2. Clean the CRT screen with a soft, damp cloth. Do not spray window cleaner directly on the screen; just spray the cleaner on a cloth and use the cloth to wipe the screen.

3. There is no conclusive research to prove or disprove that use of a CRT screen causes eyestrain, headaches, or permanent damage to the eyes. Tests have proven that a green screen is easiest on your eyes when working for extended periods of time with a computer.

You will be pleased with the Centurion Computer, because it is the leader of personal computers for business applications. All our new software will be Centurion Computer-compatible.

Please stop by our showroom for a demonstration of the Centurion Computer. We look forward to having you join our many satisfied customers.

Sincerely,

Answering "Yes" to Persuasive Requests

It's easy to answer a persuasive request when you can say "Yes." A smiling "Here it is" or "I'll be glad to" just about sums up the reply. Follow the direct plan on page 57 and use these suggestions:

1. Start With a Cheerful "Yes." Open your letter with the good news that will make your reader happy.

I'll be at the seminar to help in any way I can. The solution to the school dropout problem is important to me, too, and I'm glad you planned the seminar.

If the request is granted grudgingly or with reservations, you will probably lose the goodwill you could expect to gain by saying "Yes."

2. Confirm Details of the Request and Acceptance. The confirmation can be included with the "Yes" in the first paragraph, as in this opening sentence:

> We are pleased to enclose a copy of our annual report.

Otherwise, the confirmation should follow in the next paragraph and should repeat the details of the request to be sure the reader and writer agree. For example, a letter accepting an invitation to give a talk at a meeting should confirm the date, time, and place and the subject and length of the talk. Or if a contribution is enclosed, the letter should state the amount and purpose.

3. Ask for Any Additional Information Needed to Comply with the Request. For instance, a speaker accepting an invitation to conduct a seminar wrote, "Can you provide a screen and overhead projector so I can show transparencies during my presentation?" A vendor agreeing to act as coordinator of the annual Instrument Society of America Vendor's Night Show wrote, "Will you help me out by sending me a copy of last year's budget, timetable, and invitation list?"

4. Show Special Friendliness by Giving Something Extra When the Gesture Seems Appropriate. If you give more than is expected, the reader will feel good about coming to you and you will have increased the goodwill that is the ultimate goal of every letter you write.

The "something extra" may be an offer to do more than requested, as in these examples.

a. An Eastern Illinois University professor accepts an invitation to speak at the Indiana Vocational Association (IVA) convention in Indianapolis, with expenses paid but no fee, and offers to come at no expense to the nonprofit organization:

> Since I will be in Indianapolis that week on other business, I shall be happy to speak to the IVA convention on Monday, May 1, or Tuesday, May 2, at no expense to your organization.

b. A college graduate sends a contribution to the Alumni Fund and writes:

> I'll be glad to call the members of my class and add a little personal persuasion to the fine letter you sent them.

Or the "something extra" may be an expression of interest and willingness to help further if asked, as in these two excerpts.

a. A travel agent sends the brochures requested by a student and closes the letter with:

> Just write me if I can give you any more help. I certainly want that geography report to earn an "A."

b. A business executive sends an author the sample letter requested, with permission to reproduce it, and closes the letter with:

> Please let me know when I can help you again. When will your book be published? I'm interested in purchasing a copy for my library.

Answering "No" to Inquiries and Requests

When you must say "No," use the indirect plan on page 57, and deliver the bad news gently and tactfully. Strive to let courtesy and thoughtfulness shine through your letter. A gracious refusal is much like a persuasive request—you are asking your reader to accept your decision as the only fair answer under the circumstances.

You have already seen these principles applied to writing letters in which it was not possible to say "Yes." Do you remember how tactfully a store said "not now" to the customer who asked it to stock Petite sizes (Unit 5, page 44)? How a firm said "No" to a request from one of its dealers to purchase advertisements in two suburban telephone directories (Unit 6, page 54)?

Remember that this type of letter has two purposes: (1) to say no, while (2) keeping the goodwill of the reader. To accomplish both purposes, consider these suggestions.

1. Approach the Letter as an Opportunity to "Talk It Over" and to give whatever encouragement you can—not as a plain "No." If you think, "I must decline this invitation or this order or refuse this request," you will probably write negatively. But you will probably write constructively if you think, "What can I do to encourage this person even though I have to say 'No'?"

2. Start with a Friendly, Pleasant Buffer Paragraph. If you receive a letter that begins, "It is my unpleasant duty to inform you that . . . ," or, "I'm sorry to tell you that we cannot grant your request . . . ," don't you immediately close your mind to whatever else the writer may say? You will think that the writer is not interested in helping you, in building goodwill, or in keeping your friendship. The writer seems concerned only with saying "No" and getting an unpleasant task completed. But suppose the letter begins, "Your proposal for a joint meeting of Phi Beta Lambda (PBL) and Future Business Leaders of America (FBLA) is exciting, José." Aren't you more likely to read the rest of the message with an open mind?

3. Tell the Reader Why You Cannot Say "Yes." In your explanation, imply that you would rather say "Yes" than "No." And try to compliment the reader in some way. The PBL president who received the following explanation certainly felt that she had chosen a worthwhile film.

Many PBL groups throughout the nation have enjoyed *Preparing for Your First Job Interview*. In fact, Lisa, it is our most popular film. Last March we had three additional prints made so that it would be available to more clubs, but even these are booked well in advance.

4. Avoid a Negative Refusal. Explain before you refuse. A blunt "No" should be avoided. If your letter does a good job explaining, the reader realizes that you cannot do what he or she has asked—the "No" is inferred. If you must state your refusal (to be sure your reader realizes you are not granting the request), avoid emphasizing it or putting it in negative terms. Sometimes limiting expressions, such as *only* or *exclusively*, may substitute for negatives such as *regret, apologies, cannot,* and so on. Notice how this actual business letter dwells on the negative and almost obscures the positive points.

Dear Sir:

We are very sorry that your portrait has been damaged. This rarely happens to Pixie photos.

I regret to advise that we cannot hold negatives for a long period of time, because we lack sufficient storage space; therefore, we will not be able to reprint your portrait. I am, however, processing a refund in the amount of $15.95, which you should receive within the next six weeks. I am also returning the damaged 5 by 7 portrait to you with a free coupon.

Please accept our apologies for this problem, as we greatly value your patronage.

With kindest personal regards.

The following letter shows interest in the reader and tries to keep his business while refusing the request.

Dear Mr. Brooks:

We were happy to hear that your family was so pleased with your portraits. And we are sorry that one was damaged. Since our storage space is limited, however, all negatives are destroyed ten days after an order has been filled.

Your 5 by 7 portrait is being returned, along with a refund of $15.95. You should receive both in about three weeks.

Please use the enclosed coupon for a complimentary 5 by 7 color portrait when Pixie Photos returns to Amarillo on December 1.

---

5. Give Encouragement—And When You Can, Give Help. Sometimes you can take the sting out of a "No" with a helpful suggestion. For example, a department store representative, in declining an order for an article not carried by the store, may tell the customer where he or she can make the purchase. The reservations manager of a New Orleans hotel, not able to make the reservations requested, suggested:

> If you can conveniently defer your arrival in New Orleans until May 15, we shall be glad to reserve a double room for you and your wife. If you must be here on May 10, you might write for help to the Greater New Orleans Hotel Association, at 105 Poydras Street, New Orleans, LA 70112.

6. Close Pleasantly With a Look Toward the Future. In your last paragraph, *don't stress or repeat the negatives*. For example, closing with "We hope our inability to grant your request does not inconvenience you too much" would leave the reader thinking how dissatisfied he or she is about your refusal. Also, *do not include an apology* in your last paragraph. Saying "We are sorry that we couldn't send the information you requested" accents what you *can't* do. Instead, emphasize what you *can* do in the last paragraph. Some possibilities include (*a*) a substitute suggestion, (*b*) an expression of your desire to cooperate further, (*c*) a wish for the reader's success, and (*d*) a pleasant off-the-subject remark.

Would you agree that the following letter says "No" graciously to a job applicant?

Dear Miss Diamant:

It was certainly a pleasure to meet you this week and have the opportunity to discuss career opportunities at Holiday Inns.

Because of its position as the number one hotel chain in the world, Holiday Inns offers unique public relations challenges and opportunities. I think you would find the hotel industry an exciting one to work in . . . and being associated with the industry leader would be an especially nice bonus.

Although there are currently no openings in public relations, I will keep your résumé in our active file. I'll be sure to give you a call if a job opening develops here at Holiday Inns that fits your skills and abilities. Thank you for thinking of Holiday Inns as your employer.

Cordially,

Writing Form Replies to Inquiries

Form letters and cards are often used in business to reply to inquiries. These forms may be prepared in connection with advertising campaigns to take care of the flood of inquiries expected.

The form letter below was prepared to answer inquiries about lodging and tours at Mammoth Cave National Park.

In today's electronic office, a form letter can be prepared on a word processor by keying in only the inside address and salutation and recalling the rest of the letter from storage. And presto, the form letter becomes an individually typed letter, which is always more impressive than a photocopied or printed form letter.

Writing Cover Letters

Printed advertising leaflets, price lists, catalogs, checks, reports, and business forms are often sent to customers, dealers, and others. Sending one of these items without comment would be a bit abrupt, like walking in without knocking. Writing a short, friendly cover letter to accompany such items is both courteous and helpful. Usually the cover letter accompanies the item being sent. If the item is bulky, the cover letter may be attached to the outside of the package or mailed separately.

A cover letter also tells the purpose of and points out pertinent details about the item sent. The sender can stress how the receiver is to use the accompanying item and can stimulate interest and prompt action. A cover letter also becomes a file record of the date and the reason something is sent or received.

A cover letter that accompanies a shipment of merchandise can create personal contact with customers and lay the foundation for future sales. Just sending

Dear Prospective Visitor:

We are pleased to answer your request for information about Mammoth Cave National Park. The enclosed material should answer many of your questions about the area.

We appreciate your interest in Mammoth Cave and look forward to having you visit the park soon.

       Sincerely yours,

       Ron Hartley

       Superintendent

Enclosures 2

A form letter, already prepared, can be especially useful if you have a flood of inquiries.

the merchandise would be enough, but the cover letter is that "something extra" that can strengthen the goodwill between the organization and its customers.

Mail-order houses often receive requests for their catalogs, which are usually offered free in advertisements. When people ask for a catalog, a selling opportunity is created. A cover letter can focus attention on the catalog. Such letters may be form letters that have been prepared to generate interest in specific products or in categories of products.

Here are suggestions for writing a cover letter for merchandise or literature.

1. Start With a Short, Direct Identification of the Item Being Sent. Introduce the enclosure pleasantly by identifying the item and your reason for sending it (which may be in response to the reader's request).

2. Stress the Reader's Use of the Item. The fact that *you are sending something* isn't important. The fact that *your reader can use or enjoy it* is important. Avoid the selfish-sounding *I am enclosing* and the obvious *You will find enclosed, Enclosed please find,* and *Enclosed with this letter is (are)*.

3. Be Specific But Choose Details Carefully. Arouse the reader's interest in the enclosure by referring to specific advantages he or she may gain from it. Mentioning page numbers and marked excerpts in a booklet can stimulate reading and encourage buying. Remember, though, that the letter is only one part of the message and should never overshadow the enclosure.

4. Close With a Forward Look. Write a closing designed to promote goodwill and future business. Even when there seems no immediate possibility of a sale, try some sales promotion. And be sure to stress the service attitude.

ASSIGNMENT: Complete Section A of the Worksheet for practice in improving poorly worded replies to inquiries. Then plan, compose, and prepare (preferably type) replies to the inquiries and requests in Section B.

Name _____

Date _____

Unit 13 Worksheet

WRITING REPLIES TO INQUIRIES AND REQUESTS

A REVISING A POOR REPLY TO AN INQUIRY

1. On the lines below, improve the following reply to a prospective customer's letter:

   We received your May 2 letter. As requested, we are sending a sample of our new toothpaste called BRIGHT AND WHITE.

   _____

   _____

   _____

2. The writer of this poor reply probably lost a customer as well as a promotional opportunity. On the lines below, improve the following reply.

   Referring to your letter of January 15, I am sorry to tell you that the nuclear war video game, First Strike, about which you inquired, is currently out of stock and will not be available until early January. We deeply regret that you cannot receive this game in time for Christmas, but perhaps you would like to try ordering some of our other games. You will find several in our current catalog.

   _____

   _____

   _____

   _____

   _____

   _____

   _____

   _____

   _____

   _____

B PLANNING AND WRITING REPLIES TO INQUIRIES AND REQUESTS. *In the space provided, make a plan for each message. Follow the suggestions in the "Letter Planning Chart," Unit 6, page 55. Then write a rough draft from each plan, edit your rough draft, and prepare (preferably type) each letter in an acceptable format.*

3. *Answering "Yes" to an Inquiry Letter.* You are an assistant to Mr. Cecil Neff, Sales Manager. Write a reply to the letter below from Mrs. Myler. Base your reply on the catalog information provided.

```
                              519 Sherman Street
                              Meadville, PA 16335
                              March 25, 19--


          The Picture Place
          315 South Steward
          Iola, KS 66749

          Ladies and Gentlemen:

          The manager of our local Camera Club suggested I
          write you about making pictures from slides.  I
          would like to have several prints of a recent slide.

          How much would these prints cost?

                              Respectfully,

                              Martha Myler

                              (Mrs.) Martha Myler
```

```
          50 reproductions    49.99
          30 reproductions    29.99
          12 reproductions    12.00


     finished photographs 2 1/2'' X 3 1/2''

  Kansas Residents add 6 percent sales tax

           postage prepaid

         remittance with order

Your photographs will be the same high quality that won four
National Awards for us!
```

Letter Plan:

_____

_____

_____

_____

_____

_____

_____

4. *Answering "Yes" to an Inquiry Letter.* As Commercial Exhibits Manager for your annual Business Club Show, write a reply to the following letter. Send application forms and an information brochure for prospective exhibitors. Deadline for reservations is April 1, cost per exhibit booth is $75, and this year's show will be May 2 from 8 a.m. to 5 p.m. in the Student Union ballroom. You expect 500 people to attend.

PUBLISHING COMPANY
516 EAST 42 STREET, LAS VEGAS, NV 89104   PHONE (702) 446-1152

March 1, 19--

Dear Commercial Exhibits Manager:

   I would like to exhibit at your annual Business
Club Show this year. Please send me an application
form and any other information I will need.

                    Sincerely,

                    USA PUBLISHING COMPANY

                    Sally Pifer

                    Sally Pifer
                    Convention Coordinator

Letter Plan:

_____

_____

_____

_____

_____

5. *Answering "No" to an Inquiry Letter.* Write a reply to the letter in Problem 4 turning down Sally Pifer because you have sold all the space. Offer to put her on the mailing list to receive an invitation to exhibit at next year's show.

Letter Plan:

_____

_____

_____

_____

_____

6. *Answering "Yes" to a Persuasive Request.* Write a reply to this persuasive request and send your Check 354 for $20. Also, offer to distribute some of the Association's pamphlets to all members (30 people) of your bowling league.

ALA
AMERICAN LUNG ASSOCIATION

Dear Friend:

We are writing to you because the American Lung Association is very much in need of your help.

Your gift of $5 in the last campaign was put to good use in vital health programs fighting emphysema, bronchitis, asthma, tuberculosis, smoking, and air pollution.

Today, the need for your assistance is even greater. Lung disease--especially emphysema--is a serious threat to the health of the people in your area.

We hope you will consider a gift of $5 or more--but any amount will be greatly appreciated.

Sincerely yours,

Lois Morrisey

Lois Morrisey, Volunteer

Letter Plan:

_____

_____

_____

_____

7. *Answering "No" to a Persuasive Request.* Write a "No" answer to the letter in Problem 6. Explain that you cannot contribute this year because you were injured in a car accident a few months ago and you have many expenses related to the accident that are not covered by insurance.

Letter Plan:

_____

_____

_____

_____

_____

Unit 14

WRITING AND ACKNOWLEDGING ORDER LETTERS

To stay in business, every organization needs orders for its products or services. That is the premise around which the business world operates.

Order Letters

Order letters are easy to write because (1) getting the attention and interest of your reader is no problem and (2) no convincing or persuading is necessary. All you have to do is write an order letter that will be quick and easy for the recipient to read and fill. If you write clearly enough to let the recipient know what you want and make satisfactory plans to pay for it, you'll get an answer.

Most companies include order forms with their catalogs because they are faster and easier to read than order letters, they help the buyer give complete information, and they are convenient for the buyer. If no order form is available or if you need to include explanations that will not fit the form, you will need to write an order letter. Such letters should be organized like an order form, and they should contain the same information.

You need to give every order letter the familiar *who, what, when, where, why,* and *how* test to be certain it will accomplish your purpose.

Here are five suggestions for writing effective order letters.

1. Make Them Orders, Not Just Hints. Legally, an order letter is the "offer" portion of a contract. The "acceptance" portion of the contract is completed when the seller sends the merchandise. Use specific and direct openings such as *Please send me . . .* or *Please ship . . .* rather than vague phrases such as *I'm interested in . . .* or *I'd like to. . . .*

2. Give a Complete Description of Each Item You Are Ordering. Include the following information in your order letter:

a. Quantity desired.

b. Catalog (or model or stock) number.

c. Name of product.

d. Description of product, including as much of the following as is appropriate: (1) color, (2) size, (3) material, (4) grade or quality, (5) pattern, (6) finish, and (7) any other details available.

e. Unit price.

f. Total price for desired quantity.

g. Any other information that you have, including where you saw the product advertised.

3. Give the Information in a Clear Format. To make your letter easy to read, do one of the following:

a. Write a separate, single-spaced paragraph for each item, with double spacing between paragraphs.

b. Arrange your order in a tabular form similar to an order blank.

When several sets of numbers, items, and prices are given, tabular form is clearer than writing the information in sentences.

4. Tell How You Will Pay for the Order. Give the form of payment (personal check, COD, money order, or credit card). Be sure to add shipping charges and sales tax that may be part of the total cost. If you want the item charged to a credit card, give the credit card number and the expiration date. Also, if the printed name on the card differs from the signature and typed name on the letter, be sure to give the exact name of the cardholder.

5. Tell Where and When and How You Want the Merchandise Shipped. Give the shipping address, or say that you want the merchandise sent to the address above (your return address) or below (if your address is typed below your typed signature).

If you need the order by a certain date, be sure to include that date in your order letter. And if you have a preference, include the method of shipment. Otherwise, the seller will choose the method of transportation and will ship the merchandise when it is convenient. For example, you may need the merchandise in a hurry and be willing to pay the extra cost of air express.

Merchandise is shipped *FOB destination* or *FOB shipping point.* The initials FOB stand for "free on board." If merchandise is shipped FOB shipping point, the buyer pays shipping charges over and above the cost of the merchandise. If merchandise is shipped FOB destination, the seller pays the shipping charges and they are included in the price of the merchandise.

A good order letter is illustrated below.

Form Replies to Orders

Legally, an acknowledgment letter completes the contract of a sale, but its major purpose is to encourage future orders. A letter acknowledging an order is an excellent opportunity to resell your product and your organization. Some organizations think acknowledgments are unnecessary—they take orders for granted. However, orders may not be routine for the buyer. The way the seller handles the present order may determine whether the buyer will send future orders.

An acknowledgment should always be sent promptly and is usually sent as a form reply in one of these forms:

1. Postal Card. Acknowledgment cards with "filled-in" descriptions are particularly favored by large

```
                                        1216 E. Garden Drive
                                        Cromwell, CT 06416
                                        October 5, 19--


        Citrus Hill Grove
        Bonded Shipper
        183 North Oak Street
        Tavares, FL 32778

        Gentlemen:

        Please send me the following, as advertised in the October issue of Time
        magazine on page 53:

                    Quantity           Description        Price
                1/2 bushel, 30 lb    All grapefruit      $13.75
                1 bushel, 55 lb      All oranges          18.75

                Subtotal                                 $32.50
                add shipping and handling charges          3.60
                Total                                    $36.10

        Please ship the fruit by UPS to the return address.  I would appreciate
        receiving it before November 15.

        Also, send to my sister:

                    Quantity           Description        Price
                1/2 bushel, 30 lb    All oranges         $13.75

                add charges                                1.80
                Total                                    $15.55

        Please hold her order until after December 1, then ship by UPS to:

                Mrs. Minnie Smith
                2641 East Elm Street
                Denver, CO 80232

        Enclosed is Check No. 421 for $51.65 to cover both orders.

        I am looking forward to trying your Florida fruit.

                                Sincerely,

                                Jean Whittington
                                Jean Whittington

        Enclosure
```

A good order letter is clear, quick to read, and makes it easy for the reader to fill the order.

organizations doing business with customers by mail, such as catalog houses and large department stores. Some firms send printed general acknowledgments; but most firms use printed form cards with space provided to write in the order or a description of it and the expected date of shipment. Such cards can be filled in and mailed quickly.

2. Acknowledgment Form. Acknowledgment forms are usually set up like a letter with several different items listed and a box in front of each. The sender simply puts a check mark in front of the items that apply to the particular order.

3. Invoice (Duplicate). When an order is processed, the seller must sooner or later type an invoice or a bill. If it is done sooner, one extra copy can be made, marked "Acknowledgment—This Is Not an Invoice," or something similar. The acknowledgment copy is sent to the customer immediately. When the customer receives it, he or she knows not only that the seller has the order and is working on it but also how much is due and what the terms are. Often the shipping date is shown too. A duplicate invoice is the least effective method of acknowledgment, however, because many customers resent receiving a copy of the bill prior to receiving the merchandise.

4. Individual Letter. The individual letter does the best job of building goodwill and is becoming economically feasible, with the increased utilization of computers and word processors. The content and outline for letters like this will be discussed in the "Acknowledgment Letters" section of this unit.

There is nothing wrong with a form acknowledgment as long as it reflects the same care in its preparation that the organization is giving to filling the order. A poorly printed or mimeographed card or letter can give the customer the impression that you are going to be as sloppy with his or her order. The cold, formal acknowledgment can make you seem cold, formal, and uncaring. You can use form acknowledgments successfully if you remember that no matter how many orders you get each day, every order is unique to the customer who sent it. When form letters are used, they should be revised and updated periodically so your frequent customers will not feel that they are being taken for granted.

Acknowledgment Letters

There are several situations where an acknowledgment letter is a must. These situations include the following:

1. When a Customer Sends a First Order.

2. When the Order Is Not Clear. When this happens, it is important not to throw the mistakes of the writers in their faces. Don't tell your customers they forgot—just ask for the information you need to fill the order and encourage a quick response by enclosing a reply envelope.

3. When You Receive an Unusually Large Order from a customer.

4. When You Receive Orders for Discontinued Items. Here is a real opportunity for some selling by suggesting an alternate product. When you do not have the exact item a customer has ordered, you may send a form message to the customer, with a clipping about the substitute item. The form acknowledgment shown on page 152 is part of a wraparound to hold the enclosed clipping; the back page of the form is the order blank mentioned in the message.

5. When There Will Be a Delay in Shipment. Occasionally an item will be out of stock and shipment will be delayed.

6. When It Is Your Policy to Sell Your Products Only Through Dealers. It is never a good idea to use the phrase "it is our policy" because a customer's reaction may be that you should change your policy. Just explain what your policy is; but if you must get this idea across, say "it is our practice" instead. That phrase isn't quite as strong.

7. When You Must Refuse an Order Because of the Unsatisfactory Condition of the Account of a Customer Buying on Credit. You can offer some alternative such as sending the order COD or having the customer send 50 percent of the payment before you ship the merchandise.

Routine Acknowledgment

When a complete and accurate shipment can be made, your acknowledgment letter should follow the direct or good news plan.

1. Start With the Good News by telling when and how the merchandise will be shipped. Assure the customer that you are handling the order promptly and efficiently. Be careful not to promise that the

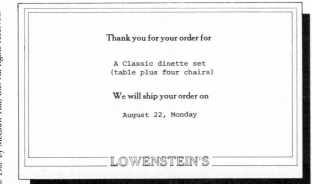

Thank you for your order for

A Classic dinette set
(table plus four chairs)

We will ship your order on

August 22, Monday

LOWENSTEIN'S

Acknowledgement cards may be filled in and mailed right away.

LOWENSTEIN'S

THANK YOU FOR YOUR INQUIRY...

We have something similar to what you are looking for—a picture and a description of it are enclosed.

Also enclosed are an order form and a return envelope that will make it easy for you to let us know your decision.

LOWENSTEIN'S money-back guarantee insures your satisfaction.

This acknowledgment shows how an order for a discontinued item can be handled by suggesting an alternate.

goods will be delivered on a specific date. It is safer to state when you *shipped* the merchandise. Remember that *order* is the word for what the buyer sends; the seller sends *merchandise*—not an order.

2. Repeat the Essential Details of the Order, such as the date of the order, order number, product name, quantity, size, and cost. Remember that a listing is much easier to read in a tabular form.

3. Build Goodwill. Thank your customer for the order and emphasize your service attitude by stressing how your product or service can help. Use a sincere and friendly tone. To be sure your letter projects the best image of you and your organization, make your letter look professional.

4. Resell Your Product and Your Organization by reassuring the reader about the quality of the merchandise and the reliability of your organization. Show genuine interest in the customer and a desire to serve. Avoid using self-centered phrases like *Our product . . . , We also make . . . ,* and *We'd also like to sell you. . . .* Use the "you" attitude, and be specific. Tell

the customer that you are looking forward to future orders.

Special Acknowledgment

Sometimes you cannot fill the order as you receive it because the order is incomplete or you no longer carry the item; or perhaps shipment will be delayed. A letter in this type of situation calls for an indirect plan. Place the emphasis on what you *can* do rather than what you can't. Avoid negative words such as *can't, delay, unable, won't, failed, forgot, error,* and *mistake.* Include the items that are appropriate for the situation from the list below. Your content will depend upon the circumstances.

1. Thank the Customer for the Order, or say something favorable about the merchandise.

2. Repeat the Order. List the essential details of the item(s) ordered.

3. Ask for the Necessary Information so that you can complete the order (avoid emphasizing the customer's error); or state the reason for delayed shipment; or suggest an alternate product. If you ask for a response from the customer, including a reply card or a return envelope will help you get a prompt, complete answer.

4. Give Shipping Information. State when and how shipment will be made.

5. Resell Your Product and Organization by mentioning the quality of your products and the reliability of your organization. By reselling the merchandise, you remind the customer that delivery is worth waiting for.

6. Promote Goodwill in the Closing with a statement indicating your desire for the reader to be satisfied with the merchandise or your desire to give good service to your customer, or both.

Read the example of a letter acknowledging an incomplete order on page 153.

Acknowledgment Refusing an Order

Some orders must be refused. It may be the policy of your organization to sell only through dealers. Or the customer's account may be in unsatisfactory condition for you to ship the merchandise on credit.

Letters refusing orders call for the indirect plan, or the "sandwich approach," with the bad news in the middle. Use the following outline for these letters:

1. Start With a "Buffer." Thank the customer for the order, and repeat the details.

2. Give an Explanation. In a positive way, tell *why* you cannot complete the order and stress what you *can do,* along with the advantages to the reader. Offer to help the reader in any way you can—give the

REDI-CHECK

2100 Minutemaker Boulevard
Waltham, Massachusetts 02154

Phone (201) 983-7746

March 15, 19--

Mr. Bob Jones
693 Gilbert Street
Hampton, VA 23366

Dear Mr. Jones:

Thank you for your order for 200 Deluxe Checks,
Stock No. 54, which we received today.

Please sign the enclosed order form and return it
to me in the enclosed postpaid envelope. Your signature is only a formality but a necessary one.
Your Deluxe Checks will be mailed as soon as I
receive this order form.

This new style of check has been very popular, and
I am sure you will be pleased with your selection.

Sincerely,

Steve Hughes

Steve Hughes, Manager
Customer Services

jm
Enclosure

If the order is incomplete, your reply should avoid negative words and emphasize what you can do rather than what you can't.

name of the nearest dealer, explain credit terms, or offer an alternate solution.

3. Say "No." Many times your explanation will imply the "No" that is coming. Be sure the refusal is clear.

4. End With a "Buffer." Resell your organization and your products.

Notice how this outline is followed in the following letter to Mr. O'Reilly.

Dear Mr. O'Reilly:

Thank you for your order for one pair of Bostonian shoes, size 10D.

The Bostonian shoe is well made and has been
the best-selling shoe in America for many
years. It is made by craftsmen who take pride
in their work. Only the finest materials are
used in manufacturing Bostonians.

Bostonian shoes are sold nationwide through a
very fine network of distributors. These out-
lets carry a complete inventory of the styles
and colors available.

Because we want you to be perfectly happy with
your new Bostonians, we are returning your
money order for $70 and requesting that you
contact Bob Surdell at:

Style Step Shoes
3356 Monroe Street
Spokane, WA 99202

Bob is one of our leading dealers, and he will
see that your shoes are perfectly fitted for
comfort.

We are sending you a flier showing our latest
styles, along with a coupon worth $5 on your
new Bostonians.

Remember, Mr. O'Reilly, Bostonians are known
as ''The Shoe That America Walks In.''

Sincerely,

Rich Lanter

Rich Lanter

mc
Enclosures
cc: Mr. Bob Surdell

This letter will make Mr. O'Reilly feel that the refusal is actually advantageous to him. When you explain the reasons for saying no, a reasonable customer will understand.

Acknowledgment letters provide an excellent opportunity to build goodwill and encourage future orders.

ASSIGNMENT: The Worksheet will give you practice in writing order and order-acknowledgment letters.

Unit 14 Worksheet

WRITING AND ACKNOWLEDGING ORDER LETTERS

A WRITING ORDER LETTERS. For Problems 1, 2, and 3, refer to the ad below from the fall catalog of the Rex Harriet Company. Prepare (preferably type) each letter in correct format on a separate sheet.

FALL CATALOG

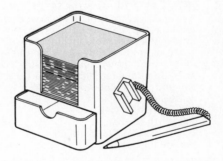

MUG FOR COMPUTER PEOPLE, with an inscription almost anyone can relate to, has special meaning for those who must deal with computers on a daily basis. Ceramic mug holds 10 ozs.
No. C2521 Old Computer Mug   **$3.50**

Rex Harriet Company
P.O. Box 75
Pittsburgh, PA 19545

3-IN-1 MEMO CUBE IS PERSONALIZED! Keep handy unit near phone, on desk or countertop. Cube comes with attached pen on curly cord and pull-out drawer for paper clips, etc. 600 rainbow-hued sheets included. We'll personalize with 3 golden initials. 600 sheet refills available. Smoke color acrylic. 4" × 4".
No. P2284 Memo Cube
    (Initials?)   **$3.98**
No. P2287 Additional Refill
    (600 Sheets)   **$1.98**

COMPUTER TERM-A-DAY CALENDAR FOR 19-- has a different computer related word and its definition for each day of the year. Example: "byte — a basic unit of storage in the memory of most computers." A great learning tool for those who want to know more about computers, a perfect gift for those already in the field. Calendar can hang on wall or stand on included easel back. 5".
No. B2682 Computer Calendar   **$5.95**

Enclose check or money order, charge to VISA or MASTERCARD, but no stamps or CODs please.

Pennsylvania residents, add 6% sales tax.

All orders FOB shipping point.

Money back if not delighted with your purchase.

PLEASE INCLUDE FOR SHIPPING AND HANDLING
Orders up to $10.00 . . . . add $1.95
Orders from $10.01 to $15.00 . . . add $2.95
Orders from $15.01 to $25.00 . . . add $3.65
Orders from $25.01 to $35.00 . . . add $3.95
Orders from $35.01 to $50.00 . . . add $4.65
Orders over $50.00 . . . . add $4.95

1. Order two computer term-a-day calendars—one is for you and the other is to be shipped as a birthday gift to Bob Bonnewell, 2121 Evergreen Road, Barrington, RI 02806.

2. Order a memo cube and one refill for yourself. Send a personal check.

3. Order the Mug for Computer People for Sam Smith, who is Supervisor of the Information Processing Department in your organization. You want it for his birthday. Charge it to your VISA card.

4. You are the office manager of Young, Adams, and Turin, Attorneys at Law, 3933 Crary Drive, Lindsborg, KS 67456. To help ensure the confidentiality of clients' legal and personal records, you decide to purchase a paper shredder for the office. After looking through several office supply catalogs, you decide on the paper shredder and accessories described below. Order one Shredmaster 2000, one cart, and a box of 100 plastic bags. Enclose a check for the down payment.

Powerful electric shredders reduce private papers to unreadable ¼″ strips!

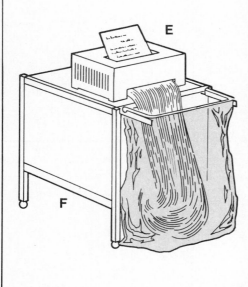

SHREDMASTER 2000
(E) FOR LETTER & LEGAL SIZE
The perfect shredding system for regular size paperwork. Materials up to 10″ wide are destroyed by ⅓ h.p. motor—up to 10 sheets of 20 lb. bond paper per pass! Even handles light cardboard, computer cards. 60 cycle, 110 volt, 1 phase, AC reversing type motor, circuit breaker equipped, cable and plug supplied. U.L. approved. Lightweight for portability, has rubber feet. For desk top use, position waste paper basket below machine to catch shredded papers. 10 h × 16¼ w × 17 d. Beige finish.
H19–1120–100
Shpg. wt. 51 lbs. $749.00

(F) CART FOR SHREDMASTER 2000
Heavy-duty chrome plated legs with walnut formica top and sides. Concealed bag holder holds clear plastic bags (16 × 11½ × 30 d), and attaches to frame beneath cart—no unsightly mess. When used deskside, Shredmaster 2000 and cart are conveniently desk high. Cart size: 22 h × 18 w × 18⅝ d.
H19–1120–875 Cart
Shpg. wt. 25 lbs. $195.00
H19–1120–876 Plastic bags,
box of 100 . . . . $36.00

Order from:

The Electronic Wastebasket
23 North St. Clair Street
North Newton, KS 67117

Terms:

20% down payment with order, balance due 30 days after receipt of invoice

Kansas residents, add 6% sales tax

All orders shipped FOB destination.

B WRITING LETTERS ACKNOWLEDGING ORDERS

5. *Acknowledging a First Order.* You're the public relations manager at The Fashion Closet in Paragould, AR 72450. Lisa Mann (Route 1, Box 42, Paragould) has ordered a pair of Jack Weather slacks, size 14 tall, in white. You granted Mrs. Mann credit just last week, and this is her first order. Write an acknowledgment letter to build goodwill. Tell her the slacks are being sent in tomorrow's mail and will be charged to her new account.

The Fashion Closet is planning a summer clearance sale in two weeks. Think up some big bargains you'll have, and mention them to Mrs. Mann. Use this opportunity to promote The Fashion Closet and its merchandise.

6. *Acknowledging an Incomplete Order.* You are sales manager of Video House and you receive the following order letter from George Green:

```
                      202 McKinley Street
                      Concord, NC 28025
                      October 10, 19--


Video House
5661 Western Avenue
Charleston, SC 29411

Ladies and Gentlemen:

Please ship one of the videocassette recorders you
have on sale this month for $400.  Ship it to me at
my address in the heading.  Please charge my Master-
Card No. 234-56-789 which expires March 19--.

            Sincerely,

            George Green

            George Green
```

You have two videocassette recorders (they have identical features) on sale this month for $400—one is Beta (smaller tapes) and the other is VHS (larger tapes). Mr. Green failed to indicate whether he wanted Beta or VHS. As sales manager of Video House, write Mr. Green a tactful letter asking his preference of Beta or VHS. Make it easy for him to reply, and use this opportunity to build goodwill and resell your product. This month you are also sending two free blank videotapes with each recorder.

7. *Acknowledging a Large Order.* One of your customers, Shick Office Furniture and Supply, 6248 Randolph Street, Ames, IA 42809, normally orders six Model A-25 secretarial chairs per month and always pays promptly. The chairs are well built and come with a ten-year guarantee. Today you receive an order for 72 of the secretarial chairs. Write an acknowledgment letter to the store owner and manager, Mr. Lester Shick. You are shipping the merchandise truck freight via Ryder/PIE today on your regular credit terms of net 30 days (no interest charges if paid within 30 days).

8. *Acknowledging an Order for a Discontinued Item.* You are employed as sales manager at Tasco Distributors, and you receive the following order letter:

```
                            13 Lincolnshire
                            Spokane, WA 97321
                            April 3, 19XX


Tasco Distributors
2042 Main Street
Seattle, WA 97401

Ladies and Gentlemen:

     Please ship one 8-digit display/print calcu-
lator, Model 3H5810, to:

          Sue Frazier
          152 Virginia Street
          Seattle, WA 97401

     Enclosed is my Check No. 189 for $45, which
includes shipping charges.

                            Sincerely,

                            Heidi Meeker
                            Heidi Meeker


Enclosure
```

You discontinued carrying this calculator about four months ago because you had a lot of complaints about it. Write to Heidi Meeker and recommend the following calculator to her:

10-digit display/print calculator
Model 4T361J
fully addressable 4-key memory
full one-year warranty
price: $52 (including shipping)

9. *Acknowledging an Order That Must Be Refused.* You are marketing manager at Stuck-on-You Designs, Inc., and you receive the following order letter:

```
                        Jon Thomas, M.D.
                           Pediatrics
                       1355 Winnette Drive
                       Cleveland, Ohio 44102



                          February 8, 19XX


        Stuck-on-You Designs, Inc.
        3800 Ala Moana Avenue
        Honolulu, HI 96822

        Ladies and Gentlemen:

        Please send 5,000 assorted smelly stickers to me at
        my office address.

        Charge the order to my VISA account No. 1234-567-891-234,
        or send me an invoice.

        Since stickers (especially smelly ones) are so popular
        with children, I've decided to give a sticker to each
        patient rather than a balloon.

                          Sincerely,

                          Jon Thomas
                          Jon Thomas, M.D.

        JT/cs
```

It is your organization's policy to sell your products exclusively through local dealers. Write a letter of acknowledgment to Dr. Jon Thomas. Refer him to Miss Gina Goerlich, Manager, The Sticker Gallery, 1743 East Main Street, Cleveland, OH 44106. Explain that The Sticker Gallery carries a complete line of your stickers. Include a sentence of commendation of the store and send your current catalog, which illustrates over 700 stickers.

Unit 15

WRITING GOODWILL LETTERS

Most business letters have two purposes:

1. To do a specific job, such as ask for or give information, transmit literature, make a sale, or collect an account.

2. To build goodwill.

Goodwill letters have only one purpose: to promote a friendly feeling between the reader and the writer. As you learned in Unit 5, all letters should try to build and maintain goodwill. Goodwill letters are special because they are letters that *do not have to be written* (but should be). If such letters were not sent, no material change in the situation would result. But when someone takes the time to send a goodwill letter, it is appreciated and remembered, and valuable improvements in human relations result.

What is goodwill? It is an intangible commodity that ultimately will result in increased business for you and your organization. Goodwill means the favorable attitude and feeling that people have toward an organization. Basically, people feel that an organization either is or is not interested in them. When they feel that an organization is interested in them, respects them, and considers their welfare important, then that organization has their goodwill.

People in progressive organizations know that the personal touch of goodwill messages builds good human relations. Goodwill letters to employees and other associates make the organization's work go more smoothly. Goodwill letters to customers show interest—and that is the best way to keep customers. About two-thirds of the customers who stop buying at a store drift away because of the store's indifference.

Recipients of goodwill letters especially appreciate them because they are unexpected. Business people seldom take time to write letters they don't have to write. So when some do, they and their organizations are remembered for their interest in people. This kind of reputation pays off in more satisfaction among customers and employees and in more sales and profits.

Typical goodwill letters include:

Letters to say thanks.
Letters of congratulation.
Letters that announce, invite, or welcome.
Letters that express get-well wishes or sympathy.
Letters that maintain or reactivate business.

All these letters share one purpose: to gain the reader's goodwill by showing interest in the reader. They also share these characteristics: reader approval, friendliness, naturalness, enthusiasm, and sincerity. Sincerity is probably the most important characteristic, because a goodwill letter that does not sound sincere becomes only lip service.

The goodwill letter you write will probably be successful when you can answer "Yes" to the following:

1. If you were the reader, would you honestly like to receive this letter? A goodwill letter hits the target only when it strikes a welcoming response.

2. Will the reader feel that you *enjoyed* writing the letter and that you *mean* everything you wrote? If the reader detects a gushy, bored, or indifferent note, he or she may doubt your sincerity and interest.

3. Did you keep the spotlight on the reader? To make the reader feel important, put *your* organization and yourself in the background and convince the reader you wrote the letter *just for him or her.*

4. Did you omit specific sales material? The reader will feel let down if your personal good wishes are only a prelude to a sales pitch.

Writing Thank-You Letters

Just as you can find many occasions for writing personal thank-you messages, you will also find many opportunities for writing thank-you letters to build goodwill in your organization.

Letters of appreciation are often sent:

1. To a new customer for a first order.

2. To an established customer for a particularly large order, or for the payment of an overdue bill, or for the last installment of a special-account purchase.

3. To an individual or an organization that responds to a special appeal or completes a spectacular job; or to someone in your own organization who makes a suggestion that proves worthwhile.

Occasionally (it should happen much more often!) such letters are also sent:

4. To customers who order regularly and pay their bills as they come due.

5. To employees who continually do their work well but unspectacularly.

6. To individuals and organizations who cooperate on the everyday jobs but get little attention.

Anniversaries and holidays are also occasions for sending thank-you messages. The letter from 24 Karat Jewelers shown below projects a warm tone. Who would guess it's a form letter produced by a word processor? The variable data (inside address and salutation) stored in the computer's memory was merged with the basic letter.

The letter quoted on the next page was written by a professor who wanted to encourage professional relations with the department members at another university:

---

24 Karat Jewelers

1365 Chatham Road, Springfield, Massachusetts 01106   Tel. (413) 555-3500

December 28, 19--

Miss Lucille E. Baker
10880 Collins Avenue
Springfield, MA 01106

Dear Miss Baker:

    As the new year begins, 24 Karat Jewelers thanks you for your friendship and for the business you have given us during the past year.

    The expansion of our store will be completed in a few weeks. We can then offer you the largest selection of fine jewelry in the city.

    During the coming year we will do our best to serve you in every way.

    We hope that the new year will be a happy and successful year for you.

             Cordially,

             Jason P. Buzanne

             Jason P. Buzanne

JPB/mtb

Note the warm tone in this end-of-the-year thank-you letter from 24 Karat Jewelers.

Dear Dr. Woodall:

I enjoyed visiting your campus and attending your excellent conference last weekend. That was my first visit to Georgia, and I was impressed! I got to know several Georgians, and they made me feel right at home.

The small-group session on typewriting was especially helpful to me, since I teach intermediate and advanced typewriting. And Dr. Glover's workshop on trends in business education was very worthwhile. I am enrolled in a graduate course called ''Issues and Trends in Business Education'' this semester, so I was able to share several ideas from the workshop with my classmates.

Thank you, Dr. Woodall, for inviting me to be part of the conference, and please thank the other members of your faculty for making me feel welcome and for helping to make your conference very successful.

Sincerely,

Have you ever worked as a salesclerk during the Christmas season? If you have, you can understand how pleased Jane O'Neill was to receive this letter of appreciation when she completed her temporary job. The letter was signed by the president of the organization.

Dear Miss O'Neill:

Thank you, Jane, for a job well done during your service with Toys ''R'' Us this past Christmas season.

Your enthusiastic cooperation was an important factor in making this Christmas successful not only for the many customers who rely upon Toys ''R'' Us to help them play Santa, but also for our store.

Although your temporary employment with Toys ''R'' Us has ended, I hope that we may benefit from your services in the future. Please drop in at our Personnel Office at any time. You are always welcome.

Appreciatively,

Another opportunity for a letter that does not *have* to be written is acknowledgment of a special service by a supplier. Your organization could just take the service for granted, but you build goodwill by writing an unexpected thank-you letter. Your supplier will be pleased to receive the friendly message.

Dear Mr. Kwatra:

You really give your customers service!

We were just about out of the 16-ounce chocolate Statue of Liberty gift boxes when you arrived—in person and on a Saturday—with an emergency delivery for us. Because you did ''more than was expected,'' many Chocolate House customers will have their Statues of Liberty earlier.

Mr. Kwatra, we appreciate such special cooperation. You confirm what we suspected: we're dealing with a company that <u>cares</u> about its customers.

Sincerely,

Many organizations use routine customer cooperation as an occasion to send a goodwill letter, as illustrated in the following letter to a new customer who has just made the final payment on a special 90-day account. The credit manager did not *have* to acknowledge the payment, which Mrs. Foster made on a visit to the store, but he showed interest and built goodwill by writing.

Dear Mrs. Foster:

You took care of your special account in top-notch form! We appreciate your check for $79 that enables us to write ''Paid in full'' and ''Thank you.''

Customers like you have made possible our growth and success during the past 37 years and will determine our future progress.

Of course, you are welcome to call on our Credit Department as well as any of our other departments whenever we can help. Won't you do this—at any time and often, Mrs. Foster?

Cordially,

Sometimes a message of appreciation is the only "pay" a person gets for accepting an extra responsibility. Such a thank-you letter is a must. The following letter was written by the president of a college to an instructor, with a photocopy sent to the instructor's immediate supervisor.

Dear Ron:

Thank you for the time and effort you put into your presentation for the Personnel Managers Association meeting yesterday. Professionalism and productivity in our offices are timely subjects of interest to all, and I felt your talk was very well received by the members of the Association.

I appreciate your willingness to make this public appearance as a representative of the Business Division of Navajo Community College. You handled it very well, Ron, and your own professional approach was exemplary.

Sincerely,

Writing Letters of Congratulation

A message of congratulation or commendation is much like a message of appreciation. Each recognizes and expresses interest in a worthwhile achievement. A letter of appreciation says "thank you" and implies "well done"; a congratulatory letters says "well done" and implies "thank you." Read the sample congratulatory letter shown below.

When your friends celebrate special events or receive honors, you want to congratulate them. In the same way, business people see opportunities for congratulatory letters on such occasions as anniversaries, graduations, births, marriages, new businesses or homes, promotions, elections, retirements, and various awards and rewards.

For instance, this brief congratulatory note was sent to an executive who recently became president of the company:

Dear Mrs. Plotner:

Congratulations on your recent promotion to president of the Whitehouse Industrial Company. I am sure that the business will grow and prosper under your capable leadership.

Sincerely,

516 Emerald Parkway
Tulsa, Oklahoma 74120
Tel. 918-237-9692

BRADFORD SHIPPING COMPANY

January 4, 19--

Mrs. Edna Whittier
Senior Vice President
Allied Oil, Inc.
One Allied Plaza
Tulsa, Oklahoma 74115

Dear Mrs. Whittier:

Congratulations on being named to the Governor's Task Force to Study Equal Opportunities in Business, Industry, and Government. I was very pleased to read that Governor Poole has chosen you as one of the ten executives for this task force.

If anyone at Bradford Shipping can help you and the other members of the task force, please let me know. We should be delighted to be of service.

Sincerely,

James E. Odle

James E. Odle
Vice President
Personnel

The writer expresses the best wishes of the entire organization in this congratulatory letter.

And notice the encouragement in the following letter sent to a new encyclopedia salesperson who has just made the first sale.

Dear Terry:

When a new agent makes the first sale, it's important news. That's why I'm sending my congratulations to you.

You've cleared the biggest hurdle. You've enjoyed the thrill every salesperson knows--the feeling of real accomplishment. You're off to a great start, and nothing can stop you now.

I expect to see you in New Orleans next May for the Advanced Sales Training School. Until then, here's to many ''repeat performances'' for you!

Sincerely,

You should distinguish goodwill messages from sales letters in which congratulations are used as an attention-getting gimmick for sales promotion. Emphasis is on goodwill when a leading child care service sends a beautiful baby diary to new parents and attaches this message: "Congratulations to the proud parents from The Cradle Club—the child care service that has the most loving and reliable babysitters in town!" But on the other hand, emphasis is on sales promotion when a retail store sends the parents a letter that begins "Our sincerest congratulations on the new arrival in your home" and then plunges into specific sales talk about strollers or baby clothes.

Certainly the contractor who received the following sales message was not fooled into thinking it was a sincere, personal message simply because it began with:

Dear Ms. Kimball:

Congratulations on being selected as contractor for the new White Oaks Shopping Mall in Cincinnati!

You, as the contractor, will be interested in selecting material that will be permanent and still economical. We assure you that Constantino's pipe and plumbing supplies have both these qualities. . . .

A letter like this one is unadulterated sales promotion with a gimmick opening and is not likely to build

goodwill. An organization's goodwill message should focus attention on the occasion that inspires it. If the writer seems more interested in his or her own organization than in the important events in the reader's life, the reader naturally feels tricked.

Remember that when you write a letter on your organization's letterhead, it is your organization talking as well as you. Perhaps saying it is your organization talking *through* you would be more accurate. Thus when you write a congratulatory message on letterhead stationery, whatever good feeling is aroused in the reader's mind will be for your organization as well as for you personally. Your organization will be remembered (because you used its letterhead); don't spoil the good impression with an unnecessary sales pitch.

Writing Letters That Announce, Invite, or Welcome

Goodwill announcements and invitations include:

1. Announcements of a new business, a new location, or an expansion or reorganization of facilities. These usually include an invitation to visit.

2. Announcements of the appointment of a new official or a new representative of the organization.

3. Announcements of a new service or policy, often inviting the reader to use it—for instance, when a store announces that it will be open an extra evening each week, or when a bank announces a new direct deposit plan, as in the example below.

Dear Suomi College Employee:

For your convenience, you can now have your paycheck deposited into your checking account automatically.

Arrangements have been made with the Suomi College and the First National Bank of Hancock to set up a direct deposit plan.

The plan is confidential and very convenient, because it deposits your paycheck directly into your checking account every payday. Of course, you'll still receive your paycheck stubs--even when you're away from school or out of town.

To make your paycheck deposits automatic, simply complete and sign the authorization card and return it in the enclosed reply envelope. That's it. We'll see that the college business office gets the card.

Sincerely,

More formal announcements and invitations may be printed and written in a formal style. Consult a reference manual or an up-to-date etiquette book for the proper wording.

Welcoming letters are written for many occasions. These messages may be morale builders, like the letter on page 167 welcoming a new employee. Usually they have a definite sales flavor, as do letters welcoming new residents of the community, new members of a club, new customers, new subscribers, new charge account customers, and new dealers. These messages discuss organization services and products and invite readers to call or visit; but they avoid specific sales promotion.

For example, letters welcoming new residents of a community can benefit both the receiver and the sender. Many retail stores and service firms use them regularly to build goodwill and gain new customers. A typical letter begins with a statement of welcome, comments favorably on the newcomer's choice of a place to live, mentions what the firm has to offer, and perhaps even includes an inducement such as a special discount to encourage the customer to come into the store.

Notice the friendly tone and service attitude of this letter from a bank president to a new customer:

Dear Mr. and Mrs. Barnes:

I was pleased to learn this morning that you have opened an account at the Mid American National Bank.

In extending to you my warm personal welcome, I wish to emphasize that all the service facilities of the bank are at your disposal.

We sincerely appreciate your confidence, as expressed in the opening of your account, and we shall do our utmost to make your association with us both pleasant and profitable for you.

Cordially yours,

Writing Get-Well Wishes and Sympathy Letters

When someone you know, either as a personal friend or as a business acquaintance, is ill, a letter from you will be appreciated. If the illness is not serious and there is no doubt about the recovery, you can send a humorous get-well card or a cheerful, happy letter. If the illness is serious or the person is getting over a major operation, then send a more subdued letter. That person will not be in a mood for jokes!

Be optimistic when you write to someone ill. Mention once at the beginning how sorry you are that the person is ill. From then on talk about a return to normal life, as the following letter did.

Dear Larry,

We are sorry to hear that you're in the hospital and hope that with rest and care you'll be up and about again soon.

Meanwhile, if there's anything we can do for you, just give us a call. We wish you a speedy recovery and a quick return to the office.

Sincerely,

Letters expressing sympathy or condolence are often the hardest letter-writing tasks because they have so many negative aspects. Many people tend to put these letters off until it is too late to send them.

The usual occasions for sympathy letters are death and serious illness. Sympathy letters are usually short. You don't want to seem curt (and so seem unfeeling), but you should be concise. As a rule, limit your letters of sympathy to two paragraphs. The first paragraph expresses sympathy. The second paragraph is a calm and optimistic look toward the future. Here is an example:

Dear Mrs. Barnocki:

We were all saddened to learn of the death of your president, Mr. Samuel Gaber. For many years we enjoyed a close and pleasant business relationship with him. Few banking executives earned greater respect and admiration.

We know that his memory will be with you through this difficult period of adjustment and that it will be a comfort to you in the years ahead.

With sympathy,

Notice how hard it would be to add another paragraph to the letter without being morbid.

Note one other thing. The letter uses the word *death*. The more you use euphemisms to avoid *die* and *death* and the dead person's name, the more you will string out your talk of the death, and the longer you will dwell on the reason for grief.

If you knew the deceased personally, use the *magic formula* in your condolence letter. The magic formula is to cite a personal incident, some small thing the deceased said or did that showed him or her to be a kind, considerate, and thoughtful person. This intimate touch, something personal that you alone are able to share about the deceased, will mean more than all the flowery phrases and fine-spun sentiments you can write. The fact that you are writing and expressing sincere sentiment is the important thing.

Writing Letters That Maintain or Reactivate Business

Letters to customers that follow up on products and services build goodwill because they show the organization's interest in customers' reactions and its desire to improve its products and services. Read in the next column what a beauty salon wrote to a new customer:

Dear David:

We really appreciate your recent visit to Klassic Kuts for your grooming needs.

We hope you found our receptionist's greeting friendly and our stylist prompt in taking care of you. That's the way it should be! But the most important thing we hope we achieved is that your stylist cut your hair in a style you like and can wear with pride.

Actually, we hope everything was to your liking, because we want you back as one of our regular customers.

      Sincerely,

HYSTER COMPANY
P.O. BOX 334 • DANVILLE, ILLINOIS 61832
217/443-7000 • TWX: 910-244-0703
CABLE: HYSTER PARTS, DANVILLEILL

MARKETING CENTER

September 19, 19--

Mrs. Karen Hall
1200 North Logan Avenue
Danville, IL 61832

Dear Karen:

      Welcome to HYSTER COMPANY! Beginning today, HYSTER is your company . . . a company made up of friendly people who are willing and eager to help you with your new job. You are important to us, both as an individual and as a member of a great team.

      To answer some of the questions you may have about your new job and your new company, I have enclosed a copy of Hyster and You, which will introduce you to the management team and tell you about employee programs and benefits and various company activities.

      As an employee of HYSTER COMPANY, you will have the opportunity to use your ability and initiative. You--and your work--are important to the company and to our customers. I hope you will find satisfaction and happiness in your work with us.

      Sincerely yours,

      Douglas A. Campbell

      Douglas A. Campbell
      President

DAC:lek
Enclosure

Lift Trucks • Winches • Compactors • Personnel Lifts • Trailers • Straddle Carriers • Mobile Cranes

A letter welcoming new employees helps foster their sense of "belonging" to the organization. (Courtesy of Hyster Company)

Letters are also often sent to customers whose accounts have been inactive for a long time. This is a way of finding out why former customers are no longer using their charge cards—whether some failure on the organization's part is responsible for lost business. Or the letter may try to persuade customers to start using their charge cards again, as the letter shown below does.

Principles for Goodwill Letters

Here is a quick-check reminder of the principles you should emphasize in writing a goodwill letter:

1. Write sincerely and with feeling.

2. Make the reader feel important.

3. Keep the message as natural and friendly as a person-to-person chat.

4. Send the letter promptly. Avoid putting the letter off until it is too late to send it.

5. Avoid the use of humor in a goodwill letter, because there is a very fine line between humor and sarcasm. Don't take any chances your goodwill letter will be misinterpreted. You're safer to stick with a straightforward message that is sincere.

Clothes Closet

4900 University Avenue Cedar City, Utah 84720 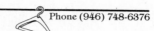 Phone (946) 748-6376

Dear Charge Customer:

A special treat is in store for you. It's Clothes Closet Days! A sale so big it only happens once a year. This year we have reduced much of our regular merchandise from ALL departments for this sale.

We invite you to take advantage of all our services--including your charge account. To let you know how much we've missed you, we're sending along a welcome-back gift--a certificate good for $10 off any purchase of $75 or more.

This year's sale starts on Wednesday, November 16, but we've designated Tuesday, November 15, as charge customer courtesy day. This will give you an opportunity to make your selections before we advertise the sale to the general public.

Mark your calendar--November 15--and join us for the charge customer courtesy day.

Sincerely,

Melody Mathews

Melody Mathews

Enclosure

The Clothes Closet reactivates business with a special discount for charge account customers.

ASSIGNMENT: *The problems in the Worksheet for this unit cover various goodwill letters that you may write.*

Unit 15 Worksheet

WRITING GOODWILL LETTERS

In each problem, prepare a message that will build goodwill. Make a plan for each message, write a rough draft, edit the rough draft, and prepare (preferably type) each letter on a separate sheet. Supply details to make your letters cordial and interesting.

1. Write one of the following appreciation letters, substituting a more original approach for the usual "thank-you for" opening.

   a. Thank the viewer who has donated an oriental rug for the auction to be held as part of the semiannual fund drive to support WKLL, the public broadcasting television station in your county.

   b. As president of the Student Advisory Council, write a letter to a nationally known tennis personality to express appreciation for the inspiring statements given at your college convocation to discuss drugs and alcohol.

2. Write one of these two letters of congratulation:

   a. Write to one of your former high school teachers who has been named Citizen of the Year in your hometown.

   b. As president of your town's Economic Development Corporation, write a congratulatory letter to Mary Mervis, owner of Mervis Industries, on the recently completed addition to the plant and the new production line, which will provide 60 new jobs.

3. Write one of these two welcoming letters:

   a. As president of Panasonic Corporation, welcome Gail Timmons, owner of The Now Sound, as a new dealer. She has just agreed to handle Panasonic products in her community.

   b. As mayor of your town, welcome Mike Street, director of the new minimum-security prison (now under construction), and his wife to your town.

4. Write one of these two form announcements to promote goodwill for your organization:

   a. Write a form letter to go along with the brochure your college is sending to guidance counselors in the high schools throughout your state. The pamphlet *Choosing a College* is not slanted in favor of any college or type of college, but the letter may include some low-pressure selling of your school.

   b. Write a letter for Mary Mervis announcing an open house at Mervis Industries the first Sunday of next month from 1 p.m. to 6 p.m. to show off the new addition. The letter will invite visitors on plant tours to see how Mervis operates. You will give door prizes and serve refreshments.

Unit 16

WRITING PERSUASIVE LETTERS

To some extent, every letter is a sales letter. You are selling your organization's image and goodwill. In this unit we'll talk about the letters that sell products or services.

In direct mail, especially the kind sent to consumers, some device is often used to get the "prospect" to open the envelope and read the message. "Free Gift Inside!" or "Urgent—Open Immediately!" or a similar message may be printed on the envelope. Inside are a letter (printed in color), a brochure, and a coupon, plus other items to make up an impressive package. Yes, much of it is "junk mail," but people have become so used to it in their mailboxes that even organizations with products or services of real value sometimes feel they have to "shout" for attention.

Sales letters to business people may use all the devices of direct mail but usually get to the point without resorting to gimmicks. We will focus on sales letters as they are used in business.

Sales letters have been an effective selling tool for many years—and for good reason. The cost of producing and mailing a large quantity of sales letters is often less than the cost of producing a radio or television commercial and buying time for it, or the cost of producing and buying space for a newspaper or magazine ad. Moreover, direct mail offers selectivity: the seller may select a mailing list according to the profession, geographic area, income, interests, and so on, of the people on the list. By selecting the mailing lists carefully, the seller is virtually assured of reaching a certain number of "qualified" prospects.

Direct mail sales letters do, however, have certain drawbacks. Because many people look upon all direct mail as junk mail, a sales letter may be discarded before it is read, even though it is well written and makes a spectacular offer. In addition, even a "successful" sales letter will usually draw a positive response from no more than five percent of the total number of people receiving the mailing.

Letters written specifically for direct mail selling are not the only sales letters. The writer who acknowledges receipt of a large order will write a thank-you letter that will also resell the customer. The writer who introduces a new sales representative to a customer is preparing the way for that representative to call for an order. And the writer who tries to persuade a superior to approve a project or an expense must sell that person on the reasons it should be approved. Therefore, every business writer must keep in mind these principles of writing sales letters:

1. *Know your products and services,* their advantages and disadvantages, why they appeal or should appeal to people—in fact, know as much as you can about them.

2. *Know your potential customers,* who they are, where they are, what their needs are, how to get through to them—in short, know everything you can about them.

3. *Know how sales are made,* what motivates people to buy, what appeals are likely to prove successful, how to get people to act.

4. *Remember the basics of effective writing,* especially in persuasive messages, and practice the techniques of clear communication that you have learned in this book and elsewhere.

Planning Sales Letters

Before you can begin actually drafting a sales letter, take five important steps. Until this initial planning is completed, it is virtually impossible to write an effective sales letter.

1. *Analyze the prospects in terms of the product.* First identify the characteristics that describe the most likely prospects for your products or services. From research or experience, build a "composite" prospect.

The sex, age, occupation, geographic location, financial situation, and so on, of the "average" prospect determine what appeals will be used in the letter. The answers to these and many other questions help you discover the needs and desires of the prospective buyers.

You wouldn't, for example, try to sell a "Sixty-Five Plus" insurance plan to college students. Nor would you try to sell homeowners' insurance to apartment dwellers.

2. *Prepare a list of prospects.* Next, you need a good mailing list. The obvious place to start is your organization's own list of customers. You can also buy lists from organizations that specialize in compiling and selling them. For sales effectiveness, a good mailing list must contain the correct names and addresses of people or organizations with common characteristics that make them a group of likely prospects for your products or services.

3. *Analyze the product in terms of the prospects.* What specific feature of the product or service makes it attractive or useful or appealing? What features should be emphasized? What features should be played down? (These analyses are usually made along with step 1.) Letters that present a product in terms of what prospective buyers think of it and how they can use it do more than make sales—they win satisfied customers.

4. *Decide on the central selling point (CSP).* The central selling point should be the item of information that will help the prospect most in reaching a decision about buying. After analyzing the prospects and the product, build your letter around this central selling point. The CSP might be appearance, durability, comfort, convenience, price, or any other positive feature that will have the greatest influence on your reader.

5. *Make a plan for the letter.* One formula for a sales presentation is AIDA—attention, interest, desire, action. Review "The Persuasive Approach" in Unit 6, page 57. By promising a benefit, try first to get the prospect to read the letter. Then arouse interest by helping the prospect to imagine using the product or service. Next, try to convince your reader of the desirability of buying it. Finally, attempt to get your prospect to act, to send in an order and a check.

Many good sales letters will not fit a set pattern. Do not let a formula dictate the letter, but rather link the product or service with the prospect's desires and needs by giving sufficient factual information to be convincing.

Writing Sales Letters to Customers

The purpose of your sales letter is to give the reader information needed to buy and use your product or service. After you have planned the letter, follow these suggestions when you actually write a sales letter.

1. Get the Reader's Attention and Interest in the Opening Sentences.

The beginning of a sales letter is critical. If the prospect doesn't read the letter, then no matter how good the offer is, no sale will result. To get the letter off to a fast start and to get the prospect reading, the central selling point (CSP) and the promise of a benefit to the buyer should be woven together at the beginning.

The opportunities for different forms, styles, attention-getting ideas, gadgets, devices, and so on, are limited only by your active imagination. Often you can capture the reader's attention in one of the following ways:

1. By arranging the first sentence as a headline—perhaps in all capitals or in color—or as a faked address block, as illustrated in the Metropolitan and F Stop letters on pages 173 and 174.

2. By presenting a humorous cartoon or striking color display.

3. By attaching a simple gadget such as a coin, stamp, piece of string, or button.

But some tricky openings are like the bang of a door. The noise gets attention, but the attention doesn't last unless the person is interested in finding out why the door has banged.

If you use an attention-getting device, be sure it leads right into the heart of the message. For instance, the cartoon may be a pictorial presentation of the CSP of the letter and the stamp may be introduced as "the postage needed to send for a Passport to Adventure." Remember, any unusual opening should point *toward the reader benefits you stress in the letter.*

Here are some popular sales-letter openings with sufficient "you" appeal to capture the reader's *interest*—not merely attention:

a. An Answer to a Problem, Need, or Desire of the Reader. Almost all successful sales-letter openings are variations of this basic opening. It is usually a winner, because all of us are interested in finding answers to our problems. It is also a natural opening, because the answer offered is always the use of the product or service advertised.

A sales letter introducing a vacuum cleaner began:

You can double your cleaning power *free* for 15 days with America's most advanced vacuum cleaner! We'll include a year's supply of bags *plus a valuable mystery gift free!*

Want to revolutionize your cleaning methods? It's easy—with the amazing new . . .

Metropolitan

```
YOU MADE THE RIGHT CHOICE...

when you bought term insurance from Metropolitan.

Is it still right?  Or is now the time to consider
something more permanent?  Perhaps today you should
expect more from your insurance plan.  You might
want the security of lifetime protection.  Or cash
values building up for an education fund or your
retirement.

To decide if term is still the answer, we should
review together your present insurance needs as well
as your financial goals.  I will call you soon for
an appointment to review your insurance program.

Sincerely,

Bill Satterwhite

G. W. Satterwhite
Registered Representative

ha

PS:  Your present term plan includes a valuable
option--the right to convert to permanent insurance
without a medical examination.
```

Life/Health/Annuities
Metropolitan Life Insurance Company
Home Office: New York, N.Y.

Because the beginning of a sales letter is critical, Metropolitan uses a special headline to get the letter off to a fast start and to get the prospect reading. (Reprinted with permission of Metropolitan Life Insurance Company)

b. An Unusual Headline, News Item, or Statement of Fact. An obvious statement, like *Spring is just around the corner* or *School will be starting again in a few weeks,* lacks imagination and attracts no attention or interest. But an unusual headline, news item, or statement of fact usually leads the prospect to read on to discover why it is true or how it applies.

The following three openings are excerpts from successful sales letters:

Every issue in government and politics has three sides—the *pro* side, the *con* side, and the *inside.* GOVERNMENT JOURNAL gives you *all* sides.

ATTENTION: PEOPLE WHO HAVE SUBSTANTIAL MONIES IN SAVINGS ACCOUNTS, CERTIFICATES OF DEPOSIT, ETC.

URGENT REMINDER:
The deadline is 12:01 a.m.

c. A Thought-Provoking Question. A question with an obvious "Yes" or "No" answer—like *Could you use more income?* or *Do you like people to laugh at you behind your back?*—is usually boring. But a question that challenges the reader to do some thinking is an excellent way to arouse interest in a message. Often, a question is better than a statement because it gives the reader a share in the idea. Instead of telling the reader, you ask him or her to think. And in answering, the reader may sell himself or herself on your idea. Naturally, the idea, the answer to the question, involves the use of the product or service you are selling.

the F stop

112 Garvey Boulevard
Los Angeles, California 90024
Tel. 213-674-9292

June 2, 19--

Make The F Stop
Your First Stop . . .

. . . Whenever you need camera or photographic equipment.

Whether you want a highly sophisticated sound movie system
or a simple pocket camera, whether you're an amateur photographer
or a professional,

                    The F Stop

                    is for you!

Nikon, Minolta, Canon, Yashica, Hasselblad, Kodak--all these
famous brands and more are available at The F Stop. Every type
of camera, lens, film, and darkroom equipment is in stock at
The F Stop, because we have the largest inventory on the West
Coast.

The enclosed brochure describes some of the many items now on
sale at The F Stop. For an extra discount, just bring this
letter with you and you will get $10 off on any purchase over $30!
(Offer ends July 30.)

                    Sincerely,

                    Mario Fermi

                    Mario Fermi
                    President

*This effective sales letter
from the F Stop offers the
reader a special discount
just for bringing the letter to
the store.*

MORE INFLATION AHEAD . . .
WHAT CAN *YOU* DO ABOUT IT?

Notice the opening question of the Sunburst Mortgage Company letter on page 175. This letter is general enough to be set up on a word processor and used as a form letter to be mailed to your entire list of mortgagees. The only change you need to make is to substitute the term *spouse* for *wife* in the postscript.

d. A Clever Quip or an Adaptation of a Familiar Saying. A clever phrase, a play on words, or the quotation of a familiar saying usually gets attention. It has particular appeal if the interpretation suggests disagreement with an accepted idea. But such openings must be closely related to the central selling point.

Here's an illustration from a Hart Drug Corporation letter about cold medicines:

A HART TO HEART TALK
    ABOUT A COLD PROPOSITION

Another example is on a letterhead in which the organization name—Dartnell—appears as skywriting:

Skywriting soon disappears . . . but withholding tax
is here to stay.

e. An Anecdote, a Fable, or a Parable. A story opening—if the story is a good one—usually arouses interest. It is effective as a sales letter opening if it relates to the central selling point of the letter and doesn't overshadow the message itself.

Sunburst Mortgage Company

4000 Parkway Drive, P.O. Box 3412, Raleigh, NC 10755   (409)-382-3231

November 14, 19--

Mr. Dwayne R. Shelby
2954 Dunedin Cove
Germantown, NC 10755

Dear Dwayne:

   Would you be interested in a mortgage policy that pays
off whether you live or die?

   Most policies will, of course, pay off the remaining
mortgage on your home if you die . . . but what if you live?

   Sunburst has a plan that works both ways. If you die,
it's insurance; and if you live, it's savings.

   This unusual policy may enable you to have the funds
available to pay your mortgage off early, thus saving many
months of house notes. Or it could be used to build a cash
reserve fund to make house payments in case of financial dis-
tress. Or it could be used for your children's education.
Or for your retirement.

   Take a moment now to fill out and return the enclosed
postpaid card. After looking over the figures we'll be
showing you, you'll be glad you did.

                          Sincerely,

                          George S. List

                          George S. List, CLU
                          Manager
                          Life Insurance Department

GSL/dwm
Enclosure

   PS: Do both you and your wife work? If so, you may
prefer to have mortgage insurance that provides coverage on
both of you. Drop the card in the mail, and you will receive
information on the most modern type of insurance now being
written--Joint Mortgage Insurance.

This persuasive letter is effective because it arouses the reader's interest, encourages the reader to see how he could benefit from the offer, and makes it easy for him to respond.

As a youngster, did you ever toss a stone over a cliff or down a very deep well—then wait and wait to hear it land?

We tossed a stone down your well, in the form of a quotation on March 14, and it hasn't landed yet.

2. Keep the Message Interesting and Informative.

Skillfully build the interest your opening sentences arouse. A sales letter in which even one paragraph drags usually means one more letter in a wastebasket. Your letter about a product or service succeeds when it leads the reader to say: "I didn't know this product [or service] would do that for me. I want [or need] it."

3. Build the Message Around the Reader.

What benefits the reader *thinks* a product or service offers will influence his or her decision about buying. Often a prospective customer knows little or nothing about the product or service you offer and has no interest when starting to read your letter. Bring your reader into the picture by showing how he or she can enjoy your product or service in a special way or how it can save time, energy, or money.

Your sales letter will *hold* the reader's interest when it gives information on how to live more happily or do a better job. Specifically, your message may appeal to one or more of the basic wants of people everywhere—such as the desire to be comfortable, healthy, and attractive to others; to have attention, praise, material possessions, relaxation, and enjoyment; to avoid pain, trouble, and criticism; and to protect their reputations and families.

Your message may stress an appeal to reason—*the rational appeal*—or to desire—*the emotional appeal*. Most successful sales messages combine rational and emotional appeals. People seldom buy something just because they have a logical reason for buying it or just because they desire it. Usually their buying depends upon both reason and desire. You *need* a car for transportation. But you make decisions about style, color, and other features on the basis of what you *like*.

One of the benefits your product or service offers usually appeals forcefully to one group of readers. Make this benefit the *central selling point* of a letter. As you develop this leading appeal, back it up with discussion of other benefits that may also appeal to the prospect. Suppose you are selling shoes. In one letter your CSP may be long wear. In developing this theme, you would certainly bring in such factors as good fit and comfort. In another letter your CSP may be style. While stressing that the shoes are stylish, you may mention that they fit well, are comfortable, and keep their fine appearance with continued wear.

In every letter, develop the appeal from the reader's viewpoint.

4. Be Sure Your Information Is Accurate and Your Interest in the Reader Is Sincere.

Concentrate on facts, not opinions or exaggeration. Misinformation in a sales letter is unethical and can endanger the success of the message. Your reader may be fooled by misrepresentation and buy once, but not twice. And most organizations depend on *repeat sales* for their profits.

Sincerity in selling includes confidence that the service you offer will be useful, practical, and economical for the buyer. Your sales message will not reflect sincere interest in the reader unless you believe that *when you make a sale you will make a friend*. Remember that making friends is the key to making *repeat* sales.

5. Forestall Objections and Procrastination— Convince Your Reader That the Time to Respond Is Now.

Imagine yourself talking with, instead of writing to, the prospective buyer. Think of the reasons that might be given for not buying or for waiting until later to decide. Then answer those objections in your letter *before* the reader has a chance to think of them.

At times the reader may object or hesitate because it is difficult to accept everything you say the product will do. So you must present *evidence* to back up your statements. Here are three kinds of evidence often used effectively in sales messages.

a. A Vivid Picture of the Use the Reader Can Make of the Product or Service. This is basically a problem-solving approach. You recognize a problem that the reader has. You present your product or service as a solution to that problem.

b. An Offer of a Sample, a Trial Use, or a Money-Back Guarantee. Sometimes you can offer tangible evidence—a free sample or a trial use of the product or service—so that your reader can personally test the claims. Or you may convince the reader that all you say is true by giving a money-back guarantee or suggesting that no payment is necessary unless or until the customer is satisfied that the purchase lives up to the promises made for it. Notice how well the writer of the following excerpt from a sales letter understands the importance of evidence:

> Perhaps you are skeptical. It's natural for you to want proof about a sales claim. I want to prove mine by having you try the SAFEGUARD system in your own home without me around to put on any pressure. In short, you be the judge. Either the SAFEGUARD system is good—and will work well—or I get it back.
>
> You don't need to make up your mind now. Just mail the enclosed postpaid card. In a few days the SAFEGUARD system will be there for you to try.

c. Performance Facts and Endorsements by Users. Facts based on actual experiences with a product or service or testimonials of people who have tried it offer strong sales support. Both performance facts and testimonials are sometimes included in the letters. More often, though, the surveys and tests on which the facts are based, as well as authentic endorsements, are included in brochures or other literature enclosed with the letter.

If your reader puts off a decision to buy until later, enthusiasm for the product may cool off. So give the advantages of *deciding now*. Suppose you are trying to persuade a reader to buy an air conditioner in January. What two objections might the prospective customer have? "Why should I buy now—why not wait until summer when I'm ready to use it?" and "I just haven't that much money to spend right now." You wouldn't mention these objections in the letter, of course. But you can anticipate them by writing about (1) the reduced January sale price, which will go back to the regular price in February; (2) the storage plan, which includes keeping the air conditioner until delivery and installation are requested; and (3) extended credit arrangements, with the first payment delayed until April 1.

6. Avoid High-Pressure Selling and "Knocking" Competing Products.

Never try to force the reader to buy. Don't even say the reader needs what you are selling. Most people resent being ordered around. You will usually get better results by telling what the product or service can do and then leaving the decision to buy to the reader.

7. Introduce the Reader to the Enclosure.

If you send a brochure or other enclosure—and you usually do—you can make it an integral part of your sales message if you keep two ideas in mind: (*a*) Refer to the enclosure *only after you have given the reader sufficient information* to develop interest in reading the rest of the letter before making a decision about buying. (*b*) Refer to your enclosure *specifically* by suggesting that the reader observe something interesting about it. *I have attached a reply card* sparks nothing. To spark a desire to do what you ask, say, "All you have to do is check your choices on the enclosed postpaid reservation certificate, fold, seal, and drop it in the mail."

8. Talk About Price at the Best Psychological Moment, and Make the Product Sound Worth the Cost.

Naturally, somewhere in your letter you talk about the cost of the item you are selling. Few people decide to buy before they know the cost. If you feel the reader will consider the article a bargain at your price, stress the price—as good news—by mentioning it near the beginning of the letter. It may even be the central selling point headlined in the opening sentences. But if you think the price may seem high to the reader, talk about cost toward the end of the letter. Make the reader want the article before you mention cost. And make the cost seem less by telling how much the reader is getting for the money. Notice how cost is linked to benefits in these excerpts from next-to-last paragraphs of letters:

> Teachers and parents have discovered the tremendous value of *Nature Magazine* in educating youngsters through the fun and reading found only in this fantastic nature-oriented magazine. It's filled with great pictures and stories about other children around the world, science and adventure, games and puzzles—everything a child loves. A gift subscription to *Nature Magazine*, 12 issues a year, is only $11.

Here's another excerpt:

> Cook with this 21-piece set for 15 days. Fry with it . . . braise with it . . . boil with it. Try your old favorites and take a stab at something new. You're under no obligation. But if you're as delighted as I'm sure you will be . . . keep it—for just $12.95 a month for the next 12 months.

9. Close With a Request for Action That Is Specific, Easy, and Rewarding to the Reader.

The closing paragraph of your letter often is the key to getting the reader to act. He or she may think about buying the article mentioned in the letter but may not do anything about buying it unless the letter tells exactly what to do. Be specific; for instance, (*a*) tell the reader to fill out and send in the enclosed order form; (*b*) ask the reader to come into the store for a demonstration—tell where and when one will take place and what it will include; or (*c*) tell the reader to invite a representative to call—after you give the representative's name, phone number, and office hours. Whenever you can, mention a reason for acting at once. The longer the reader waits before acting on your suggestion, the less likely he or she is to act at all.

Even when the reader is interested in the product advertised and wants it, a little push for action is usually needed. Your closing paragraph can give this if it uses this *three-way call for action*, which tells the reader:

a. What to do.

b. How to do it (make it easy).

c. Why it should be done promptly.

Notice how the words in italics in these closing paragraphs from an effective sales promotion letter use the three-way call for action.

> Take just a moment to *jot your name on the enclosed postpaid order card, drop it into a convenient mailbox*, and we'll see that your Roll King is on the way in less than a week.

> If you send a check or money order, we'll pay all express charges. Or, if you prefer, we'll send the Roll King c.o.d. Just check the appropriate box on the order card.

> *With a Roll King your next round will be the easiest and most enjoyable you have ever played!*

Short closing paragraphs often combine the three persuasive elements in one or two sentences:

> There's no need to bother with a check at this time— I'll be glad to bill you later—but do *avoid missing a single exciting issue* of TRAVEL by *returning the postpaid card today*.

You can't prepare an effective sales letter if you think of the recipients merely as names on a mailing list. Instead write to a group of people who are alike in at least one aspect—their need for your product or service. And the more attributes the members of the group have in common, the easier it is to relate your sales information to the individual reader's interests.

Notice that the Motorola sales letter on page 178 is not a high-pressure sales approach but does ask for action in the last paragraph.

Writing Sales Letters to Dealers

Before preparing a sales promotion letter to send to a prospective customer, ask yourself, "How will this customer use the product or service I'm selling?" Then plan your letter to show how your reader can

MOTOROLA INC.

October 8, 19--

Mr. Charles H. Gold
One Logan Terrace Court
Palatine, IL 60067

Good Morning:

Your business demands a great deal of you. Your time is limited. Your
decisions are often critical. When you need answers, you need them NOW.

MOTOROLA understands that ... and we can help you put the resources you
need within fingertip reach, anywhere you travel. How? Through car
telephone service. You can maintain constant contact with your office
and important clients and you can make those necessary decisions and
meet those crucial deadlines ... from the convenience and privacy of
your own car.

Literally thousands of excutives, just like you, are using car telephone service every day to improve their business by converting wasted
travel time into productive travel time.

Give me a call today at (517) 472-5536, or fill out and return the
enclosed reply card. I'll be happy to answer any questions you may
have and provide you with a personal demonstration on the cost savings
of a car telephone.

Don't let another day go by. Call today and stay in touch tomorrow.

Sincerely,

M O T O R O L A
Communications and Electronics, Inc.

Jeff Loomis

Jeff Loomis
Personal Communications Representative
Mobile Telephone Sales

dmc
Enclosure

Communications Sector
1301 E. Algonquin Rd., Schaumburg, Illinois 60196 (312) 397-1000

Note how this effective sales letter from Motorola asks for action in the last paragraph. It can easily be individualized by merging the letter with a mailing list of prospective customers.
(Courtesy of Motorola Communications Sector)

have more fun, do a better job more quickly and easily, or save money by using your product.

When the prospective customer is a dealer, you ask the same question. However, the answer will be different. Dealers are interested in products and services that will help them play their role better, increase profits, and decrease expenses. So you will use a somewhat different sales approach in these letters.

You can stress two important reader benefits in sales letters to dealers:

1. Turnover. Naturally, a retailer is more interested in how much or how many can be sold in a short time than in any other fact about the product. No matter how much potential profit can be made on each item sold, an article is of no value to the dealer if it stays on the shelf. Letters to dealers should stress how fast the product will sell and give facts to prove its popularity with the dealer's customers.

2. Markup. After salability of the product, the dealer's next interest is markup, the difference between the price paid for the article and the price at which it is sold. (This is not profit, because there are other selling expenses that must be deducted before the dealer makes any profit. But turnover and markup are important factors in determining the profit.) Your sales letter should convince the dealer that the difference between buying price and selling price is large enough to ensure a worthwhile profit.

The opening paragraph in letters to dealers usually gets attention and interest if it tells what the product or service can do for the reader. A successful opening often is a direct comment about the salability of and markup on the product, like the following:

A quick sale and a 60 percent markup are yours
 When a customer spots
  ARNOLD PALMER GOLF CARTS
   On your showroom floor!

Adapt the whole letter to the dealer. Talk about customers' use of the article and the features they will like. Talk about prices and about the advantages of buying in quantity. Stress the ways in which you can help the dealer increase the sale of your products. The dealer aids you may suggest include your national advertising, which will bring customers into the store asking for the articles advertised; mats for the dealer's newspaper advertising; display materials and suggestions; and envelope stuffers, posters, catalogs, and other publicity items.

A variation of the dealer sales letter is seen in the following letter about a promotional package offered by Promotions Unlimited:

Dear Mr. DeLourdes:

How do your customers react to the words ''FREE'' and ''WIN''? The TREASURE CHEST (shown in detail in the enclosed brochure) will appeal to passersby because you offer them the opportunity to WIN it! All the prospective customer has to do is complete an entry blank with name and address and drop the blank into a box!

In one package, you get everything you need for a successful promotion: the TREASURE CHEST, containing prizes for the whole family; a giant colorful window poster; 1000 entry blanks; and an entry box.

The cost? Only $49.95 each! The result? The TREASURE CHEST will bring shoppers inside your doors!

Take a moment to fill in the postpaid order card and drop it into the mail. Your TREASURE CHEST will be shipped the day we receive your order. If you're not completely satisfied, just return the package within 10 days, and you owe nothing.

If you enclose your check with your order, we'll prepay all freight charges.

Sincerely,

Writing Replies to Inquiries as Sales Letters

Every inquiry about your products or services is important, since it opens a door for your sales message.

Sales promotion letters written in answer to requests for information about advertised products and services are often called *invited* or *solicited* sales letters.

The big difference between invited sales letters and other sales promotion letters is that you start invited sales letters with a direct answer to one of the questions asked. You do not need—and therefore do not use—an attention-getting opener. The reader is interested in the answers to his or her questions. You can best hold that interest by answering all questions—direct and implied—completely and promptly.

In invited sales letters you should, of course, stress the advantages to the reader of using the product or service. And you should close with a three-point request for action.

For help in writing a sales letter in reply to an inquiry, refer to Unit 13.

Writing Cover Letters as Sales Letters

Cover letters are often successful as sales messages and may be as effective for that purpose as answers to inquiries or as uninvited (cold-turkey) sales letters. The Pilot Life letter shown on the next page illustrates this type of letter. For a review of cover letters, reread "Writing Cover Letters," page 129.

Writing Sales Letter Series

A series of sales promotion letters may be sent to prospective buyers when the seller feels that one letter won't accomplish the job of selling the product or service. The two most frequent ways of using a sales letter series are described below.

1. *Wear-out series.* A number of sales letters are prepared. Each is complete in itself and independent of any other letters or advertising plans. The first letter is sent to a selected list of prospects. Then other letters are sent to each prospect at intervals as long as there is reason to believe the prospect may still be in the market. Every letter in the series tries to get an order. This type of letter series is used chiefly for selling *inexpensive* merchandise.

2. *Campaign series.* A number of sales letters are prepared, each one building on the preceding one. As you plan these letters, decide on the number of letters to be sent and the intervals—often 10 to 15 days—at which they will be sent. Plan to send a complete series of letters to each prospect; ordinarily, you do not expect an order from your prospect until all the letters have been received. Frequently this direct mail advertising is coordinated with newspaper, magazine, radio, and TV publicity. This type of letter series is used primarily for selling merchandise which is *expensive.*

C L McComas, CLU
Senior Associate

Pilot Life
Insurance Company
Suite 122
1255 Lynnfield Rd
Memphis, TN 38119
Telephone Bus 901 767 1151

October 9, 19--

Mr. Gary Cooper
153 Peabody Avenue
Tupelo, MS 39488

Dear Mr. Cooper:

RE: PILOT LIFE POLICY NO. AB9022

Do you have questions about your Pilot Life insurance policy? If so, I would like to answer them.
I have been assigned to service Pilot Life policy-
owners in Mississippi who are without the service
of an active Pilot Life agent. This service is
free!

Please review the enclosed list and check any of
the 11 questions you would like to have answered.
If you have others, send them in also. This service will not cost you a cent--even the reply
envelope is free!

Sincerely,

C. L. McComas

C. L. McComas, CLU

asc
Enclosures

Pilot Life Insurance Company · Greensboro, North Carolina 27420 · A Jefferson-Pilot Company

*This sales letter is a cover
letter for a policyowner
service request form. (Courtesy of Pilot Life)*

ASSIGNMENT: In the Worksheet for this unit, plan and prepare effective sales messages.

180 *Writing Persuasive Letters*

Unit 16 Worksheet

WRITING PERSUASIVE LETTERS

A ANALYZING PERSUASIVE LETTERS

1. Collect three pieces of direct mail advertising, and mark the AIDA parts of each letter (attention, interest, desire, action).

2. On a separate sheet of paper list the appeals (both emotional and rational) used in each of the letters in Problem 1.

B WRITING PERSUASIVE LETTERS. *Plan and prepare (preferably type) sales promotion letters that will present the products described in Problems 3–7 to prospective buyers in terms of their needs and desires. Supply sufficient specific details to make each letter an effective sales message.*

3. Your product is a subscription to a newspaper or magazine. Select a newspaper or magazine that you read regularly. Compose a sales letter to persuade your readers that they will find it as enjoyable and as worthwhile as you do.

4. Write a letter to convince the readers of your monthly magazine that they should buy a special publication featuring ten great mystery stories. The reader receives a free bonus gift but may return the mystery book within seven days if not satisfied. The hardbound volume consists of 931 pages and 61 full-color illustrations. It costs $19.98, payable in three monthly installments of $6.66 with no charge for interest, postage, or handling.

5. You are a representative of a large mail-order house. One of your direct mail jobs is to write a letter to promote insulated boots made of water-resistant leather. They are ideal for work or sport. They come in men's sizes 7–12, widths B-E and sell for $72.99 (5 inches high) or $82.99 (7 inches high). They also have a one-year warranty: If a leak occurs because of defects in material or manufacture, the boots will be replaced. You are enclosing an order form. Payment may be made by check, charge card, or c.o.d.

6. Plan and write a letter in which you try to sell at least 100 leather pocket appointment books (for the coming year) to a retailer for Christmas stock. They make good-looking gifts at a price that the dealer's customers will appreciate—and a markup the dealer will like. Be sure to describe the books' features and uses as the customers will see them. You are enclosing an order form. The retail price is $3.97; the dealer's cost is $1.99 each, or $1.79 each for an order of 100 or more.

7. As sales manager of Posters 'n' Cards Printing Company, write a letter to be prepared on the word processor and sent to the managers of campus book stores. Persuade the managers to stock your posters and greeting cards. The colorful 14- by 21-inch posters are laminated with permanent plastic so they won't rip or wrinkle. They have self-adhesive peel-off strips on the back for easy mounting. The suggested retail price is $2.50 each and the wholesale cost is $1.25. The cards—for all occasions—cost 50 cents, with a suggested retail price of $1. Enclose a catalog and an order blank.

Unit 17

WRITING CREDIT AND COLLECTION LETTERS

The majority (over 90 percent) of buying and selling in the United States is done on a credit basis, which means "buy now and pay later." Several million dollars' worth of business is done on credit each year; only 1 percent becomes "bad debt." When the customer does not "pay later," the seller must start the collection process to minimize the bad debts. In this unit you will learn how to write the numerous letters that are used in the credit and collection process.

Writing Credit Letters

Letters concerning credit fall into four basic categories. Since credit is such a large part of the operation of most organizations today, form letters are often used to keep the cost down and the productivity up. Today, with word processing equipment, these form letters can be quickly prepared to look like individually written letters.

Requesting Credit

Customers wishing to establish credit will write or telephone your organization's credit department for a credit application form. The form usually requests both personal and business information such as:

1. Name, address, social security number, telephone number, and date of birth.

2. Name and address of present employer, position, length of employment, and monthly compensation.

3. Bank and other credit references.

4. Rental or mortgage and auto payment information.

The major reason customers wish to establish credit is *convenience.* Consumers can (1) buy now and pay later, (2) avoid carrying cash with them or writing checks, (3) exchange and buy on approval more eas-

ily, and (4) receive advance notice about sales, promotions, and other special events.

Investigating Credit

When the credit application is received, your credit department will investigate the application by sending a form letter, such as the one below, to the banks and credit references listed by the applicant.

Ladies and Gentlemen:

SUBJECT: Credit Inquiry

The following applicant has given your name as a credit reference:

> Mr. Raymond C. Williams
> Suite 301
> Windy City Towers
> 4802 North Sixth Street
> San Francisco, CA 94100

We would appreciate your giving us the confidential information requested below:

1. The date the applicant opened an account with you

   _____

2. The terms of the account are

   _____

3. The credit limit on the account is

   _____

4. The amount now owed is

   _____

5. The amount past due is

   _____

6. The date of the last transaction was

_____

7. Normal paying habits of the applicant are

_____

8. Remarks

_____

Please use the back of the letter if more room
is needed.

A postpaid return envelope is enclosed for
your convenience. Your help will certainly be
appreciated, and any information you give us
will be kept confidential. Please call on us
when we can reciprocate.

Sincerely,

_____

A local credit agency is usually contacted also for a
report of the credit history of the applicant.

Evaluating the Credit Information. Once the replies
to these letters have been received, your credit department will decide whether to extend or refuse
credit on the basis of the applicant's credit standing
or credit rating. *Credit standing* means the reputation
for financial responsibility. *Credit rating* means a
credit agency's appraisal—based on reports from
creditors—of a credit standing at any one time.

Traditionally, the following *three Cs of credit* form
the basis for extending credit privileges:

1. *Character* refers to a sense of honesty and ethical
dealings with others. It means meeting obligations
and is demonstrated by *willingness to pay.*

2. *Capacity* is the *ability to pay.* It is evidenced by income or potential income.

3. *Capital* refers to tangible assets in relation to debts.
Capital also determines the *ability to pay* if the debtor
does not pay willingly.

A fourth C—*conditions*—refers to the general business trends, local business influences, or current
demand for particular products and is frequently considered in evaluating an applicant for credit.

Extending Credit

Few letters are more welcome than one extending
credit. Writing one is a pleasant task. You are telling
someone who has applied for credit, who has filled
out an application form, and whose credit standing
has been investigated that he or she rates high
enough to be given credit privileges. That's good
news to anybody!

When writing a letter extending credit, use the direct approach and the following outline as a guide:

1. Welcome the new charge customer and express
the wish for a pleasant association.

2. Outline the special privileges that are available.

3. Explain the terms of payment.

4. Encourage the customer to use the new charge
account, and enclose some sales material.

5. Build goodwill by indicating your eagerness to
serve the new customer well.

The letter from Markham's on page 185 exempli-
fies the "good news" approach and fulfills these five
outline goals. Notice how the writer begins with a
welcome and the good news that the customer's
credit account is ready for use. The second paragraph
calls attention to the significance of the enclosed
credit card. The writer might have added other privileges that charge customers receive, such as advance
notice of sales. Details about terms and payment,
which must be explained to new charge customers,
are placed in the middle of the letter, after the good
news and before the light sales promotion appeal and
pleasant ending.

Many retail stores notify credit applicants of acceptance by a form message and explain monthly
statements and add-on purchases. However, a personalized credit acceptance letter such as the one illustrated on page 185 goes much farther in strength-
ening a credit relationship, building goodwill,
minimizing collection problems, and increasing sales.

The major reason organizations sell on credit is *to
increase profits.* Sales figures go up because credit customers buy more merchandise of better quality on a
regular basis.

Refusing Credit

Your organization cannot afford to extend credit to
every customer who asks for it. After you evaluate
the credit information you've gathered, you must
decide whether the account would be more likely to
(1) increase sales and profits or (2) become an uncol-
lectible account. If the information gathered indicates
that an applicant for credit is a poor credit risk, a
credit-refusal letter is a must. It is a difficult letter to
write, since you are telling the applicant that credit
cannot be approved. Use the indirect approach when
writing this letter.

Every credit-refusal letter has two objectives: (1) to
say no tactfully, and (2) to keep the goodwill of the
credit applicant. Your goal is not to discourage credit
buying but to convince the applicant that buying on a
cash basis now will be advantageous.

There are various reasons for refusing credit. The
main ones are (1) lack of a credit record (no credit
rating is just as bad as a poor credit rating), (2) over-
extension in credit buying, which will result in an
inability to pay obligations on a timely basis, and
(3) unwillingness to pay that which is owed. Regard-

MARKHAM'S
DEPARTMENT STORE

382 Melrose Avenue
St. Louis, Missouri 63147
Tel. 314-555-3900

March 8, 19--

Mrs. Deborah Ruiz
212 Maple Avenue
Dayton, Ohio 47382

Dear Mrs. Ruiz:

Welcome to your place of honor among the many satisfied customers who say "Charge it, please" at Markham's. Your account is ready for use when you next visit our store. Our staff will do everything possible to make your shopping here pleasant and satisfying.

The enclosed "Charga-Plate," your personal identification, is the key to happy shopping. Markham's offers a wide selection of practically everything for you, your family, and your home--at reasonable prices.

You will receive a monthly statement of purchases made shortly after our closing date, the 25th of each month. Then you may have until the 15th of the next month to pay your bill. From the fine way that you have handled charge accounts at other stores, we know that you will make prompt payments.

We invite you, Mrs. Ruiz, to enjoy the convenience of your charge account to the fullest by taking advantage of Markham's many special services, such as telephone shopping with the help of Sara Friendly, our personal shopper; free parking at the back of the store; prompt and efficient delivery throughout the city and suburbs; and even a nursery for the preschool set.

Come in often to shop or just to browse around. You are always welcome at Markham's.

Sincerely,

Jack Wallensky

Jack Walensky
Credit Manager

JW/dc
Enclosure

The letter granting credit to a customer is similar to the one extending credit to a dealer. Note how this letter fulfills the five goals listed on page 184.

less of the reason(s) for refusing credit, the letter that refuses must be clear about why credit is not extended. A harsh credit refusal can lose the customer's present cash business. It can also discourage the customer from reapplying for credit later.

Consider this credit refusal written to a college student who applied for credit at an oil company:

Dear Miss Davenport:

Regretfully, we do not issue credit to college students.

Please reapply after you are employed full-time. Until then, we want to encourage you to remain a cash customer. We will do all we possibly can to make your purchases of our gasoline and related products worthwhile.

Yours very truly,

How would you react to this curt turndown? It fails to keep the goodwill of the credit applicant! How could you rewrite this credit refusal, de-emphasizing as much as possible the reason for the refusal? Here's a letter that does a better job.

Dear Miss Davenport:

Your credit application is a clear indication that you are satisfied with our efforts to serve your automobile needs. Thank you for sending it to us.

Because college students have a difficult time building a credit rating while they are committed to getting an education, we would like to make a suggestion to you.

Once you are employed full-time, please send us another credit application. We'll be happy at that time to welcome you as a new addition to our growing family of charge customers.

In the meantime, Miss Davenport, let us continue to serve you on a cash basis. Our gasoline and related automotive products are designed to extend the problem-free life of your car.

Sincerely,

The opening statement serves as a cushion because it is positive in tone. The reason for refusal is indicated clearly enough, although not stated outright. The key to this turndown is the interest shown in reevaluating the applicant's credit status later. And of course, there is a cordial "pay as you go" invitation.

Writing Collection Letters

The goal of every credit department is to keep customers paying on time. When payments are not received on time, letters are sent to remind customers that their payments are past due. Messages which attempt to collect are referred to as *collection letters*; they are written because of the need to persuade customers to pay.

The purpose of collection letters is twofold: (1) to get the money owed and (2) to keep the customer's goodwill and future business.

Collection Letter Series

Most organizations use a series of collection letters to be sent at predetermined intervals, beginning with a statement of account and ending with a last call for payment.

Statement of Account. Most organizations send statements each month to their credit customers. These statements provide the customers with a record of their charges and the total amount due.

If the payment is not received, a duplicate copy of the statement is usually sent with a printed statement. The statement will be a friendly reminder, such as, "If you haven't sent us your payment, please do so today!"

Impersonal Reminder. If payment is still not received, a printed letter is sent without personalization. At this early stage you want to maintain the position that the customer is trustworthy and intends to pay. The tone of the message is friendly, as illustrated in the reminder at the bottom of this page.

Another impersonal reminder might be a form letter in which you fill in the date, inside address, and account information. It can be given a more personal touch by having it prepared on word processing equipment, as illustrated on page 187.

Personal Reminder. This message is a personal letter, usually no more than a couple of paragraphs. Care is taken to ensure that the customer will consider it a reminder—not a *demand* for payment. It attempts to persuade the person to pay and does not intimidate. The following message illustrates the tone used in such a reminder:

ANCHOR LIFE INSURANCE COMPANY
328 BENNINGTON DRIVE, LANSING, MICHIGAN 48917   TEL. (517) 542-6000

Please . . .

          . . . Don't forget the payment that is now due!

As you know, your Anchor insurance policy is designed to protect your family from financial difficulty when you are gone. Because missing a payment can cancel this protection, we urge you to send us the amount due as soon as possible.

Please don't delay! Keep your policy working for you and your family by sending us your payment before the cancellation date.

A gentle reminder such as this one may be sent with a duplicate statement.

Markham's
DEPARTMENT STORE

382 Melrose Avenue St. Louis, Missouri 63147 Tel. 314-555-3900

October 19, 19--

Mr. Wayne Dye
432 Lake Drive
St. Louis, MO 63147

Account Number	Type	Balance	Amount Due
644-83312-7	GRC	$170.49	$30.00

Dear Customer:

We value having you as one of our charge customers.

It is important, though, that payments be made promptly each
month. Your good credit reputation is very important to you.

The "Amount Due" shown above should be paid before your next
billing date.

If you've already paid the amount due shown above, please
disregard this letter and accept our thanks.

Sincerely,

Bill Byers

Bill Byers
Collection Department
529-4732

Preparing form letters like this one on a word processor means you can fill in all the individual information and make the reminder more personal.

Dear Mr. Bounty:

Enclosed is a duplicate list of your credit
charges from December 19--.

It is sent to you as a friendly reminder that
the balance on your account with us is past
due. Please take a few minutes today to send us
your check for $224.76.

Use the postpaid addressed envelope provided for your use.

Sincerely,

Request for an Explanation. When a credit customer
does not respond to personal reminder messages,
you can assume that something is preventing the customer from paying. It may be that the customer is
unhappy with the purchased merchandise or there is
a financial difficulty. Whatever the reason for holding
up payment, you want the customer to (1) explain
why the payment hasn't been made or (2) settle the

account. The following letter illustrates the approach
generally used in requesting an explanation:

Dear Mrs. Levander:

We are a bit concerned about your overdue
account. Several reminder notices have been
mailed to you, and we expected to receive your
$384.32 check in the mail. But so far we
haven't.

There may be a circumstance beyond your control that prevents you from settling this account. If so, please write me about it. I'm
certain we can work out a payment arrangement
after we know what your situation is.

Just think how good you will feel, Mrs.
Levander, when your account with us has been
paid in full.

Sincerely,

Note that the writer of this message did not threaten. The tone reflects the assumption that the customer is basically honest. The object of the message is to get the money owed and to keep the customer's future business.

Appeal(s) for Payment. The next collection message is an appeal to the credit customer to pay before you turn the past-due account over to a collection agency or an attorney. This is a stern letter, but calmly written. Typical appeals are to the customer's pride or sense of fair play.

The appeal for payment should not threaten to take the debtor to court unless you actually plan to. Give the person another chance to save a good credit standing by sending payment before the deadline—usually 10 to 12 days from the date of the letter. The following letter is an example of a courteous request for payment which appeals to both the customer's pride and his sense of fair play.

Dear Mr. Davis:

Your good credit reputation enabled you to purchase a $198.99 suit from us over three months ago. We were glad to place your name on our credit list at that time, and we made it clear that accounts are due on the 15th of the month following the purchase. When you bought the suit, Mr. Davis, you accepted those terms.

Your credit reputation is a valuable asset. We want you to keep it that way because of the advantages it gives you. You have enjoyed a liberal extension of time; but to be fair to our other customers, you must pay the amount that is past due by March 2.

Won't you please send us your check for $198.99 today?

Sincerely,

Last Call for Payment. The final message is an appeal to customers to pay so the delinquent account doesn't have to be turned over to a collection agency or an attorney. In this letter customers are given one last chance to save a good credit standing by sending payment before the deadline—usually five to ten days from the date of the letter. Never threaten the customer; state the consequences simply and regretfully. Notice that the following letter tries to keep the friendship of the customer by stressing interest in playing fair.

Dear Mrs. Haskell:

Your credit reputation is important to you, Mrs. Haskell.

For some time now, we have been writing to you in an effort to clear up your balance of $303, explained in the attached statement. So far you have not sent us either a check or an explanation, although six messages have called the debt to your attention.

Can't we still settle this account in a friendly way? If you send your check for $303 now, you can continue to buy luggage and accessories on our regular credit terms. The agreement with our collection agency, however, does not allow further delay. We must turn your account over to the Pipkin Collection Agency unless it is taken care of within ten days.

The choice is yours. If your check reaches us by November 16, your credit standing with us will still be good and our friendly business relations will continue.

Please mail your check for $303 today. Protect your credit reputation.

Sincerely,

Payment Acknowledgment

When a customer writes you about a past-due account, answer with a personal letter. Don't send any more letters from the collection series. A special thank-you message should be sent when the customer responds to a collection letter with payment in full.

Dear Miss Wright:

Thank you for your check for $324.18. Your account has been marked ''paid in full.''

Your cooperation in this matter enables us to continue to serve you in every way we can.

Sincerely,

ASSIGNMENT: Complete the Worksheet to check your understanding of the credit and collection letters discussed in this unit.

Unit 17 Worksheet

WRITING CREDIT AND COLLECTION LETTERS

A APPLYING FOR CREDIT

1. Complete for yourself the VISA credit application on pages 190 and 191.

B WRITING CREDIT LETTERS. *Prepare (preferably type) the credit letters below.*

2. *Extending Credit.* In January, Mrs. Linda Stafford, 146 North Front Street, Grand Junction, CO 81501, applied for a credit account at Chaney's Interiors, 443 Shelby Drive East, Grand Junction, Colorado 81501. She wished to buy on credit two Tiffany-style lamps costing a total of $364.

   After checking her credit rating and finding it highly satisfactory, the store opened an installment account for her. Mrs. Stafford agreed to pay $44 down and $44 (including finance charges) on the 15th of each of the next eight months.

   Write the credit approval letter which Chaney's might write to welcome Mrs. Stafford as a new credit customer. The letter should be brief and appreciative with a hint of reselling and sales promotion. The approach should be direct, the confirmation of terms exact, and the closing should be specific and forward-looking.

3. *Refusing Credit.* Reply to Miss Rose Tutwiler's application for a charge account at Donna's Boutique, 3291 Austin Peay Highway, Hartford, CT 06501.

   Donna's checked Miss Tutwiler's credit record and found that she had charge accounts in eight other stores in the city—each with an unpaid balance. Miss Tutwiler's credit history during the last few years was one of irresponsible buying, of continued difficulty in making payments, and of numerous past-due accounts.

   Write the message that Donna's might send her. The letter should be tactful and persuasive and should leave the door open for a different decision later (but no promises). Reflect the credit manager's understanding of the customer's problems and desire to be fair and helpful while trying to keep her business on a cash basis. Miss Tutwiler's address is 1468 Chicago Street, Hartford, CT 06501.

VISA Services Application

Please print or type all information

Purpose of Application:

I am applying for: ☐ **Regular VISA Account** – Credit limits from $1000-$5000. Annual fee is $15 per account.

☐ **VISA Preferred** – Annual income requirement $35,000; annual fee is $45 per account.
Credit limits $5000 and up. Credit limit requested _____ .

Applicant Information:

Name	last	first	middle	Social Security Number	Date of Birth	Country of Citizenship

Home Address (number and street) / city / state / zip code / Home Telephone Number

Residence own ☐ rent ☐ buying ☐ monthly payment $_____   Length of time at present address years months   If less than 2 yrs., give previous address under additional information.

Present Employer (If self-employed, send proof of income) / Position / Yearly Net Salary

Employer's Address / Telephone Number / Years Employed / If less than 6 months, give previous employer under additional information.

Other Income and Source   **IMPORTANT:** Income from alimony, child support or separate maintenance payments need not be revealed if you do not wish the bank to consider it in its credit decision.

Nearest Relative (name, street address) Not Living with You / city / state / zip code / Relationship to Applicant

Additional Information

Co-Applicant Information:

Name	last	first	middle	Social Security Number	Date of Birth	Country of Citizenship

Home Address (number and street) / city / state / zip code / Home Telephone Number

Residence own ☐ rent ☐ buying ☐ monthly payment $_____   Length of time at present address years months   If less than 2 yrs., give previous address under additional information.

Present Employer (If self-employed, send proof of income) / Position / Yearly Net Salary $

Employer's Address / Telephone Number / Years Employed / If less than 6 months, give previous employer under additional information.

Other Income and Source   **IMPORTANT:** Income from alimony, child support or separate maintenance payments need not be revealed if you do not wish the bank to consider it in its credit decision.

Nearest Relative (name, street address) Not Living with You / city / state / zip code / Relationship to Applicant

Additional Information

Financial Information:

Cash and Deposits:
(Include cash value of life insurance):   Total Balances $

Institution Name	Account Number	Balance	Pledged ☐ Yes ☐ No

Securities Owned: Total Loans $ Total Market Value $

Name	Number Shares	Loan Balance	Market Value

Real Estate Owned: Total Loans $ Total Market Value $

Location/Description	Monthly Payment	Market Value	Loans

Vehicles and Equipment: Total Loans $ Total Market Value $

Description	Creditor	Monthly Payment	Market Value	Loans

Other Assets:
(Furnishings, jewelry, fur, inventory, etc.)   Total Market Value $

Other Loans:
(Any balance owed not listed above.)   Total Loans $

Institution	Account Number	Credit Limit	Monthly Payment

Total Loans $		Total Market Value $		Net Worth $	

Please indicate if there is any obligation to pay:
Child care ☐   Alimony ☐   Child support ☐   Separate maintenance ☐   Amount $ _____   Frequency _____

Are all obligations up to date?   Yes ☐   No ☐
If no, please describe.

Other Account Information	Number of Cards Requested	Authorized user(s) other than Applicant/Co-Applicant	Relationship to Applicant

☐ Yes, I want Overdraft Banking Services. If funds are not available in my Indiana National Checking Account, the bank can automatically deposit the necessary funds up to my unused VISA credit limit. | My Checking Account No. _____

VISA Preferred Account Applicants   Emergency Identification Code (A confidential 5 position code used for the purpose of customer identification. The code is to be supplied by the cardholder. Example: maiden name.) | Approximate Monthly Billing Date   ☐ 5th   ☐ 20th

If I do not qualify for the Preferred Account and I do qualify for the regular VISA, I authorize you to open a regular VISA Account, if I do not already have a regular VISA Account. If I do not qualify for the Regular VISA Account, I authorize you to open a VISA Line of Credit account with a limit of less than $1,000 and no fee.

The above information is given to obtain credit privileges, I (we) hereby authorize the obtaining of information concerning any statements made herein, and I (we) agree to be bound by the terms of the VISA Cardholder Agreement. Signers shall be jointly and severally liable.

Applicant's Signature _____   Date _____   Co-Applicant's Signature _____   Date _____

(A.) NO APPLICANT MAY BE DENIED A CREDIT CARD ON ACCOUNT OF APPLICANT'S SEX OR MARITAL STATUS; NO APPLICANT MAY BE DENIED A CREDIT CARD ON ACCOUNT OF RACE, COLOR, RELIGION, NATIONAL ORIGIN, ANCESTRY, AGE (BETWEEN 40 AND 70), SEX, MARITAL STATUS, PHYSICAL OR MENTAL HANDICAP UNRELATED TO THE ABILITY TO PAY OR UNFAVORABLE DISCHARGE FROM MILITARY SERVICE (ILLINOIS LAW). (B.) THE APPLICANT MAY REQUEST THE REASON FOR REJECTION OF HIS OR HER APPLICATION FOR A CREDIT CARD. (C.) NO PERSON NEED RE-APPLY FOR A CREDIT CARD SOLELY BECAUSE OF A CHANGE IN MARITAL STATUS UNLESS THE CHANGE IN MARITAL STATUS HAS CAUSED A DETERIORATION IN THE PERSON'S FINANCIAL POSITION. (D.) A PERSON MAY HOLD A CREDIT CARD IN ANY NAME PERMITTED BY LAW THAT HE OR SHE REGULARLY USES AND IS GENERALLY KNOWN BY, SO LONG AS NO FRAUD IS INTENDED THEREBY.   **Form #575-8195 Rev. 10-83**

Courtesy of Visa

 C WRITING COLLECTION LETTERS. *You work in the Credit Department at Karney's. Mr. Martin Reed, Rural Route 2—Box 83, Covington, IN 47932, opened an account at Karney's six months ago. He paid each month as agreed until the June 1 payment was due. It didn't arrive. You billed him on July 1 for the overdue balance of $181.69 ($179 plus interest of $2.69) and included an impersonal reminder.*

4. On July 15 you still have not heard from Mr. Reed. Prepare (preferably type) a personal reminder for $181.69.

5. On August 1 you have had no response to the letter you sent in Problem 4. Prepare (preferably type) a letter requesting an explanation. The amount due is $184.41.

6. On August 15, since you've not heard from your letter in Problem 5, prepare (preferably type) a letter using a firm appeal. The amount due is $184.41.

7. On September 1 you've still received no response to any of the letters you've written to Mr. Reed. Write (preferably type) the last call for payment of $187.17.

Unit 18

WRITING CLAIM AND ADJUSTMENT LETTERS

Ideally, everything runs smoothly in the operation of an organization—no mistakes, no problems, no defects, and no misunderstandings. However, even in the best-managed organizations, because they are run by human beings, dissatisfactions are bound to occur. In recent years consumer movements and federal legislation have made both buyers and sellers more aware of problems caused by business errors. When a product or service does not meet the expectations of customers, they are disappointed and usually complain.

Their complaints should not be called "complaints," because that word has a negative connotation and could lead to a bad attitude toward customers. Letters about such complaints should be called *claim* or *adjustment* letters. *Complaint* connotes irritation, unpleasantness, negativism, and even anger. *Adjustment* is a more positive term, suggesting resolving the problem in a fair and equitable manner.

Consider these questions:

Would you rather have satisfied customers spreading good reports about your organization than unhappy customers complaining about your products or services?

Can you satisfy unhappy customers unless you know why they are dissatisfied?

Unless someone tells an organization that something is wrong, the organization may never know it and the error may be repeated. It has been estimated that every time the average customer is offended or feels he or she has been wronged, 125 people will hear about it—either directly or indirectly. With this potential negative publicity, reputable organizations are eager to discover, analyze, and correct defects in their products and services. An organization's primary source of information about such defects is through requests for adjustment from its customers.

Many organizations actively seek information about potential problems by sending a checklist-type questionnaire to customers with a postpaid, preaddressed envelope. The questionnaire McAlpin Appliance Co. uses is shown on page 194.

Customer satisfaction and goodwill are such important assets that some progressive organizations have established a customer services, consumer affairs, or customer relations department to handle adjustments promptly and graciously. Adjustment executives should strive to solve customer dissatisfactions fairly, quickly, and tactfully, because business success depends on customer satisfaction. Whether a claim is granted or refused, the adjustment letter should be used to build and keep customer goodwill.

Writing Requests for Adjustments

A letter requesting an adjustment will be easy to write if you think of it as a three-step process and follow these three steps:

STEP 1: Give identifying information.

STEP 2: Explain what's wrong.

STEP 3: Ask for a specific adjustment.

Here is a clear, complete, concise, and courteous request for an adjustment. Notice that it follows the three steps just listed.

Dear Customer Services Manager:

On May 15, we ordered a framed original Salvador Dali lithograph, Catalog No. 49367, for our newly remodeled Conference Room. We sent our Purchase Order 3861 with our Check 8639 for $775, which included shipping and handling.

When the lithograph arrived on June 1, the glass was broken and one corner of the lithograph was torn.

We are returning the damaged lithograph to you today via United Parcel Service. Please send us a replacement or a refund.

Sincerely,

McALPIN APPLIANCE CO.

Dear Customer:

Our shipping department reports that your recent purchase has been delivered.

So that we may know whether you are pleased with your purchase or whether the merchandise needs further service or adjustment, please fill out and mail the attached card.

We appreciate your business and want to do everything we can to make sure that you enjoy shopping at our store and that you are satisfied with your purchases.

Sincerely,

Ashlea Wilson

Ashlea Wilson
Customer Service Dept.

	YES	NO
Was your visit to our store pleasant?	☐	☐
Was the sales representative helpful?	☐	☐
Did the delivery truck arrive on schedule?	☐	☐
Were delivery persons careful?	☐	☐
Did they place or install your appliance as you requested?	☐	☐

If you have suggestions for ways we can improve our service, please write them below.

_____
_____
_____
_____
_____
_____
_____

McAlpin shows its service attitude and helps to maintain its business by sending a follow-up questionnaire.

Here is another well-written letter requesting an adjustment. Notice that this writer reverses the order of the three steps, but the letter gets the job done just as well.

Ladies and Gentlemen:

Please repair or replace my calculator watch, Model C863, and send it to me at the address above.

After six months of use, the musical alarm has quit working.

Enclosed is my watch, a copy of the sales receipt showing the date of purchase, and your warranty, which guarantees material and workmanship for one year.

Sincerely,

Follow these suggestions when you write a request for an adjustment:

1. Assume That the Problem Was Unintentional. Reputable organizations will want to keep your goodwill and do the fair thing. Whenever you write an adjustment letter, don't show anger or disgust; don't argue or threaten; don't even try to persuade. Just tell your story calmly and clearly, with confidence that you will be treated fairly.

2. Present All Facts and Details Clearly. Give your reader a complete and unbiased picture on which to base the adjustment decision. Follow the three steps for adjustment requests and include in your message:

a. *A description of the original transaction with all pertinent facts,* such as date and place of purchase, from whom purchased, terms of payment, a copy of the sales slip or other evidence of purchase, an account number, and an invoice number.

b. *A clear, concise explanation of the problem* which brought about your request for an adjustment.

3. Ask for the Adjustment You Think You Deserve. Tell the reader what you think should be done. If you are not sure what the adjustment should be, ask the reader to study the circumstances and determine the fair solution.

Writing Letters Granting Adjustments

When a request for an adjustment is being granted, follow these steps:

STEP 1: Give the good news.

STEP 2: Give an explanation and a "thank you."

STEP 3: Resell the product or the service, and your organization.

These three steps are used effectively in the following letter:

Dear Mr. Kietzmann:

Your new patio umbrella is being mailed pre-paid today, Mr. Kietzmann. It should arrive in a few days.

Thank you for returning the torn one. Since a mended umbrella might not be water-resistant, we are sending you a new one, so that you can keep your new patio table protected. You will notice that the new umbrella is made of vinyl-coated nylon, which has proved superior to the polyester and cotton one you bought last year.

When you need patio furniture and accessories, you will find everything from small tables to fountains in our latest catalog. You can rely on our guarantee of high quality and ''satis-faction or your money back.''

Sincerely,

Note the organization of the letter to Mr. Kietzmann. First comes the news he wants to hear most—a new patio umbrella is on its way. Next comes the writer's appreciation for the customer's calling attention to the defect. Then the writer explains the change in materials, an explanation owed to the reader, and one that in this case can make the organization look progressive and concerned. The final appeal for another sale is appropriate because the adjustment requested has been granted and the reader will be satisfied.

Follow these suggestions when you write a letter granting an adjustment:

1. Start by Telling the Reader That Full Adjustment Is Gladly Granted. Give the good news in the first sentence. Don't let the reader feel you are doing him or her a favor, even if you feel that you are making a special concession. Instead, convince the reader that goodwill and friendship are more important to you than the money involved and that your organization can always be depended upon to take good care of its customers. Notice the difference in the tone of the two letters from Ralph's Repair Service on pages 197 and 199. Which one would you rather receive?

2. Express Sincere Appreciation for the Reader's Adjustment Request. Then your reader will know you are aware that writing the letter and waiting for the adjustment inconvenience him or her and that you welcome this opportunity to set things right. Let the customer know how his or her letter has helped the organization to improve its products or service.

3. Stress the Effort Your Organization Is Making to Prevent a Recurrence of Customer Dissatisfaction. Accept the blame and apologize if your organization is at fault. If appropriate, explain what caused the problem, but don't blame the computer. Most people know that computers don't make errors—only the operators. Don't make the mistake of telling your reader "This will *never* happen again." No one can promise that. If appropriate, explain what your organization is doing to prevent a repetition of the problem.

4. End the Letter Positively. Don't end with a negative phrase, such as *We hope you do not have any more trouble with your Valic Vaporizer*. The best ending of a letter granting an adjustment makes no reference to the incident that caused the adjustment. End on a note that implies future dealings, and don't overlook the possibility of doing some effective sales promotion for related products or at least some reselling of your organization.

Writing Letters Denying Adjustments

An adjustment cannot always be granted. Letters denying adjustments are the kind that organizations least like to send and customers least like to receive. Letters denying adjustments have two purposes: (1) to say no and (2) to rebuild customer goodwill—a difficult task.

Use the effective buffer-paragraph technique when writing bad-news letters:

STEP 1: Buffer

STEP 2: Explanation

STEP 3: No (stated or implied)

STEP 4: Buffer

You may wish to review "The Indirect Approach," page 57, and "Answering 'No' to Inquiries and Requests," pages 139–141, for other special techniques to help you write effective bad-news messages.

The writer of the following letter realizes that Mrs. Wellman must be sold on the organization's position and be kept as a customer (after all, she did buy an expensive item). Here's the answer to Mrs. Wellman's request for repair or replacement of an automatic garage door opener.

Dear Mrs. Wellman:

You are right to expect high-quality merchandise from The Automatic Door Company, Mrs. Wellman. We try to give you the best for your money and to stand behind our products when they fail as a result of defects in material and workmanship, as our warranty states.

We appreciate your sending the door opener to us for analysis. It appears that the opener has gotten wet. Excess moisture over a period of time causes corrosion to form on the integrated circuit board. After the corrosion buildup reaches a certain level, the transmitter will not work.

Our service manager estimates that cleaning and repairing your door opener would cost $47.

Since your door opener is several years old, you may want to consider buying a new one. We have made many improvements to the door openers since yours was manufactured, including a sealed circuit board that would prevent the possibility of damage from moisture. A new door opener, which costs $70 postpaid, should give you even longer service than your old one did.

Please let us know whether you want us to repair or replace your opener.

Sincerely,

These suggestions will help you when you write a letter denying an adjustment:

1. Start With the Reader's Point of View in Your Buffer Paragraph. Since the customer probably thinks he or she is right, try to coax—not force—him or her to accept the logical solution. Be sure the customer realizes that you understand the problem and that you will be fair.

2. Convince the Customer That the Request Is Appreciated and Has Been Given Individual Consideration. The requested adjustment is important to the reader. In your letter, show that the reader's point of view is also important to your organization.

3. Present the Explanation Before the Decision. Stress what *can* be done and emphasize your purpose—to be fair to all customers. Don't blame and don't argue. Avoid unfriendly, negative expressions, such as *your complaint, your error, you misinterpreted, you neglected, you claim, you are mistaken, our records show, your ignorance.* By a truthful and tactful presentation, lead the customer to accept your solution as the only reasonable one.

4. Be Courteous Even When Answering an Angry or a Distorted Claim. If you answer sarcastically, you may lose both your self-respect and your customer. Completely ignore any insults in the letter you have received; concentrate on writing an answer that is friendly, rational, and professional. Usually it costs less to keep the customer you have than to find a new one.

5. Try to Leave the Reader in a Pleasant Frame of Mind. A friendly but concise closing is even more important when the adjustment is not granted.

Writing Letters Compromising on Adjustments

You may decide to compromise on the adjustment because both the seller and the buyer share responsibility or because you are uncertain about who is responsible and want to correct the trouble to keep the customer's goodwill. Follow these steps when writing a letter compromising on an adjustment:

STEP 1: Buffer
STEP 2: Explanation
STEP 3: No (stated or implied)
STEP 4: Counterproposal or compromise
STEP 5: Buffer

In the following letter, the writer tries to retain the customer's goodwill by repairing the product with no labor charge, even though the warranty has expired.

Dear Mr. Shelato:

As a Tuthill Pump Company customer, you <u>should</u> expect satisfaction because our pledge is based upon the terms of our sales agreements, including warranties.

Since the one-year warranty on your sanitary pump is no longer in effect, it is too late to credit your account, Mr. Shelato. However, we will gladly replace the partially dissolved nylon gaskets for you at the cost of the replacement parts, with no charge for labor. Our estimate for the parts is $39.50. We now have Teflon gaskets, which are more resistant to strong acids and alkalies. The Teflon gaskets would cost $59, again with no charge for labor.

If you will please complete and return the enclosed authorization-for-repair form indicating whether you prefer nylon or Teflon gaskets, we will repair your sanitary pump and ship it back to you within ten days.

Sincerely,

RALPH'S REPAIR SERVICE

1207 GARDEN DRIVE
WACO, TX 76703

January 17, 19--

Jeri Gleichman
P.O. Box 312
Waco, TX 76703

Jeri Gleichman;

As you can see your window is repaired--at
no cost to you.

The problem did not start the day (Dec. 19)
it was in our service department for a thermostat,
because the problem was that the regulator-to-glass
attaching screws were loose. This happens from the
door and window being used over a period of time
(usually a couple of years or more). So your
blaming us for breaking your window was unfounded
and I might add not the truth as the window first
starts not to close tight then becomes worse. At
the time it was here it was down approximately 1",
so it had to start sometime before that and we were
being held responsible.

We have enjoyed many years of auto service to
all kinds of people and with many different makes
and models of cars and are not in the habit of
breaking customers cars or being accused of the same.

Respectfully,

RALPH'S REPAIR SERVICE

Max Erickson

Max Erickson
Service Manager

ME/lk

*Read the letter shown here.
Do you think it will leave
the customer in a pleasant
state of mind?*

When you write a compromise adjustment, follow these suggestions:

1. Reflect Pleasant Cooperation in the Buffer Opening. But don't imply that you are granting the request. If you grant the request in the first sentence, the customer may not read the rest of the letter.

2. Give the Explanation. State the facts and reasons thoroughly and courteously—but don't go overboard. By giving a logical explanation first, you may be able to prevent a negative reaction from the customer.

3. State or Imply the Refusal. Make the refusal clear, but de-emphasize it.

4. Offer a Counterproposal or Compromise. This offer should be given willingly and graciously or not at all. Remember to let the service attitude show.

5. Use a Buffer Closing. Suggest what action the customer should take, but leave the decision to him or her.

Writing Form Letters as Adjustments

The tone and style of the usual form letter reek of "mass production." Trite phrases, used much too often, sound insincere. Form letters are commonly used in adjustment correspondence; but even a form letter, carefully written, can stress personalized service and genuine concern for the reader.

Read the following two form letters, which are routine adjustment letters used for a problem with a magazine subscription. Both are concise, clear, correct, and complete. But which letter would you prefer to receive?

Dear Sir or Madam:

This letter is to acknowledge receipt of your recent communication relative to your subscription.

It is necessary that you fill out in detail the enclosed form and return it immediately.

We will get back to you when we have located and corrected the problem with your subscription.

Very truly yours

Dear Miss Monfredini:

Thank you for letting us know that you have not been receiving your copies of Stars and Stripes.

We are checking with our Circulation Department to see what happened. Unless we need additional information from you, you can expect to start receiving your copies of Stars and Stripes within ten days.

Your interest in our weekly news publication is appreciated.

Sincerely,

The second letter is more personalized than the first and is not so brusque, even though it, too, is a form letter. For further illustration of this point, reread the discussion, "Avoid a Formal Tone in Your Writing," on page 34.

ASSIGNMENT: *The problems in the Worksheet give you a chance to demonstrate your understanding of adjustment correspondence.*

RALPH'S REPAIR SERVICE

1207 GARDEN DRIVE
WACO, TX 76703

January 17, 19--

Jeri Gleichman
P.O. Box 312
Waco, TX 76703

Dear Jeri Gleichman:

Your car window now works like new.

The window would not close completely because
the screws attaching the regulator to the glass
were loose. This happens from the normal use of
the door and window. It usually takes a couple of
years or more before the screws can loosen suf-
ficiently to prevent the window from closing tight.

Once this starts, the window gradually gets
worse until it won't close properly. The loosening
car window develops over a period of time and not
in one day. This is apparently what had happened
the day your car was in our shop to replace the
thermostat. You, of course, would have no way of
knowing this, but we were glad to investigate and
repair the window at no expense to you.

We look forward to handling your repair needs
in the future.

Sincerely,

RALPH'S REPAIR SERVICE

Max Erickson

Max Erickson
Service Manager

ME/lk

*A friendly, rational, and
professional answer will
help you to keep your customer.*

Unit 18 Worksheet

WRITING CLAIM AND ADJUSTMENT LETTERS

A BACKGROUND. *On December 29 you ordered one pair of binoculars, Stock No. BN0374, for $24.80 (including shipping and handling) from Stevens Merchandise Center, P.O. Box 94800, Houston, TX 77290. The mail-order form advertised a 15-day free trial on all merchandise. You charged your order to your Bonus Credit Card, account 5580-466-823-009, which expires 9/—. The binoculars arrive on January 27. You try the binoculars and decide not to keep them. On January 29 you return the binoculars in the original shipping package by first class mail along with a letter asking Stevens to credit your account for $24.80.*

1. *Claim Letter.* Write (preferably type) the January 29 letter to mail to Stevens with the binoculars.

2. *Claim Letter.* Your February and March statements from Bonus Credit Card Company do not reflect a credit from Stevens. Write (preferably type) a letter to the attention of the Customer Relations Department at Bonus Credit Card Company asking their help in getting the credit.

B BACKGROUND. *Butch Walsh ordered a Watchdog Intruder Alarm from the catalog shown on the next page on September 20. The alarm was to be a gift for his supervisor's birthday on October 15. The alarm and the invoice (also shown on the next page) arrived on October 30. Butch is steaming and writes the letter on page 203.*

3. *Claim Letter.* Butch's poor claim letter is shown on page 203. Rewrite it.

4. *Granting Adjustment.* As customer relations manager at Security & Safety Co., answer Butch Walsh's angry letter and grant the half-price adjustment he has asked for.

5. *Refusing Adjustment.* Answer Butch Walsh's angry letter and refuse the adjustment. You can't resell the alarm because of the engraving. The catalog does say engraving takes three to four weeks extra. Correct the invoice. Suggest that Butch Walsh give the alarm to his supervisor for Christmas.

WATCHDOG
INTRUDER ALARM

Protect your office with this alarm system that looks like a wall plaque.

Free engraving on cover plate (maximum of 3 letters). Please specify letters desired when ordering and allow 3-4 weeks extra for engraving.

Catalog No. K1403 . . . . $36.00

Shipping and handling included in all prices. Merchandise shipped in ten days from receipt of order.

Security & Safety Co.
38 Chandler Street
Mahwah, NJ 07430

SECURITY & SAFETY CO.
38 Chandler Street
Mahwah, NJ 07430

To: Butch Walsh
705 N. Scott Street
Clarkston, GA 30021

Invoice No. D1438

Date: October 28, 19--

Customer Account No. 782-31-4982

Date	Quantity	Description	Amount
9/20/--	1	Cat. No. K1403 Watchdog Intruder Alarm Engraving LDH	63.00
		TOTAL DUE	63.00

To avoid finance charge of 1½% per month, pay balance in 30 days of invoice date.

C BACKGROUND. *Your company, Enersystem Industries, Oklahoma City, OK 73127, ships all merchandise FOB shipping point. The invoices clearly state the shipping policy, and a separate amount is shown on each invoice for shipping. In the past month several customers have deducted the shipping charges from their invoice before sending their payment. You've had to write an individual letter to each of these customers asking them to pay the shipping charges.*

```
                    705 N. Scott St.
                    Clarkston, Georgia 30021
                    11/1/19--


                    Security & Safety Co.
                    38 Chandler Street
                    Mahwah NJ

                    Dear Stupid Security & Safety Co.

                    You idiets sure took you sweet time about sending my
                    order and you also goofed it up royally!!!!

                    First--I don't appreciate being charged $63 for a
                    Watchdog Intruder Alarm that's listed in your catalogeu
                    at $36.00.  Did you think you could make a few extra
                    bucks that way and I'd never notiec3?  Well----you
                    can't cheat me cause I won't stand for it.

                    At least you got teh engraved initeals on the cover
                    write.  I wanted this for my supreviseor's birthday
                    but it is passed now and I had to buy something else.
                    Your catalogeu promised 10 day delivery and I ordered
                    this over a month ago.

                    I think to be fare you should give it to me for $18
                    which is halfprice.  I'm still

                                Boiling Mad!

                                Butch Walsh
                                Butch Walsh
```

6. You decide to write a form letter to be sent to any future customers who deduct the shipping charges before paying their invoices. The letters will be prepared on a word processor so they can be individualized and the actual amount of the shipping and invoice can be inserted in the letter. Avoid negative phrases like *you are not entitled to* or *you mistakenly deducted,* which are likely to offend the customer. In your letter, assume the mistake is an honest one. Explain to the customer what FOB shipping point means and point out that shipping this way allows you to sell the item at a lower price; even though you would like to allow him or her the deduction, it would be unfair to your other customers. Ask the customer to send you a check for the shipping charges.

Unit 19

WRITING PUBLIC OFFICIALS AND THE MEDIA

Have you ever thought about writing a letter to a public official? What about writing a letter to the editor of a newspaper or magazine? Writing these kinds of letters is one of the most meaningful ways you can participate in our democratic system and be sure your "voice" is heard. Good citizens and progressive organizations take an interest in the world around us because it affects our lives and the organizations we work for.

Writing Letters to Lawmakers

Lawmakers represent the people who elect them. The latter are called *constituents* of the lawmaker. Lawmakers are very interested in how their constituents feel on issues before the legislative bodies. Many lawmakers seek our opinions on current issues through periodic questionnaires mailed to constituents with their newsletters. However, the best and most convincing way to express your opinion is through an individually written letter.

Does your letter really make a difference? With rare exceptions, lawmakers not only read their mail but are very interested in the contents. Those letters that aren't read by the lawmaker are handled by key staff personnel who relay the contents to the lawmaker. Your letter, just like your vote, does count. While your letter alone may not change or add a law, your opinion combined with the opinions of many other constituents can make a difference. There have been several instances over the years in which Congress has repealed a law because of the avalanche of mail opposing it. Many lawmakers receive over 6,000 pieces of mail each week, and they are unanimous in their view that letters are an important aspect of learning the feelings of their constituents.

Characteristics of a Good Legislative Letter

When writing a lawmaker, follow these suggestions:

1. Address Your Lawmaker Properly. Consult a good reference manual for correct titles and salutations. Many newspapers publish a list of names and addresses of area lawmakers at least once a week. The library is another good source for this information.

2. Use a Subject Line. Identify the topic you're writing about. If it is a bill, include the bill name and number, if known, or the popular title. Remember, there are over 20,000 bills introduced each year, so this identification is important.

3. Be Concise. Discuss only one issue in each letter, and do it briefly. Organize this letter using the direct plan, and present your points in a clear, logical order.

4. Use Your Own Words. Form letters and postcards with identical wording have less impact than a carefully thought-out individual letter. A telegram is immediate but impersonal. Petitions with dozens of signatures carry little or no weight, because lawmakers know many of these signatures are from disinterested people who have signed a petition because they were asked, not because they feel strongly about the issue.

5. Tell Why and How. When expressing your opinion about a bill under consideration, tell *why* you feel the legislation is good or bad and *how* the legislation affects you, your coworkers, your profession, your community, or other people in your district or state. Give factual personal examples and observations to strengthen your case. Give facts and figures, and include copies of pertinent articles and editorials from newspapers and magazines.

6. Be Courteous and Rational. Avoid starting your letter with *As a citizen and a taxpayer.* . . . Your lawmaker assumes you are not an alien, and we all pay taxes. Don't be rude to your lawmaker or threaten him or her with a statement such as *If you don't vote for this bill, I won't vote for you in the next election!* This makes you appear emotional, unstable, and irrational. If you are perceived this way, then what you have to say will have little or no credibility. Logical reasons work much better than threats.

7. **Watch Your Timing.** Write early in the legislative session before a bill has been introduced to give your ideas on the bill. Once a bill has been introduced, write to the committee members when the hearings begin and to your lawmakers before the bill comes to the floor for debate and vote. Your lawmakers are glad to hear from you any time, but obviously your letter is more effective if it arrives while your lawmakers are still deciding how to vote.

Almost all lawmakers answer their mail. If your reply is just a brief acknowledgment, write again to ask for more specific information, asking, for instance:

How do you stand on the issue?

Do you support or oppose the bill?

A follow-up letter will show you're really interested and you'll find persistence pays off when it comes to getting a reply.

Don't send a photocopy of your letter to other lawmakers who represent you. Courtesy dictates that you write each one individually—an easy task with word processing.

Construction of a Good Legislative Letter

Type your letter, if at all possible, because a typed letter looks more businesslike and more professional.

Be sure to include your address so you can receive a reply. Use your organization stationery only if you are representing the views of your organization. Otherwise, use your personal stationery or use plain paper with a complete heading.

There are two general categories of letters that are written to lawmakers.

1. **Legislative letters,** which deal with legislation. Use the direct approach in these letters. A typical outline for a legislative letter is given on page 207.

2. **Service letters,** which deal with helping individuals cut through the red tape when they have inquiries about social security, veterans and black lung benefits, immigration and passports, or other state or federal government agencies and benefits. These letters also use the direct approach. A typical outline for a service letter is given on page 208.

Follow-Up Letters

Even though your lawmakers are paid to represent you and help you, common courtesy requires a thank-you letter when they have voted the way you want on legislation and when they have helped you

as a result of a service letter. Review "Writing Thank-You Letters" in Unit 15.

Writing Letters to Editors

Nearly all groups in the media encourage their readers, listeners, or viewers to send written responses to their publications, programs, and editorial comments. People who write these letters are people who are eager to share their convictions, knowledge, and concern with others.

Concerned citizens and conscientious organizations write these letters to share a view, express a concern, correct an error, suggest an improvement, or give information. These letters become an obligation when an article is erroneous or misleading, because readers tend to accept as fact anything that is in print.

Characteristics of a Good Letter to the Editor

When writing an editor, follow these suggestions:

1. **Get Right to the Point.** Say outright why you're writing the letter. Give enough details that your letter is meaningful to all readers, even those who know nothing about the topic. Answer the obvious questions that will be in readers' minds.

2. **Be Brief.** Short words and sentences make your letter more readable. Your letter should be short; but do include all the important points, and limit your letter to one topic.

3. **Be Rational.** Even though you may be responding to something that really angers you, skip the temptation to write a sarcastic rebuttal. Emotionally charged letters help increase readership at your expense. You'll be embarrassed when you see the letter in print showing your temper. Your letter should be polite and professional.

4. **Use Good Taste.** Avoid insulting a race, religious group, political faction, ethnic group, or minority. Letters that are libelous or contain personal attacks are not published by reputable editors.

5. **Be Fair.** There are two sides to every story, and it doesn't weaken your argument to indicate an awareness of another approach. Be certain all your data and facts are accurate.

Construction of a Letter to the Editor

1. **Follow the Rules.** Most publications have an editorial page where letters to the editor are printed along with some guidelines for these letters. Space is limited, so letters should be a maximum of 200 to 300 words. These letters may be edited for length, accuracy, and good taste.

2. **Type Your Letter** (if at all possible). Ideally your

```
              (Letterhead with current date)

                            or

                    (Complete heading)




The Honorable _____ _____
House of Representatives
Room Number and Building Name
City, State ZIP Code

Dear Representative _____:

Subject:  (Identify the bill or issue)

1.  State your support of (or opposition to) the
    issue you're writing about.  Include the bill
    number, if known, and popular title.

2.  Tell why you support (or oppose) the issue, giving
    local and/or personal examples, experiences, and
    observations.  Quote statistics (and their source),
    if available, to back up your view.  Explain the
    consequences of the bill's success or failure
    to you and to other constituents.

3.  Ask the lawmaker to sponsor or support (or op-
    pose) the legislation discussed above.

4.  Express appreciation for the lawmaker's having
    considered your views, and ask for a reply that
    gives the lawmaker's views.

                    Sincerely,
                    Your signature
                    (Your name)
```

This plan for a letter to a lawmaker is used for a legislative letter.

letter should be double-spaced with indented paragraphs and wide margins.

3. Meet the Deadline. If your letter is triggered by a recent news story or editorial, write your letter the same day while the topic is still "news" or your letter may not be considered for publication.

4. Identify Yourself. Always sign your letter with your full name, title (if pertinent to the topic), and address. And include a telephone number where you can be reached in the daytime. Your name and address will be published with your letter. A few newspapers will withhold signatures if the editor feels the circumstances warrant it, but not many. Anonymous letters are considered to lack credibility and are not published.

The outline on page 209 can be adapted to most letters to the editor.

Writing News Releases

The news release, also called a press release, is prepared for the media and reports something that has happened or that will happen. The news release, like a letter, is used to build goodwill and promote your organization. News releases that appear along with other news and business articles are more convincing and get more attention than advertisements.

Larger organizations have a public relations department to handle this aspect of promoting the organization, but all employees have a responsibility to contribute to good public relations and to the high visibility their organization has with the public. You may be responsible for writing the final copy of a news release or writing a draft for someone in the public relations department to edit and forward to the media. You may also write a news release for a ser-

```
                    (Letterhead with current date)

                                or

                       (Complete heading)




The Honorable _____ _____
House of Representatives
Room Number and Building Name
City, State ZIP Code

Dear Representative _____:

Subject:  (Name the agency and give
             your identification number.)

1.  Give background concisely and in chronological
    order.

2.  Explain your problem and what you've done to
    attempt to solve it.

3.  Give written permission for the lawmaker to
    examine your records.

4.  Ask for what you need to solve the problem, and
    ask for a reply.

                    Sincerely,

                    Your signature

                    (Your name)
```

This plan for a letter to a lawmaker is used for a service letter.

vice or professional organization to which you belong.

News releases may be written to announce a new or improved product or service, the appointment or promotion of a top executive officer, new or expanded facilities, awards earned or community services donated by employees or the organization, financial activities, or other items that indicate that yours is a positive, progressive organization. Subjects that promote an organization's positive image are appropriate.

Characteristics of a Good News Release

Since a news release is really a news story, write it in a journalistic style with the most important information first.

Give the relevant *who, what, why, when, where,* and *how* information in the first paragraph. In the following paragraphs give the information in descending order, with the most newsworthy items first and the least important items last. Then if the release has to be cut, the least important information can easily be cut from the end of the article. You also want your reader to read what you consider to be the most important information first. If you put your major points at the end of the release, your reader might stop reading before he or she gets that far.

Construction of a News Release

Avoid starting your news release by naming your organization or its chief executive officer. (You don't

```
Date


Letters to the Editor
Name of newspaper or magazine
Street address or P.O. Box
City, State ZIP Code

Editor:

1.  Tell what topic your letter is covering and

    your stand.

2.  Give your explanation, facts, reasons, and/or

    examples.

3.  Give your summary or conclusion.


Your full name
Title (if pertinent to the topic)
Organization name (if pertinent to the topic)
Street address or P.O. Box
City, State ZIP Code

Phone number (where you can be reached during the
day)
```

This plan is used for an effective letter to the editor.

want the editor to view your news release as an advertisement in disguise.) The media will probably be more likely to use your news release if you start with a local-news, human-interest, or public-service angle.

Editors welcome brief, concise news releases, but they would rather have too much information than too little. "Too much" can be edited; "too little" may involve time-consuming telephone calls and could result in the release's going into "File 13" as an alternative.

Follow these suggestions when preparing a news release:

1. Either use special news release letterhead or plain paper.

2. In the heading or closing include the name, title, organization name, address, and phone number of the person to get in touch with for further information.

3. Provide the release information, such as "FOR IMMEDIATE RELEASE" or "FOR RELEASE ON JUNE 2, 19—."

4. Give your release a title in all capital letters.

5. Type the release double-spaced with generous margins and indented paragraphs.

6. If the release is more than one page, type MORE in the lower right corner of each page and number the continuation pages. Center # # # or END two or three lines below the last line of the release.

Observe how these suggestions were followed in the following release:

From: Susan Robenson   April 18, 19—
        Illusions International, Ltd.
        2543 Beechway Boulevard
        Colby, KS 67701
        301-835-6000

FOR IMMEDIATE RELEASE

          ILLUSIONS INTERNATIONAL, LTD.
              NAMES VICE PRESIDENT

Denise Marble has been named vice president of operations and educational supervisor at Illusions International, Ltd., in Colby, Kansas. The announcement was made by Ashlea Browning, company president.

Ms. Marble will supervise 15 color analysts and 20 hairstylists. Her professional affiliations include serving two years as president of the Kansas Hairdressers and Color Analysts Association. Currently she is on the board of directors of the National Hairdressers and Color Analysts Association.

Her training and expertise are in all phases of hair design and color analysis, including wardrobe analysis, makeup, and skin care.

Ms. Marble, a native of Topeka, Kansas, is a graduate of the University of California at Los Angeles. Her career interest began when she was a summer intern with the Merle Norman Studio in Hollywood.

                    END

ASSIGNMENT: *The problems in the Worksheet will give you an opportunity to write some of the communications discussed in Unit 19.*

Unit 19 Worksheet

WRITING PUBLIC OFFICIALS AND THE MEDIA

 LETTERS TO LAWMAKERS

1. Look up the names and addresses of the lawmakers who represent you. Pick an issue that is of interest to you, and write (preferably type) a letter to the appropriate lawmaker. Remember to write to your state lawmakers about state issues and to your federal lawmakers about national laws and issues. Do a little research on the topic you choose by reading articles in newspapers and periodicals. In addition to current topics in the news, here is an A to Z list of ideas for your letter:
   a. social security
   b. one six-year term for the President
   c. the selective service system
   d. the draft
   e. our court system
   f. public aid
   g. aid to dependent children
   h. mail service
   i. state lotteries
   j. illegal aliens
   k. violence and sex on television
   l. our prison system
   m. the death penalty
   n. financing for our public and private schools
   o. drugs and drug abuse
   p. drunk driving
   q. gun control
   r. missing and/or abused children
   s. changing the national speed limit
   t. nuclear weapons and nuclear war
   u. military spending and military strength
   v. the space program
   w. the economy
   x. medical care and/or medicare
   y. government spending
   z. any topic that concerns you

2. *Letter to the Editor.* Ten years ago your city replaced (with local tax dollars) four blocks of street in the downtown area with a landscaped mall. Now there is a proposal before the city to tear out the mall and replace it (with local tax dollars) with a street to provide on-the-street parking. There are two parking garages within one block of the mall area, as well as some side-street parking. On a few busy days each year, the parking garages are full.

Write (preferably type) a letter to the editor of your local newspaper telling why you are for or against the proposal to replace the mall with a street.

3. *Writing a News Release.* Your local symphony orchestra has received an unexpected gift of $50,000 from an anonymous donor to be used where needed. Assume you are the advertising director of this symphony orchestra, and write (preferably type) the news release.

Part 4

EMPLOYMENT COMMUNICATIONS

How do you get a job, or a better job?

Statistics show that you will be faced with this question more than once during your working life. It is a "job" to get a job, and it takes more than formal education, previous experience, and availability to get you on a payroll. You need to prepare a résumé and set into action a plan for securing employment. In today's competitive world, even the best-qualified people need to know the techniques of getting a job. That's our goal in Part 4 of *Modern Business Correspondence*—to help you get an interview that will lead to a job.

In a recent survey, employers were asked what people can do to make themselves more employable. Employers suggested taking business and technical courses to keep up with new technology and acquiring recent business experience, perhaps through summer or part-time jobs. You should also investigate a cooperative or work-study program through your school. The employers indicated that you need to develop more definite career goals and a better knowledge of business and how it works, and to have more flexibility in the types of work you will consider. A willingness to relocate, travel, or work variable hours is helpful. They also stressed the importance of your meeting the requirements for entry-level jobs, having a strong academic background, and mastering communications skills.

According to employers, the top five areas that you need to improve to succeed on the job are:

1. Ability to write and speak effectively
2. Work habits
3. Concern for productivity
4. Dependability
5. Ability to read and apply printed matter required for the job

Job hunting is hard work—it takes just as much effort and skill as a job does once you've been hired. You can make your job hunting easier if you take the time to do some advance planning and careful preparation. You can't "whip up" a good résumé and letter of application in an hour or two. It takes time, research, careful planning, and analysis to prepare a résumé and a letter of application for your "sales campaign."

Most personnel managers prefer a one- or two-page résumé with a one-page cover letter, or letter of application. This combination gives you an opportunity to explain in detail how your qualifications fit the job you are applying for. And it reveals a great deal about your personality.

You will find this two-part message effective in applying for a job. A prospective employer is certainly interested in what you can do right now but is even more interested in what kind of person you are, how well you work with others, how you will respond to on-the-job training, and what you will be able to do for the organization in five, ten, or more years. The employer can judge these points best from your application letter, which interprets the facts that you have listed on your résumé.

The main thing is to sell a product—yourself—to a customer—the prospective employer. Your résumé and letter of application should therefore be planned much like a sales campaign.

Unit 20

PREPARING RÉSUMÉS AND EMPLOYMENT APPLICATIONS

Let's start your "sales campaign" to sell yourself to an employer by preparing your résumé and employment applications.

Before you can sell your ability and services to an employer, you must identify your best traits, attitudes, and skills. Try to get a complete and objective picture of yourself as an applicant by standing back and looking at your qualifications as though they belonged to someone else.

The first step is to take inventory of yourself—your experience, education, personal qualities, and special interests and abilities.

Jot down everything: part-time, temporary, and even volunteer work; subjects you did best in; school and community activities; hobbies and interests; memberships and offices in professional and service organizations; awards, achievements, and honors. Writing these down (in any order) will help you think about what you have to offer your prospective employer. It will also give you clues about the kind of work you should be looking for.

Take the selling points you have and make the best of them by emphasizing them positively.

ASSIGNMENT: To help you take inventory of yourself, complete Section A of the Worksheet for Unit 20.

Preparing a Résumé

Once you have analyzed yourself in Section A of the worksheet, you're ready to take the next step: Prepare a written summary of your background—your résumé. *Always* prepare your résumé *before* you start to write the application letter. The application letter should not repeat details in the résumé but should interpret them in terms of the job applied for. Putting your résumé together should help you organize your thoughts about yourself and see yourself realistically in relation to the job you want.

Rearrange the notes you've already jotted down into categories. Then pick out the key points (a résumé is a summary, not a biography) and present them in a way that will give an employer a truthful and persuasive picture of who you are and what you can do. The résumé is probably your most helpful job-hunting tool because it focuses attention on your strong points and can be left behind as a representative of who you are and what you offer.

You'll probably be asked to fill out a regular application form too, and we'll discuss that later in the unit. But the résumé, if properly prepared, is more likely to catch the eye and help the employer gain a favorable impression of you quickly. A good résumé must be tailored to suit you and your background as well as the specific type of job you are applying for.

The following guidelines will help you decide what to put in your résumé, what to leave out, and what form and tone to use.

There are literally dozens of books, pamphlets, and articles written on how to prepare a résumé, and they all have different approaches. Likewise, all personnel managers are different and have their own likes and dislikes concerning résumés. Consequently, there is no "right" format for a résumé. A takeoff on the words of Abraham Lincoln sums up the situation: You can please some of the people some of the time, but you can't please all of the people all of the time.

The suggestions in this section—based on the likes and dislikes of many employers—will help you prepare an effective résumé that will impress most personnel people. First, let's examine the blocks of information that most résumés contain.

The Heading

Begin with your identification: your full name, complete mailing address (both permanent and temporary, if applicable), and telephone number. These should stand out at the top of the page. Be sure the telephone is one at which messages will be taken during business hours. It is unnecessary to type a heading such as "DATA SHEET" or "RESUME" (it will be obvious).

Job or Career Objective

This should be a concise statement indicating the type of job you are looking for and reflecting your goals for the next five or six years. Avoid a job objective such as "Position as sales person with eventual goal to become president of the organization." That's a bit presumptuous! Also avoid a job objective that is too general, such as "An interesting job with a challenging opportunity," or "A job working with people." Everyone wants a challenging opportunity and practically every job requires working with people.

Some people change the job objective on each résumé to fit the particular position they are applying for. This can be done with minimal retyping if you have your résumé stored on a word processor.

Experience

Work experience is usually the key part of a résumé. Begin with your present or last job, and work backwards to your *first* job.

List All Pertinent Work Experience. Give the organization name and complete mailing address, and list your job responsibilities and accomplishments.

Emphasize what you have accomplished. List part-time jobs such as baby-sitting, delivering newspapers, mowing lawns, retail sales, stocking shelves, fast-food service, and waiting on tables. If your paid work experience is limited, list volunteer work you have done. Work experience doesn't have to be paid to be valuable to a prospective employer.

You Learn Something of Value From Every Job. A baby-sitter is wholly responsible for the life of a helpless human being. A newspaper delivery route offers good training in meeting a schedule whatever the weather, in managing other people's (the newspaper's) money, and in selling. Mowing lawns means caring for other people's property, running an expensive machine, and being reliable in your service. A salesclerk and a person stocking shelves have to keep records, work with inventories, and follow directions. People who work in the food service industry

write orders, run a cash register, and make change. All of these jobs offer experience in meeting the public and dealing with people.

If you have lots of work experience, you might choose to omit the less important part-time jobs.

Give Concise but Complete Facts About Each Job. Include positions held, names of supervisors, organization names, complete mailing addresses, brief descriptions of your duties, and dates for each job.

Emphasize previous job duties that pertain to the job you are applying for (even though they may not have been your primary job responsibilities). Present your job duties in the best light you can. It is better to say "Responsible for filing and finding correspondence and customer orders" than to say "Did some filing." Start with *action* verbs that describe your job responsibilities, such as *analyzed, conducted, coordinated, created, developed, established, expanded, handled, implemented, improved, increased, initiated, maintained, managed, operated, organized, planned, prepared, produced, reorganized, saved, sold, supervised,* and *trained.*

Education

Begin with your present or most recent education and work backward to high school. Give the names of the schools, complete mailing addresses, dates attended, year(s) graduated, degrees, and majors. If you have not completed a degree, list what you have completed, such as one-year certificate in word processing, or 18 semester hours in business. If your grade point average is B or better, you may wish to include it.

If education is your main selling point, include a subheading called "Educational Highlights" and list:

1. Courses (a few major courses with most important ones first).

2. Skills (such as typing speed, letter composition, ability to operate special equipment).

3. Knowledge (such as programming languages).

4. Specialized training (such as seminars, workshops, and special courses).

List these items in the order of importance to a prospective employer, with the most impressive first.

Additional Information

Develop a category to include any other information on your résumé that you consider a selling point, such as leadership and your leisure activities (your interests and hobbies), special honors and accomplishments, military service and current status, and membership in professional and service organizations. If you've been out of school more than ten years, don't include school extracurricular activities—only honors and awards.

Personal details such as age, weight, height, marital status, dependents, health, and social security numbers are optional. If you feel they are assets, include them; otherwise, omit them. Many recruiting firms recommend omitting your age if you are over 35 years of age. Also, if you wish to include marital status, use single or married. If you are any other status, omit it. If you are female and have pre-school-age children, do not include that information on your résumé.

References

List your references in an easy-to-read arrangement as the last block of information on the résumé. Name as references only people who know you well enough to report on your work habits and on the quality of work you do in school or on the job. Include both school and job references when you can. Ask permission before naming any person as a reference. Since you want to list only people who will give you a favorable recommendation, ask for permission in this way: "Do you feel you know me well enough that I could use your name as a reference?" That gives people a tactful way to decline if they can't honestly give you a good recommendation.

When listing references, follow these suggestions:

1. Give three or four references (maximum of one character reference), putting them in table form for easier reading.

2. Use a courtesy title (Mr., Miss, Ms., Mrs., Dr., and so on) before each name.

3. Follow the name with the person's title (Manager, Accounting and Collection Department; Professor of English; Sales Manager; Word Processing Supervisor).

4. Give a complete mailing address (business rather than home address) for each reference.

5. Give a telephone number (including the area code) for each reference. Many people would rather telephone than write to a reference. Not only will they save time, but they can also tell a good deal from the person's tone of voice as he or she describes you.

Instead of listing the references, many résumés have a statement "References available on request." This may be necessary if you wish to limit your résumé to one page. If you choose this option, you should prepare a separate sheet with the heading "References for (your name)" at the time you prepare your résumé.

Signature and Dateline

Some employers like a handwritten date and signature on a résumé, as illustrated on page 221. That personalizes even a printed résumé. If you wish to provide a place to date and sign your résumé, type a line with the word *date* under it and a second line (either under or to the right of the dateline) with the word *signature* under it.

Now that we've examined the basic categories of information for your résumé, let's look at some other aspects of writing and preparing the finished product.

What to Include and What to Omit

Borrow a trick from the professionals who write advertisements and sales letters. Have you ever seen an ad for wood siding for a house that points out it will have to be painted every four years? We don't think so. Do the same with your résumé; avoid the negative. If your typing speed is good or your grade point average high, include it. If not, don't mention it.

The statement "Federal law prohibits discrimination because of race, color, religion, age, sex, or national origin" is on most employment forms, and these forms have no questions about this information. There is, however, no law that *you* can't include this information on your résumé. As a general rule, omit any information that gives your race, religion, political preference, salary, or reasons for changing jobs. However, if you feel any of this information could be an asset to you in securing a particular job, include it.

Stress the Qualifications That Seem Most Important to the Job

Remember that a personnel manager reads résumés the way you read a newspaper article—you start at the beginning and you read until you lose interest. After your heading and job objective, put the category (education or experience) that is your strongest selling point for the job you want. Personal details, if used, should follow the education and experience blocks.

Writing Style

Think of your résumé as an organized summary in outline form highlighting the facts (not opinions or interpretations) about your abilities and your training. These facts should be tabulated—listed in columns, *not* explained in sentences and paragraphs. Use a telegraphic sentence style: "Responsible for setting up and maintaining central filing system for regional office" rather than "I was responsible for. . . ." The meaning is just as clear, and you eliminate the overuse of "I."

Format and Appearance

Your résumé is probably the first glimpse a prospective employer has of you and how you do things.

Make it attractive, uncluttered, neat, and correct. Use good-quality (20-pound) paper, 8½ by 11 inches. Never use letterhead; plain white paper is the most common, but some people use a buff color and a few people use a pastel color for attention. The envelope should match the paper used for the résumé in weight, finish, and color.

Leave sufficient white space around and between columns so that all information stands out and is easy to find and read. Center all the headings, or use all side headings. Arrange all the data on one page if you can without crowding. If you need to include more details than will fit on one page, arrange the information attractively on two sheets (use only one side of the paper). The second page should include your name at the left margin and "Page 2" at the right margin.

Your résumé should be as long as necessary to effectively do the job—but no longer. And before you make copies, proofread it very carefully for typing errors, misspelled words, and inaccurate details such as dates, ZIP Codes, and phone numbers. A prospective employer will consider your résumé a sample of your best work.

Résumé data can be arranged in these three styles:

1. Chronological Résumé. This style gives information in reverse chronological order with dates. It is the easiest to write and prepare and works best for people with a steady employment background. Personnel people like this style best. The résumés on pages 218 and 219 illustrate this style.

2. Functional Résumé. This style highlights skills and qualifications. It is convenient for hiding breaks

---

DAVID S. DOUGLAS
3166 Logan Terrace
Glasgow, Kentucky 42141
Telephone (606) 555-8826

CAREER
OBJECTIVE
Position in motel/restaurant management with opportunity for advancement.

EXPERIENCE
6/85 - now   Mando's Italian Food, 4023 Summer Avenue, Glasgow, KY 42141. Duties: Worked as cook six nights a week (about 45 hours a week). Responsible for closing restaurant Mondays through Thursdays.

7/83 - 5/85   Red Apple Inn, 611 Madison Avenue, Glasgow, KY 42141. Duties: Worked as waiter (about 25 hours a week) while attending State Technical Institute.

6/81 - 5/83   U.S. Army, Fort Polk, LA 71459. Attained rank of sergeant. Supervised training for 500 men. Received Honorable Discharge and Good Conduct Medal.

9/80 - 5/81   Oscar's Grocery, 4070 Willow Street, Neon, KY 41840. Duties: Did general grocery duties including stocking shelves, arranging displays, and serving customers.

EDUCATION
9/83 - 5/85   State Technical Institute, Glasgow, KY 42141. Received Associate of Science degree in Motel/Restaurant Management.

9/78 - 6/81   Memorial High School, Neon, KY 41840. Graduated in top 15 percent of class.

ACTIVITIES
ROTC officer at State (two years). Photographer for college yearbook. President of high school senior class. Captain of high school basketball team.

REFERENCES
Mr. James P. Lucchesi   Ms. Lena Jensen
Owner, Mando's Italian Food   Manager, Red Apple Inn
4023 Summer Avenue   611 Madison Avenue
Glasgow, KY 42141   Glasgow, KY 42141
Phone (606) 555-8361   Phone (606) 555-4492

Mr. William B. Champion, Division Head
General-Vocational Technologies
State Technical Institute
Glasgow, KY 42141
Phone (606) 555-4468

This résumé illustrates a chronological style. David Douglas stresses his work experience by listing it first.

```
                        JOYCE M. KRAMER
                      405 Churchill Street
                      Blencoe, Iowa 51523
                        (515) 555-2098


        CAREER OBJECTIVE:  An office position using my Secretarial Administration
             training with the opportunity for advancement.

                             EDUCATION

        DeSoto County Junior College, Middleton, Iowa 52638, 1986-1988
             Associate of Arts Degree, June 1988, 3.82 GPA
             Major:  Secretarial Administration
             Special Skills:  Typing - 75 words a minute
                              Shorthand Dictation - 100 words a minute

             Educational Highlights:  Business English, Business Correspondence,
                                      Word Processing Applications,
                                      Records Management, Data Processing,
                                      Accounting, Economics, Business Law

             Activities and Honors:  Phi Theta (college scholastic honor society)
                                     Phi Beta Lambda (business students' organization)

        Central High School, Blevins, Iowa, 1983-1986
             Ranked fifth in graduating class
             Activities and Honors:  National Honor Society
                                     Gregg Shorthand Award
                                     Future Business Leaders of America


                             EXPERIENCE

        First National Bank, 501 Union Avenue, Middleton, Iowa 52638, 1986-1988
             Part-time Secretary to Mr. James Brown, Vice President of Marketing
             Duties:  Typing, taking dictation, filing, answering telephone

        LeBonheur Children's Hospital, 848 Adams Avenue, Blevins, Iowa 50000, 1984-1986
             Candy Striper Volunteer
             Duties:  Attending patients, under supervision of Miss Mary Greene,
                      Head Nurse

                             REFERENCES

        Dr. Carolyn Bowlin, Chairperson          Mr. Edward Jamison, Instructor
        Department of Secretarial Administration Department of Accounting
        DeSoto County Junior College             DeSoto County Junior College
        Middleton, Iowa 52638                    Middleton, Iowa 52638
        (515) 555-2958                           (515) 555-2960
```

Joyce Kramer's résumé illustrates a chronological style. She stresses her education by listing it first.

in employment or frequent job changes and does not include dates and places of employment.

3. Combination Résumé. This is a combination of the chronological and functional with the experience block divided into two sections: (*a*) job skills and qualifications, followed by (*b*) dates and places of employment. This style is especially effective when you've had several jobs with similar job duties, because it allows you to prepare a more concise résumé. This style is illustrated on pages 220 and 221.

Summary of Qualifications and Accomplishments

Although a résumé is generally used for applying for a job, it can be used when you are seeking a promotion or asking for a raise, or when you need a bio-graphical sketch for someone to introduce you or nominate you for an award. For these reasons it is important that you keep your résumé up to date even when you're not looking for a job.

You may wish to prepare a "Qualifications and Accomplishments of (your name)" report which includes your achievements, responsibilities, accomplishments, and any additional pertinent training or education. This could be used to help verify your productivity when you ask for a salary increase or seek a promotion.

Completing the Employment Application Form

Even though you have a résumé, almost all prospective employers will ask you to complete an *application form* for employment.

```
                    SHIRLEY A. KESTER

                    407 Sheridan Street
                    Danville, IL 61832
                  Telephone:  (217) 555-8213

CAREER            A medical secretarial position with a goal to become an
OBJECTIVE         Accredited Records Technician.

EDUCATION         Danville Area Community College, 2000 East Main Street,
                  Danville, Illinois 61832.  To be graduated in May with an
1/84 - 5/86       Associate of Applied Science degree, Medical Secretary
                  Major and a Certificate in Computer Programming.

EDUCATIONAL       Medical Terminology        Computer Programming Languages
HIGHLIGHTS        Medical Transcription        FORTRAN
                  Physiology/Anatomy           COBOL - I and II
                  Records Management           RPG - ASSEMBLER
                  Typewriting - 3 semesters  Terminal Operations
                  Payroll Accounting         Word Processing
                  Business Correspondence    Intro. to Data Processing
                  Secretarial Systems and    Accounting Principles
                    Procedures

                         Office Equipment Skills

                  Word Processing Equipment  Computer Equipment
                    IBM Mag Card I             CRT
                    IBM Memory                 IBM 4331
                    IBM OS6                    DOS V/SE

QUALIFICATION     Ten years in service related positions.  Extensive dealing
SUMMARY           with public and controlling service-related records.

ADMINISTRATIVE    Supervising telephone surveyors
                  Setting up file system of potential clients
                  Planning areas to be surveyed
                  Plotting maps of survey area

ADMINISTRATIVE    Filing reference information
ASSISTANT         Typing reference cards and correspondence
                  Ordering and controlling supplies
                  Making customer's appointments
                  Answering phone
                  Greeting customers

RETAIL            Keeping sales records
SALES             Taking inventory
                  Pricing merchandise
                  Selling merchandise
                  Operating several types of cash registers
```

Shirley Kester's résumé illustrates a combination style. It would become a functional résumé if the places and dates of employment were omitted (and it would fit on one page).

Why do organizations use application forms? The form requests exact data the employer needs, the interviewer may use it as a guide for interviewing you, and the data is located in the same place for all applicants. The way you complete the application form tells the interviewer how well you can follow written directions, how accurately you can complete a task, how good you are with detail, and whether your work habits are neat or sloppy.

The best preparation for completing an employment application is to know what kinds of information you will be asked. Application forms can be one page or several pages long, but all application forms ask for these basic categories of information:

1. Personal—your name and mailing address and your phone number during business hours.

2. Education—dates and the levels of education you've completed, and names and addresses of schools.

3. Experience—places and dates of previous employment. A category for volunteer experience now appears on many applications.

4. References—names, addresses, and phone numbers of at least three people who can recommend you.

5. Signature—to verify that the information you've given is accurate to the best of your knowledge.

Some applications ask essay-type questions, which are really intended to test your ability to communicate in writing and your spelling, punctuation, and grammar skills.

```
Shirley A. Kester                                           Page 2

WORK              Beautician's Assistant, full-time, Lera's Beauty Salon,
HISTORY           417 North Gilbert, Danville, Illinois 61832.
1980 - 1983       Supervisor:  Lera Barnhart
                  Telephone:  (217) 555-3929

1980              Supervisor of telephone survey, full-time, Sunset Memorial
                  Park-Gibraltor Mausoleum Corporation, 3901 North Vermilion,
                  Danville, Illinois 61832.
                  Supervisor:  James Darby
                  Telephone:  (217) 555-2874

1975 - 1978       Beautician's Assistant, full-time, Hairem Beauty Salon,
                  615 West Madison, Danville, Illinois 61832.
                  Supervisor:  Erva Combs - moved to Florida
                  Telephone:  Unknown

1974 - 1975       Sales Clerk, full-time, Goldblatt's Department Store,
                  Danville, Illinois 61832.  CLOSED
                  Supervisor:  Richard Haenel
                  Telephone:  (217) 555-1450

1973 - 1974       Sales Clark, part-time, K-Mart Department Store,
                  2721 North Vermilion, Danville, Illinois 61832.
                  Supervisor:  James Wasson
                  Telephone:  (217) 555-1100

REFERENCES        Available on request.



          November 21, 19--            Shirley A. Kester
          Date                          Signature
```

You will usually be asked to fill out an application when you apply in person for a job. So remember the Boy Scout motto and "Be prepared" by following these suggestions:

1. Take with you the information listed above (in writing). You make a poor impression if you can't remember a phone number, date, or ZIP Code. Never write "see résumé" across the application; fill it out completely.

2. Read completely through the form *before* you start to fill it out. This will help you answer the questions correctly. Once you have completed the application, reread the directions and recheck all the information for accuracy.

3. Take two pens (preferably black ink) that write and an ink eraser. A pencil can smudge and fade in time.

Write legibly—most employers won't consider an application they can't read.

4. Take a pocket dictionary. A spelling error could mean an automatic rejection when you apply for an office position.

5. Follow directions. If the instructions say print, don't write. Put nothing in sections marked "Do Not Write Below This Line," "Office Use," and "Not to Be Completed by Applicant."

6. Answer all questions. If the information doesn't apply to you, put N/A (not applicable) or draw a line in the blank to show that you have read the question.

If there is a place to put "other business skills" or "comments," put *something* there to sell yourself. Never leave it blank.

Copyright © 1987 by McGraw-Hill, Inc. All rights reserved.

7. Avoid listing the salary you expect. If this question is asked, answer with "open." This question can best be answered during the interview. You might eliminate yourself from an interview if your figure is out of line with current salary guidelines.

8. Give positive reasons for leaving previous jobs. When this information is requested, give reasons such as "better job opportunity," "career advancement," or "return to school." Answers such as "work too hard," "didn't like boss," or "hours too long" may reflect negatively on you and should be avoided.

Remember that you start applying for the job the minute you walk in the door. It is just as important to make a favorable impression on the receptionist as on the interviewer. The receptionist's reaction may de-termine whether or not you get an interview. Follow these suggestions while in the personnel office:

1. Be polite and courteous. Don't act bored and impatient.

2. Ask for only one copy of the application.

3. Have adequate supplies and information with you to complete the form.

4. Avoid asking unnecessary or obvious questions. If you must ask questions, make notes as you complete the application so you need to interrupt the receptionist only once.

Remember that this form becomes part of your permanent employment record if you are hired.

ASSIGNMENT: In Section B of the Worksheet you will put to use for an employment application the self-analysis you made in Section A. You will gain experience in preparing a résumé and filling out an application form.

Unit 20 Worksheet

PREPARING RÉSUMÉS AND EMPLOYMENT APPLICATIONS

A *EXAMINING THE JOB MARKET AND YOURSELF. Complete Problem 1. Do not hand in these planning sheets. They are for your own use in studying your job market, in analyzing your personal traits and abilities in reference to a prospective job, and in assembling some "evidence" that you may use in the employment communications you will write.*

1. *Self Analysis*
   a. What vocation do you plan to enter? (If you have not yet decided on one particular vocation, list two or three vocational choices.)

   _____

   _____

   _____

   b. List two or more specific jobs which could provide the first step in the realization of one of the vocational choices listed under item (*a*) and into which you might fit when you're ready to look for a job.

   _____

   _____

   _____

   c. List several duties that a person holding one of the jobs listed under item (*b*) would presumably be expected to perform.

   _____

   _____

   _____

   _____

   _____

   _____

   d. List several organizations in your community (or in other communities in which you would like to live and work) that employ persons in the job detailed under item (*c*).

   _____

_____

_____

_____

_____

_____

e. List in the left-hand column *a number of your personal traits* (not physical features) that could help you in carrying out the duties listed under item (*c*) in Problem 1. Use concrete adjectives such as *dependable, neat, cheerful, tactful*. In the right column, opposite each trait listed, *record any evidence* you can think of to show that you have the trait. Here are some examples to get you started.

_____ | _____

_____ | _____

_____ | _____

_____ | _____

_____ | _____

_____ | _____

_____ | _____

_____ | _____

_____ | _____

_____ | _____

_____ | _____

_____ | _____

_____ | _____

f. In the column to the left *list a number of your abilities* (things you can do well) that could help you in carrying out the duties listed under item (*c*) of Problem 1. Be specific—for instance, *ability to write computer programs in COBOL, prepare financial statements, compose effective business letters*. In the column to the right, opposite each ability listed, *jot down any evidence* you can think of to show that you have that ability. For example:

_____ | _____

_____ | _____

_____ | _____

_____ | _____

_____ | _____

_____ | _____

_____   _____
_____   _____
_____   _____
_____   _____
_____   _____
_____   _____
_____   _____
_____   _____
_____   _____
_____   _____
_____   _____
_____   _____
_____   _____
_____   _____
_____   _____
_____   _____
_____   _____
_____   _____
_____   _____
_____   _____
_____   _____
_____   _____
_____   _____

B WRITING YOUR RÉSUMÉ AND COMPLETING AN EMPLOYMENT APPLICATION

2. Select a format (chronological, functional, or combination) and prepare your résumé for the job you want. Make it an attractive, easy-reference summary of your qualifications. Assume you have successfully completed any courses you are enrolled in.

3. Complete the application blank on pages 226–228. Include part-time jobs and summer employment. Type the data or write in longhand (using a pen with black ink); in either case do it neatly, carefully, and correctly—as though you were actually applying for a job.

Ernest and Fast Associates
Employment Application

An Equal Opportunity Employer
Ernest and Fast Policy and Federal Law Forbid Discrimination Because of Race, Religion, Age, Sex, Marital Status, Disability, or National Origin.

Date_____

Personal Data

Applying for position as _____ Salary required _____ Date available _____

Name: _____
       (Last)   (First)   (Middle)   (Maiden)

Present address _____
     (Street)   (City)   (State)   (Zip)   (How long at this address)

Permanent address _____
     (Street)   (City)   (State)   (Zip)   (How long at this address)

Telephone number _____ Social Security number _____
     (Area code)

Are you a U.S. citizen? ☐ Yes ☐ No   If non-citizen, give Alien Registration No. _____

Check appropriate box for age: Under 16 ☐, 16 or 17 ☐, 18 through 64 ☐, 65 or over ☐

Person to be notified in case of emergency:

    Name_____ Telephone_____

    Address_____

Relatives employed by Ernest and Fast: Name_____ Department _____

                                             Name_____ Department _____

Will you consider relocation? Yes ☐ No ☐   Domestic Yes ☐ No ☐   International Yes ☐ No ☐

Have you ever been employed by Ernest and Fast or its subsidiaries?   Yes ☐ No ☐

If "Yes", indicate department, publication or company _____ Dates_____

Have you previously applied for employment with Ernest and Fast?_____ If "Yes", when?_____

How were you referred to Ernest and Fast? ☐ Agency ☐ School ☐ Advertisement ☐ Direct contact ☐ **Ernest and Fast employee** ☐ Other

Name of referral source above:_____

Military Data

Have you ever served in the Military Service of the United States?_____

Branch of Service_____From_____To_____Rank_____

Give details of Service duties which might apply to civilian occupations _____

Educational Data

Schools	Print Name, Number and Street, City, State, and Zip Code for each School Listing	Dates	Type of Course or Major	Graduated?	Degree Received
Grade School		From_____ To	/////		/////
High School		From_____ To			/////
College		From_____ To			
Graduate School		From_____ To			
Trade, Bus., Night, or Corres.		From_____ To			
Other		From_____ To			

Approximate scholastic average: High school _____College_____ Class rank: High school _____College_____

Percent of college expenses earned _____ How earned? _____

Activities

Do not name organizations that will reveal race, religion, age, sex or national origin.

School and college activities _____

Special interests outside 1._____   Indicate the amount of   1._____
of business.   time devoted to each.

2._____   2._____

3._____   .3._____

List any activity that might represent a conflict of interest with Ernest and Fast. _____

Skills

List any special skills you may have_____

What foreign languages do you: ☐ Speak   ☐ Speak   ☐ Speak
☐ Read _____   ☐ Read _____   ☐ Read _____
☐ Write   ☐ Write   ☐ Write

Business machines you can operate_____

Typing speed _____words per minute   ☐ Electric   Steno speed_____words per minute   Method_____
☐ Manual

Employment Data
Begin with most recent employer. List all full-time, part-time, temporary, or self-employment.

Company
name
Employed from ___ Mo-Yr ___ To ___ Mo-Yr ___

Street address
Salary
or earnings   Start   Finish

City _____ State _____ Zip code _____ Telephone (Area code)

Name and title of
immediate supervisor _____ Your title

Description of duties

Reason for terminating or considering a change

Company
name
Employed from ___ Mo-Yr ___ To ___ Mo-Yr ___

Street address
Salary
or earnings   Start   Finish

City _____ State _____ Zip code _____ Telephone (Area code)

Name and title of
immediate supervisor _____ Your title

Description of duties

Reason for terminating

Company
name
Employed from ___ Mo-Yr ___ To ___ Mo-Yr ___

Street address
Salary
or earnings   Start   Finish

City _____ State _____ Zip code _____ Telephone (Area code)

Name and title of
immediate supervisor _____ Your title

Description of duties

Reason for terminating

Company
name
Employed from ___ Mo-Yr ___ To ___ Mo-Yr ___

Street address
Salary
or earnings   Start   Finish

City _____ State _____ Zip code _____ Telephone (Area code)

Name and title of
immediate supervisor _____ Your title

Description of duties

Reason for terminating

Unit 21

WRITING EMPLOYMENT COMMUNICATIONS

Once you have a résumé (see Unit 20), there are several other employment communications you will need to prepare, which we will discuss in this unit.

Preparing to Write Your Application Letter

A résumé should never be mailed without a cover letter, which we call a *letter of application*. Even the best-written résumé has a mass-produced look because of the format. Many employers will not even look at a résumé if it comes without a cover letter. An application letter is not written like a letter of transmittal; it is your personal sales letter and should be written following the steps of a sales promotion letter in Unit 16.

An application letter may be the most important letter you will ever write, because it may determine the course of your life—at least for a time. The purpose of an application letter is to get an interview; the purpose of the interview is to get a job offer for a job that you hope will lead to a satisfying and successful career.

Yes, an application letter that will get you an interview is difficult to write. You will need to spend considerable time planning, writing, and possibly rewriting your application before it is ready to mail.

Never copy a letter that someone else writes or that you find in a textbook. The personnel people will probably recognize it, just as you recognize a movie that you've seen before or a book you've read before. You may not remember all the details, but you remember enough to know that you've seen it or read it before. You don't want to run the risk that a personnel manager will "recognize" your letter as one that sounds unusually familiar. You shouldn't even copy sentences verbatim from model application letters.

Plan and write your own letter in your own style. To be successful for *you,* an application letter should reflect *your* personality, *your* attitude toward life and work.

Prepare a Mailing List of Prospective Employers

One way to obtain names of prospective employers for your mailing list is to list organizations that have employees who do the kind of work you plan to do. You can then write an application (called a *prospecting application*) to the organizations where you feel you could be happy working. The purpose of the prospecting application is to interest the personnel directors in your qualifications so they will contact you for an interview.

A more popular way to obtain names for your list is to locate organizations that are advertising suitable job openings. You can then write an application (called an *invited application*) to each prospective employer for a job which you know is open and for which you are qualified. You can readily find out about such job openings through (1) help-wanted ads in newspapers, magazines, and trade journals; (2) school placement services; (3) public or private employment agencies; or (4) relatives, friends, or acquaintances who tell you about vacancies.

Study the Organization and the Job

You must understand both the organization and the job for which you apply before you can tell an employer how your personality, training, and experience make you a good choice—or *the* choice—for that job. Learn any information you can about what products or services the organization offers, how many employees it has, whether it is publicly or privately owned, and so on. The more you know about the organization and the job requirements, the more interesting and convincing you can make your letter.

Determine What You Can Do for the Organization

To secure attention and interest, write about doing something for your reader. Don't start your letter with *I*, and avoid overusing *I* and *my* throughout your letter. Just as sales executives do, consider your qualifications in terms of what a particular job requires. Only then can you give the employer any practical reasons for buying your services.

Remember that you are competing with many other people who are also trying to sell their services. If your application is to stand out from the others, it must highlight the specific qualifications that would make you a valuable employee. Every reply to an advertisement for a typist will probably mention the applicant's ability to type. To make your letter stand out, find out what kind of typing ability is needed and then determine what you can offer. You might learn, for example, that typing reports containing statistics is part of the job. If this is a requirement for which you are prepared, you won't just say that you can type; you will tell the employer that you can set up statistical material in attractive form and type reports rapidly and accurately.

Decide on the Central Selling Point

In the letter you may mention all your important qualifications for the job, but you can't stress them all. Ask yourself: "Of all my qualifications, which one would be most important in the job for which I am applying? Which one will appeal most to this employer?" It may be your experience in similar work; your ability to get along well with people; your college training; or a special skill, such as the ability to operate a word processor and keyboard rapidly. This most important qualification becomes your *central selling point*, around which you build your letter.

Make a Plan for the Letter

Remember, the purpose of your application letter is to get an interview. Your letter has to be convincing (because of your excellent qualifications) and persuade the employer to talk to you before filling the job.

Plan the content of your letter so it will attract the employer's favorable attention and interest, convince the employer that you have the qualifications to do an outstanding job, and persuade him or her to invite you for an interview.

Writing Your Application Letter

To interest the employer in you as an applicant—and to obtain an invitation for an interview—aim to accomplish these four purposes in your letter:

1. Show the Employer You Know How to Write a Superior Business Letter. Type your letter on good-quality plain paper (see the discussion of format and appearance on pages 105–108). Each letter should be individually addressed and typed. It should be centered on the page (left, right, top, and bottom margins equal); have the appropriate format and parts (see Unit 10); pass the five tests of effective correspondence (see Unit 1); use accurate grammar, punctuation, spelling, and typing; and be signed in blue or black ink. Omit reference initials, but include an enclosure notation (your résumé is enclosed).

2. Show the Employer You Understand the Requirements of the Job for Which You Apply. If you are answering an advertisement, read it thoroughly and know exactly what it tells you about the job advertised and the qualifications wanted. If you are not answering an ad or if the ad does not give details, determine the job requirements by applying what you have learned in school, at work, or in talking with people who have done similar work. For example, if you are applying for a job as a salesperson, think of all the duties a salesperson usually performs— calling on customers, making sales presentations, demonstrating products, handling telephone calls, writing orders, working with coworkers and a supervisor, and the like—and the abilities and personality traits that are necessary to handle these duties successfully.

3. Show the Employer You Have the Qualifications Needed to Fill the Job. Your qualifications are the heart of an application. The employer wants someone who can do the work that needs to be done and do it well. Explain in detail how your background, personality, training, and experience will help you do the job well. If you are answering an advertisement, be sure to give all information requested and to show that you have every requirement suggested in the ad. Cover all the requirements in the letter itself; don't depend on the résumé to take the place of a thorough application letter.

Explain your qualifications in specific terms. It is not enough to say, "I can do accounting work." Explain that you can do payroll, keep the records either manually or on a computer, prepare the quarterly reports, and so on.

Toward the end of the message, call attention to the résumé enclosed.

4. Show the Employer You Are More Interested in Helping the Organization Than in Getting Something for Your Own Benefit. Be sincere and enthusiastic when you talk about working, serving, and cooperating. Use the "you" attitude. You certainly won't sound as though you are interested in service to the organization if your letter is filled with questions about salary, raises, vacations, pension plans, sick leave, and overtime pay. Leave these matters for the interview.

Desirable Features of an Application Letter

Perhaps the best way to be sure the application letter accomplishes all four objectives is to develop it in three parts: (1) an interesting opening that will get the employer's attention; (2) a convincing presentation of your qualifications; and (3) a strong closing requesting action.

1. An Interesting Opening. Your opening must attract favorable attention and get the employer interested in your qualifications—interested enough to read on. Here are four ways to get your reader's attention. Use the first if you write an invited application for a job that has been advertised. Use the second, third, or fourth if you write a prospecting application for a job that is not advertised.

a. Mention the source of your information about the vacancy. Here is an opening written by an applicant who learned of a job opportunity from a college placement office:

> From the MSU Placement Office I learned that you are looking for a top-flight salesperson who can also give outstanding field demonstrations with Holtz farm equipment.

This applicant heard about a job opportunity from a teacher:

> Mrs. Martha Kendall, Director of the School of Medical Records Administration at the University of Maryland, brought to my attention your need for an Assistant Administrator in your Medical Records Department. Mrs. Kendall is confident that my college preparation and my experience in the Medical Records Department of Giles County Hospital will enable me to meet all the requirements of this job.

b. Summarize your qualifications for the kind of job you would like to have with the organization.

> As an employee in your purchasing department, I could rapidly and accurately take dictation (80 wpm) and type letters (65 wpm). I believe I would thoroughly enjoy working with my office associates and furthering Gillette's goodwill with other organizations both in the office and by phone.

Here's another example of an opening that summarizes your qualifications.

> With my college background, accounting and selling experience, and ability to get along with people, I believe that I could successfully sell Eastman Kodak products.

c. Refer to the organization's reputation, progress, or policies.

> The recent expansion of Colgate-Palmolive's research and production facilities, as reported in *Chemical Engineering*, suggests a possible opening for a chemist.

Another example of this opening is given below.

> As a recent college graduate certified to teach math and science, I would like to have the opportunity to contribute to the continued growth and success of the Randolph County School System.

d. Suggest your attitude toward the kind of work the organization engages in.

> Retailing means to me the challenge of meeting people and selling them on a product, an idea, a principle, or a goal.

2. A Convincing Presentation. To be convincing, the presentation of your qualifications must be related to the work to be done and backed by evidence.

Avoid vague, unconvincing expressions such as *I have a good personality, I am intelligent, I am dependable,* or *I am interested in working with people.* You can portray your personal traits more convincingly by presenting the evidence and letting the reader draw the conclusions. Notice how this applicant uses previous work experience to tell the employer he is a hard worker:

> After delivering newspapers several mornings a week while in high school, I'm not afraid of the long hours of work that always occur during rush periods. Hard work doesn't bother me either, since I enjoyed three busy summers assisting my father on construction jobs.

a. *Interpret your training in terms of the work to be done.* The courses you take and the school activities you participate in are not nearly as important to an employer as the lessons these experiences teach you. In your letter, instead of listing courses and extracurricular activities, try to point up ways in which you can do a better job for the organization because of something you learned in school. Notice how the successful application letters on pages 232–235 and the following excerpts relate qualifications and work experience to the work to be done.

Applicants for field representative for Timely Clothes, Inc.:

> My college courses in clothing construction and design and in salesmanship have given me a fairly broad knowledge of the makeup of men's and women's fashions and many pointers about selling that I could put to good use for Timely.

> In my basic college courses—including psychology, humanities, social science, and public speaking—I gained a broader understanding of human behavior and learned to think on my feet and win people to my point of view.

Applicants for a job in retailing:

> Among other extracurricular activities, I worked on the advertising staff of the college paper and had the opportunity to meet and talk with most of the merchants in Weston. Through this experience I learned about business problems and about what the public expects of a retail store.

```
                              P.O. Box 37
                              Neon, Kentucky 41840
                              September 6, 19--


Mr. Robert L. Jones
Personnel Manager
Consolidated Freightways
1942 Parkway Avenue
Detroit, Michigan 48236

Dear Mr. Jones:

With a recent college degree in accounting and several years of
work experience, I am confident of my ability to do excellent
work as a junior accountant.  I am applying for the job that
Consolidated Freightways advertised in the Detroit Herald.

The past three years' experience in the trucking industry has
increased my knowledge of the transportation field.  Working
in an office has increased my awareness of operations, finance,
and budgeting.  In addition, through my reading I have also become
familiar with many of the Interstate Commerce Commission's regula-
tions.

Since your company leases over 90 percent of its equipment,
proper accounting methods for leases are vital to Consolidated
Freightways' accurate financial reports.  The attention to
detail and accuracy which I have developed can reduce costly
accounting errors for you.

The enclosed resume will also give you a description of my
activities and a list of references.  Will you write me or phone
(606) 555-3327 to tell me when I may come in and talk with you?

                         Sincerely yours,

                         Rickey Lee Savarin

                         Rickey Lee Savarin


Enclosure
```

*Notice how the writer of this application letter adapts his work experience to the job
he is applying for.*

```
                                        214 Loretta Avenue
                                        Reno, NV 89502
                                        November 19, 19--




        Mr. Harry C. Potter
        Personnel Manager
        Veterans Administration Hospital
        1000 Locust Street
        Reno, NV 89502

        Dear Mr. Potter:

        The Veterans Administration has been an outstanding medical
        facility in this area for many years, and I would like to be
        considered for a position on your secretarial staff.  Several
        friends of mine are employed at the Medical Center, and they
        are quite pleased with the excellent working conditions and
        advancement opportunities.

        Communication and writing skills are extremely important in a
        secretarial position, and I feel that I could be an asset to
        your hospital in both of these areas.  Good grammar, neatness,
        accurate spelling, and precise writing have always come nat-
        urally to me.  My business courses have given me a strong
        secretarial background, and I adapt easily to people and
        methods of operations.

        Enclosed is my resume, which details my education, job expe-
        rience, and other information which may be of interest to you.

        I would like to have the opportunity to meet with you to dis-
        cuss my qualifications and the possibility of employment at
        the Veterans Administration.  I can be reached at 555-3314
        after 12:30 p.m.

                                Sincerely yours,

                                Linda K. Carson

                                Linda K. Carson


        Enclosure
```

This effective application letter is for a specific job. Note that it has an interesting opening, a convincing presentation of her qualifications, and a strong closing.

Since I have held several part-time jobs and participated in many outside activities while in college, I learned the value of budgeting my time and getting important things done first. This knowledge should be helpful in your busy office.

b. *Adapt your work experience to job requirements.* In the application letter, discuss work experience in terms of what you have learned from it. The employer is interested in how your previous jobs prepared you to do good work for his or her organization. Use the application letters in this unit and the following excerpts to help you adapt your work experience to the job for which you are applying.

Applicant for job as sales representative:

As a successful book sales representative for Lawrence Publishing Company, I have learned to get along with people in the most difficult selling situation—in the customer's home. This job also taught me time management, which is very important to a salesperson working outside an office.

Applicant for assistant in the purchasing department of a major manufacturer:

I am familiar with purchasing terms and the overall structure of a manufacturing firm. Working as an assistant in the purchasing department of Bohn Aluminum Corporation also gave me a good background in buying policies and practices. This experience would enable me to process your orders quickly and accurately.

3. A Strong Closing. Close your application letter with a specific request for action—usually that the employer name a time for a conference with you

```
                              405 Churchill Street
                              Blencoe, Iowa 51523
                              June 18, 19--


     Mr. Hugh M. Brown III
     Personnel Manager
     BSM, Inc.
     343 Oak Street
     Omaha, Nebraska 68108

     Dear Mr. Brown:

          Because of my college training in secretarial administration and my
     work experience, I believe that I can be the SUPERSECRETARY for whom you
     advertised in yesterday's Omaha Star.

          Just two weeks ago I completed, with honors, the two-year secretarial
     administration program at DeSoto County Junior College--a program that
     was both practical and thorough.

          My typing speed is now 75 words a minute; I can take shorthand dicta-
     tion at 100 words a minute.  Besides specific skills, the business courses
     I took at DCJC have given me an understanding of the business world and
     its functions.

          I learned to apply these skills to an office situation during my
     employment at First National Bank of Middleton.  During the two years I
     was at DCJC, I found my job in the Marketing Department of the bank very
     enjoyable.  And I believe that my work background will enable me to adapt
     quickly to your office routine.

          Office work is a challenge to me.  I look forward to new responsi-
     bilities, and I would like to put my abilities and skills to work for
     BSM, Inc.

          When you have reviewed the enclosed resume and contacted my former
     employers and teachers, please write or phone me and suggest a time when
     I may come to your office for an interview.  (My phone number is (515)
     555-2098.)

                              Sincerely,

                              Joyce M. Kramer

                              Joyce M. Kramer

     Enclosure
```

This application letter shows confidence and high-lights the writer's skills in relation to the employer's needs.

about the job—and give the reader a good reason for inviting you for an interview.

When you apply for a job far from your home, the organization may suggest an expense-paid trip to the job location or a conference with a representative in your vicinity. In the successful applications on this page and on page 235 and in the excerpts below, each applicant asks for an interview and adds a statement about the contribution he or she can make to the organization.

The references listed on the enclosed résumé will be glad to confirm that I can meet the high requirements of word processing specialist for United American Bank. Please call me at (701) 488-4932 or write to me at the above address to tell me when it would be convenient for you to talk with me.

I can start work for Southwestern Life Insurance Company after my graduation on August 20. I would like to have an appointment to meet and talk with you at your convenience. My telephone number is (392) 594-4951; my address is given above.

Give Your Letter a Final Check

When you have completed an application letter, ask the following questions to decide whether it is the best letter you can write.

1. Does the letter show that I know how to apply the principles of writing effective business letters?

2. Will my opening paragraph interest the employer?

3. Does the letter make clear that I understand the requirements of the job?

```
                                            407 Sheridan Street
                                            Danville, IL 61832
                                            November 21, 19--


         Mr. J. Hammer
         Personnel Manager
         Lakeview Medical Center
         812 North Logan Avenue
         Danville, IL 61832

         Dear Mr. Hammer:

         FUTURE!  Computers are the future.  I offer a degree in the
         areas of medical records, computer operations, and programming.
         Knowing the progressiveness that Lakeview Medical Center
         strives for, I would consider it a privilege to become a
         records technician with your hospital.

         The two years I attended Danville Area Community College were
         spent on a concentrated education in medical secretary pro-
         cedures combined with computer skills.  My previous positions
         gave me experience in dealing with the public and controlling
         records required for reference use.

         Details of my education and experience are in the enclosed
         resume.

         I would very much appreciate an interview with you.  I am
         available for employment immediately and can be reached at
         (217) 555-8213.

                                       Sincerely,

                                       Shirley A. Kester

                                       Shirley A. Kester


         Enclosure
```

Note the attention getting opening of this successful application letter. Her résumé, which is enclosed, is illustrated on pages 220 and 221.

4. Does the letter emphasize that I have the personality, training, and experience to fill the job?

5. Does the letter indicate that I am interested in what I can do for the organization?

6. Do I ask for specific action in the closing paragraph—and motivate the reply that I want?

Once you've determined you have written the best letter you can, proofread it several times for errors in spelling, grammar, and other areas. Then try to mail your letter so it will arrive on a Tuesday, Wednesday, or Thursday. Mondays most organizations are busy getting the week's work started and going through a heavy volume of mail. Fridays they are busy trying to get the week's work finished up.

Writing Thank-You and Follow-Up Letters

Few people are hired at the first interview. The employer usually narrows the field down to a few applicants, then calls the better ones in for another interview before making the final selection.

Postinterview Thank-You Letters

Unless you are hired at the interview, write a thank-you letter within 24 hours expressing appreciation for the interview and your continued interest in the job.

A thank-you letter is always welcome, and it serves as a written record of your good manners and your ability to communicate. It is an opportunity to mention one of your "selling points" again or one that didn't come up during the interview. Even if you applied to a local firm, send a letter rather than interrupt your interviewer with a phone call.

Sending this letter will give you a decided advantage over the other applicants. Very few applicants actually send postinterview thank-you letters.

The thank-you letter Joyce Kramer sent after her interview with a personnel manager is shown below.

Dear Mr. Brown:

Thank you for talking with me personally about the job in your Customer Service Department.

The tour of your facilities was very interesting, and I was especially impressed by the time you spent with me as a prospective employee.

I am still very much interested in the position as office assistant; you can reach me at my home telephone, (302) 555-2098.

                    Sincerely,

Write a similar thank-you letter if you have been told that your application will be kept on file for consideration when a job opening fits your qualifications.

Follow-Up Letters

If you hear nothing within a reasonable time after writing your thank-you letter, you may write a follow-up letter. Often you can make this follow-up more effective by providing additional information, such as a change of address, graduation from school, or completion of a temporary job.

Sometimes a follow-up letter will spark a response when you have had no reply to your original application for several weeks and feel that the employer has overlooked it. In this letter you should mention the date of the previous application, the job for which you applied, and your continued interest in the job. In it you may summarize and give additional information about your major qualifications, but you need not enclose a résumé.

Other Thank-You Letters

When you accept a job, you have several thank-you letters to write. Did someone tell you about the job opening? Did someone give a favorable report of your qualifications or in any other way help you to get the job? Did someone write you a note congratulating you and wishing you success on the new job? All these people deserve simple, sincere messages of appreciation (see Unit 15). You may be applying for a job again someday, and these people will be more

willing to help you the next time if you let them know you appreciated their help this time.

Requesting Information About Job Applicants

When an employer writes to one of the references given on a résumé to ask for information about the applicant, the letter follows the form of a direct inquiry (see Unit 12). The employer should mark the inquiry "Confidential" and ask questions that will obtain the facts and opinions that he or she needs. Many times a form letter is sent.

Sending Information About Job Applicants

The person who answers a request for information about an applicant should also mark the response "Confidential." The reply should be a report of facts that will give an accurate picture of the applicant rather than a biased recommendation. Opinions should be clearly separated from facts. A former employer should not say, for instance, "Miss Kester will make an excellent accountant for you." But the employer might say, "Miss Kester did superior work in my office, and I believe that she will make an excellent accountant for you."

If the recommendation is positive, use the direct approach. If the recommendation is negative use the indirect "buffer" approach. Requests for information about job applicants should be (1) answered promptly (before the position is filled with another applicant) and (2) answered honestly. This letter is important because it could affect a person's career and an organization's opinion of you.

Accepting and Refusing Job Offers

If you receive a job offer by mail, write an acceptance or a refusal just as soon as you can. If you accept, say so in a short, enthusiastic letter.

Notice the happy—not gushy—tone of Joyce Kramer's acceptance.

Dear Mr. Brown:

I am happy to accept the office assistant job in the Customer Service Department of BSM, Inc. Thank you for choosing me.

The job, as you described it, seems both interesting and challenging to me.

As you suggested, I'll report at 9 a.m. on Monday, June 6. I am looking forward to the challenge of office work at BSM, Inc.

                    Sincerely,

If you decide to decline the job offer, say "No" so graciously that you leave the door open for future employment with the organization. Someday you may have contact with the people or the organization or you may even wish to reapply.

Notifying Applicant of Appointment or Rejection

Just as a job applicant should be concerned about courtesy and sending a postinterview thank-you letter, the organization should be equally concerned about courtesy and notifying each candidate of his or her selection or rejection. If you are selected, you will usually be notified by phone. Those candidates not selected will have a much better impression of the organization if they receive a reply. Many organizations send a card or letter to let the unsuccessful applicants know that the position has been filled. These can be prepared and stored on a word processor and individualized by keying the name, address, and salutation on each letter. An example is shown in the next column; notice how the bad-news approach is used.

Just as most applicants never get around to sending the postinterview thank-you letter, many organizations do not get around to notifying the unsuccessful applicants. It is, however, just plain common courtesy to send these letters.

Resigning From a Job

When you decide to change jobs, you will need to submit a letter of resignation. Your resignation

---

Dear Miss Swenson:

Thank you for submitting your résumé in response to our recent newspaper advertisement. Although you have excellent qualifications for employment, another applicant was selected.

We will keep your résumé in our active files for one year and call you if opportunities arise for an individual with your background.

Sincerely,

---

should be in writing and should give at least two weeks' notice. Higher-level positions and some state civil service systems require more than two weeks' notice.

Even though you may be angry or dissatisfied when you resign, avoid the temptation to "lay it on the line," because this letter will become a permanent part of your personnel file. Keep in mind the old saying: Don't burn your bridges behind you. You never know when some of the same people you worked for will show up at a future place of employment. No job is perfect.

A typical plan for a resignation letter is:

1. Tell how you've benefited (in terms of experience).

2. State in a positive way that you're resigning, and give the effective date.

3. Use a goodwill closing, and offer to train a replacement.

ASSIGNMENT: *The Worksheet for Unit 21 will give you helpful experience in writing employment communications.*

Unit 21 Worksheet

WRITING EMPLOYMENT COMMUNICATIONS

Plan and prepare each of these letters thoughtfully and edit them carefully. Make them your very best—models that you can adapt quickly to actual situations when you have limited time to write and mail your own letters about employment. Type each letter on plain paper.

1. *Invited Application Letter.* Clip an ad from a newspaper or a magazine about a job you would like to have. Prepare an application letter in reply to the ad. Hand the ad in with your letter. Refer to the illustrated application letters of Rickey Lee Savarin and Joyce Kramer for ideas, but do not copy them. Address the letter to the appropriate person in the organization if you can find out his or her name and official title or position. Otherwise, address it to the personnel manager of the organization. Assume that you will enclose your résumé. If you can't find an ad for a job you like, write your own ad and hand it in with the letter.

2. *Prospecting Application Letter.* Choose an organization you would like to work for, and prepare a letter of application. Assume that you will enclose your résumé. Refer to the illustrated letters of Linda Carson and Shirley Kester for ideas, but do not copy them.

3. *Postinterview Thank-You Letter.* Assume that your application letter (Problem 1) won you an interview. Although you were told that you made a good impression and that you would hear more later, you received no job offer. Write the letter of appreciation to be sent to the personnel director the day following the interview.

4. *Requesting Recommendation Letter.* During your interview (Problem 3), assume the personnel manager asks you for a letter of recommendation from a former instructor or employer. Write the necessary request letter asking that it be sent directly to the personnel manager.

5. *Recommendation Letter.* Assume you are the former instructor or employer receiving the letter in Problem 4. Write the letter of recommendation about yourself. Give some serious thought to what you can honestly say in the recommendation.

6. *Acknowledging Job Offer.* You have been offered the job you applied for in Problem 1. Write a letter thanking the employer for the offer. Indicate that you will let the employer know within two weeks whether you will accept or reject the offer.

7. *Declining a Job Offer Letter.* Write a letter declining the job offer you received in Problem 6. You may assume any reason or reasons you wish for declining the job offer.

8. *Thank-You Letter.* You have accepted a job offer and have heard that the person you gave as a reference gave you an excellent recommendation. This was a strong factor in the decision to offer you the job. Write a letter to the person who wrote the recommendation, thanking him or her for helping you.

Reference Section

GRAMMAR

The ability to use the English language competently is an enviable skill in the business world. Speaking and writing clearly, coherently, and effectively is a goal of every business executive. The words you use in conversation, in the office, and in business letters must be well chosen so as to convey your meaning accurately. You therefore need to know which word to use—and when and why.

Studying and practicing the rules of grammar will help you to make fewer errors in your writing—and to recognize and correct your errors *before* you mail a letter or submit a report.

When you put together even two words that make a complete thought, you have formed a sentence. *I work* expresses a complete thought. The subject is *I* and the predicate is *work*. Every sentence must have a subject and a predicate. The subject must contain a noun or a pronoun. The predicate must contain a verb.

Parts of Speech

Words classified according to their use in the sentence are called parts of speech. The parts of speech are nouns, pronouns, verbs, adjectives, adverbs, prepositions, and conjunctions.

G-1. Nouns

A noun is the name of a person *(Vanessa)*, place *(Baltimore)*, thing *(mountain)*, idea *(beauty)*, or attribute *(courage)*.

Nouns may be proper *(Rodney)* or common *(book)*, concrete *(tree)* or abstract *(modern)*, or collective *(family)*.

The gender of a noun may be masculine *(boy)*, feminine *(woman)*, common *(child)*, or neuter *(piano)*.

G-1-a. Plurals of Nouns. The number of a noun indicates whether it is singular or plural. To form the plurals of most nouns, follow these rules:

1. Add *s* to the singular *(order, orders; decision, decisions; price, prices)*.

2. Add *es* to a singular that ends in *s* (or an *s* sound), *sh* or *ch*, *s*, or *z* *(business, businesses; loss, losses; church, churches; tax, taxes)*.

3. Change *y* to *i* and add *es* for words ending in *y* preceded by a consonant *(company, companies; copy, copies)*.

4. Add only *s* for words ending in *y* preceded by a vowel *(Tuesday, Tuesdays; attorney, attorneys)*.

5. Add only *s* for words ending in *o* preceded by a vowel *(ratio, ratios; video, videos; studio, studios)*.

6. Add *es* to most nouns ending in *o* preceded by a consonant *(hero, heroes)*. Some exceptions are *memo, memos; zero, zeros*.

7. Add *s* to the singular of most nouns that end in *f*, *fe*, or *ff* *(belief, beliefs; brief, briefs; proof, proofs; plaintiff, plaintiffs)*. For certain other nouns, change the final *f* or *fe* to *v* and add *es* *(half, halves; self, selves; wife, wives)*.

8. A few plurals are formed irregularly *(foot, feet; child, children; woman, women)*. If you are not sure of a plural form, consult a dictionary.

9. For a hyphenated or a two-word compound noun, change the chief word of the compound for a plural form *(account receivable, accounts receivable; brother-in-law, brothers-in-law; notary public, notaries public)*. If the compound is made up of a noun and a preposition, change the noun (not the preposition) to the plural *(passerby, passersby)*. If the compound does not contain a noun, form the plural on the last element of the compound *(trade-in, trade-ins)*. Compounds written as one word usually form the plural at the end *(letterhead, letterheads)*.

10. Add *s* to most proper nouns *(Buzan, Buzans; Romano, Romanos; Gary, Garys)*. But add *es* to a proper noun ending in *s* or an *s* sound *(James, Jameses)*. Plurals of titles and personal names are formed as follows: *the Misses Shelton* or *the Miss Sheltons; the Doctors Wilson* or *the Doctor Wilsons*.

11. Some nouns have the same form in the singular and the plural *(Japanese; deer; corps; politics)*.

12. Certain nouns are always singular *(athletics; economics; mathematics; news)*.

13. Certain nouns are always plural *(credentials; pants; goods; proceeds; statistics)*.

14. Plurals of words from other languages that have been incorporated into the English language should be looked up in the dictionary *(analysis, analyses; parenthesis, parentheses; criterion, criteria)*. Some of these words have both a foreign and an English plural; in fact, the dictionary may show that there is a difference in the meaning of each plural form.

15. Add *s* to form the plurals of most abbreviations *(Dr., Drs.; no., nos.; dept., depts.)*. The abbreviations of many units of weight and measure, however, are the same in both the singular and the plural *(oz* for both *ounce* and *ounces; ft* for both *foot* and *feet)*. A few single-letter abbreviations form the plural by doubling the same letter *(p.* and *pp.* for *page* and *pages; f.* and *ff.* for *following page* and *following pages)*. The plurals of capital letters, abbreviations ending with capital letters, figures, and symbols are formed by adding *s (P.h.D.s, 3s, &s)* unless the omission of the apostrophe would cause misreading *(A's, I's, U's)*. The plurals of words referred to as words are formed by adding *s* or *es* unless the plural form would be likely to be misread or would be unfamiliar *(ands, dos, don'ts* but *which's* and *or's)*. Add an apostrophe plus *s* to form the plural of uncapitalized letters and uncapitalized abbreviations with internal periods *(i's, c.o.d.'s)*.

G-1-b. Possessives of Nouns

1. Add an apostrophe and *s* to form the possessive of most singular nouns *(woman's* coat; *manager's* office; *assistant's* desk; *Charles's* vacation).

2. For singular nouns that end in *s* if adding the apostrophe and *s* makes the word hard to pronounce, add only the apostrophe (Ms. *Jennings'* idea; *Jesus'* teachings).

3. Add only an apostrophe to regularly formed plurals *(employees'* vacations; *ladies'* suits; *presidents'* portraits).

4. Add an apostrophe and *s* to irregularly formed plurals *(men's* shirts; *children's* toys).

5. Add the apostrophe and *s* to the final member of a compound noun (her mother-in-*law's* car; the editor in *chief's* responsibilities; the secretary-treasurer's report). It is usually preferable to recast a sentence to avoid the plural possessive of a compound noun *(the decision of all the editors in chief* is better than *all the editors in chief's decision)*.

6. To indicate joint ownership of two or more nouns, form the possessive on the final noun (MacLaren and *MacLaren's* clients). But if separate ownership is meant, make *each* noun possessive (the *secretary's* and the *treasurer's* reports).

7. To indicate the possessive of a singular abbreviation, add an apostrophe and *s* (the Harris *Co.'s* offer; Mr. Hugh Miller, *Sr.'s* resignation); of a plural abbreviation, add only an apostrophe (the *M.D.s'* diagnoses).

8. Restrict the use of the possessive to persons and animals. Do not use the possessive form to refer to inanimate things; use an *of* phrase (the format *of the letter*; the provisions *of the will*). Some exceptions are expressions of time and measure *(today's* market; two *weeks'* vacation; ten *dollars'* worth of supplies) and personification (the *company's* assets).

G-2. Pronouns

A pronoun is used in place of a noun, to avoid repetition.

> The chairperson has studied the recommendations and agrees with *them*.

G-2-a. A pronoun must agree with its antecedent (the word for which it stands) in number, person, and gender.

> One of the men left *his* keys on the desk.

G-2-b. Demonstrative pronouns *(this, that, these, those)* should plainly refer to a specific antecedent. Do not use *this* or *that* to refer to the thought of an entire sentence.

> VAGUE: Four people in our word processing department were absent yesterday. *This* accounts for the backlog today.

> CLEAR: Four people in our word processing department were absent yesterday. Their absences account for the backlog today.

G-2-c. Relative pronouns *(who, whom)* do not agree in case with their antecedents. Their grammatical function in the sentence determines their case. A relative pronoun usually introduces a clause. To determine the correct case of the pronoun, rearrange the clause in the order of subject, verb, object. Disregard any parenthetical clauses.

> She is the one whom I believe the committee will choose. (Disregard the parenthetical clause *I believe*, and the normal order of the clause is *the committee will choose whom*. The subject is *committee*, the verb is *will choose*, and the object is *whom*.)

G-2-d. Compound personal pronouns *(yourself, myself*, etc.) have two uses. They may be used for emphasis. They may reflect the action of the verb back upon the subject but are never the subject themselves. A compound personal pronoun should not be used in place of a personal pronoun.

He told me that himself. (Emphasis.)

She gave herself time to get to the airport. (Reflexive.)

G-3. Verbs

A verb states a condition or implies or shows action. A sentence must contain a verb to be complete. When the complete verb is a group of words, it is called a *verb phrase*. A verb phrase has one principal verb and one auxiliary verb (the auxiliary may include more than one word). The common auxiliary verbs are forms of the verbs *to be* and *to have*.

Marcie *works*. Marcie *has been working*. (Auxiliary: *has been*)

G-3-a. Verb Tenses. The tense of a verb tells when the action of the verb takes place.

They want. (Present.)

They wanted. (Past.)

They will want. (Future.)

They have wanted. (Present perfect.)

They had wanted. (Past perfect.)

They will have wanted. (Future perfect.)

1. The tense of the verb in a subordinate clause must agree with the tense of the verb in the principal clause unless the subordinate clause expresses a general truth.

The general manager *announced* that all employees *were expected* to attend the meeting.

Carmen *saw* a movie which *is* not *recommended* for children. (General truth.)

2. In a sequence all the verbs should be in the same tense unless any expresses a general truth.

I *went* to the university, *registered* for five courses, and *returned* home at about 2 p.m.

3. Do not use the present tense for past events.

He *came* to me and *said*, "I can explain the error."

NOT: He comes to me and says . . .

G-3-b. Agreement of Verb With Subject. A verb should agree with its subject in person and number.

Three sales representatives complete their training today.

1. Singular subjects connected by *either . . . or, neither . . . nor* require singular verbs.

Either a refund or a credit memorandum *is* acceptable.

2. When *either . . . or, neither . . . nor* connects subjects differing in number, the verb should agree with that part of the subject that is nearer to the verb.

Neither the retailers nor the wholesaler *is* liable.

Neither the wholesaler nor the retailers *are* liable.

3. When such expressions as *together with, as well as, including* separate the subject and the verb, the verb agrees in number with the real subject.

The catalog, together with the special sales brochures, *is* ready.

4. When the subject is a collective noun that names a group or unit acting as a whole, use a singular verb.

The organization *is* liberal in its promotion policies.

But when the members of the group or unit are considered to be acting separately, use a plural verb.

The committee *were* still discussing the issue.

The jury *were* still deliberating.

5. When a noun singular in form is used as the subject to indicate quantity *(some, all, none, part)* or when a fraction is the subject, use a singular verb when a singular sense is meant and a plural verb when a plural sense is meant. Whether the plural or the singular sense is meant is usually indicated by the object of the prepositional phrase used with the subject.

None of the catalogs *were* shipped today.

All of the event *was* televised.

One-half of the students *were* absent.

One-tenth of the population *are* Orientals. (Exception.)

6. When the subject is *a number*, the verb must be plural. When the subject is *the number*, the verb must be singular.

A number of students *are* being honored.

The number of complaints *is* not surprising.

7. When the name of a business firm includes *and Associates* or *and Company*, use a singular verb.

Boyle, Rickman and Associates *is* opening new offices.

8. When the subject is a group of words, such as a slogan, a title, or a quotation, use a singular verb.

Sell the sizzle not the steak is a well-known saying in the restaurant industry.

G-3-c. Verbal Nouns. Participles ending in *ing* are often used as nouns and are called gerunds. A pronoun modifying a gerund should be in the possessive form.

I shall appreciate *your* sending the check promptly.

G-4. Adjectives

An adjective describes or limits a noun or a pronoun. An adjective construction may be a single word, two or more unrelated words, a compound, a phrase, or a clause. It may precede or follow the noun or pronoun.

Five *new portable* dictating machines are needed.

The office administrator *for whom we advertised* is hard to find.

Liz, *dressed in a gray flannel suit,* was the first to arrive.

The *loss-of-income* provision is explained below.

An adjective may be modified only by an adverb, not by another adjective.

Jonathan is *extremely* (adv.) agile (adj.).

G-4-a. Comparison of Adjectives. To express different degrees or qualities, descriptive adjectives may be compared in three forms: *positive, comparative* (two things compared), and *superlative* (three or more things compared).

Shep's grades are *high.* (Positive.)

Shep's grades are *higher* than mine. (Comparative.)

Shep's grades are the *highest* in the class. (Superlative.)

To form the comparative and superlative degrees, follow these rules.

1. To form the comparative of most adjectives, add *er* to the positive: tall, *taller.* To form the superlative, add *est* to the positive: tall, *tallest.*

2. For irregular adjectives, change the form of the word completely (*good, better, best*).

3. For adjectives of two syllables, the comparative is formed by adding *er* or the words *more* or *less* to the positive, and the superlative is formed by adding *est* or the words *most* or *least* to the positive: *likely, likelier, likeliest;* **OR:** *likely, less likely* (or *more likely*), *least likely* (or *most likely*). Adjectives of three or more syllables are always compared by adding *more* or *most, less* or *least* (*more* efficient, *most* efficient).

4. Some adjectives state qualities that cannot be compared (*complete, correct, level, round, perfect, unique*). However, these words may be modified by *more nearly* (or *less nearly*) and similar adverbs to suggest an approach to the absolute.

5. The word *other* must be used in comparing a person or a thing with other members of the group to which it belongs.

Our new model is selling better than any *other* we have developed.

G-4-b. Compound Adjectives. A compound adjective is made up of two or more words used together as a single thought to modify a noun.

A compound adjective should be hyphenated when it precedes the noun if the compound:

1. Is a two-word one-thought modifier (*long-range* goals).

Exception: Very commonly used compounds are not hyphenated: *high school* teachers; *real estate* agent.

2. Is a phrase of three or more words (*up-to-date* report).

3. Is a number combined with a noun (*fourteen-day* period).

4. Has coequal modifiers (*labor-management* relations).

5. Includes irregularly formed comparatives and superlatives (*better-selling* items; *worst-looking* letter).

6. Combines *well* with a participle (*well-educated* executive).

A compound adjective that follows the noun should also be hyphenated when it:

1. Is a *well* compound that retains its one-thought meaning (*well-read, well-to-do;* **BUT NOT:** *well known, well managed*).

2. Is made up of an adjective or a noun followed by a noun to which *ed* has been added (*high-priced, left-handed*).

3. Is a noun or an adjective followed by a participle (*time-consuming, factory-installed, strange-looking, ill-advised*).

4. Is formed by joining a noun with an adjective (*fire-resistant, tax-exempt*).

Consult the dictionary for compounds composed of common prefixes and suffixes (*audio*visual, *post*script, *pre*addressed, *inter*office, *mid*-July, business-*like*).

Do not hyphenate a foreign phrase used as a compound modifier (*per capita* consumption, *ad hoc* ruling, *ex officio* member).

Do not hyphenate a two-word proper noun used as an adjective (*Latin American* conference, *Western Union* telegram, *Supreme Court* decision).

Consult a reference manual for compound adjectives commonly used without hyphens (*real estate, income tax, social security, life insurance, word processing*).

G-5. Adverbs

An adverb explains, describes, or limits a verb, an adjective, or another adverb.

Does this machine work *efficiently?* (Modifies verb.)

It is *very* efficient. (Modifies adjective.)

We drove *quite* carefully on the ice. (Modifies adverb.)

G-5-a. Place an adverb as close as possible to the word it modifies. Its position may alter the meaning of the sentence.

He met her *only* today.

He met *only* her today.

Only he met her today.

G-5-b. Verbs of the senses (*look, taste, feel, smell,* etc.)

and linking verbs (forms of *be, become, seem,* and *appear*) are usually followed by an adjective which describes the subject.

> The meat smells *bad.* (Adjective, modifies *meat.*)
>
> He looked *happy.* (Adjective, modifies *He.*)
>
> I feel *bad.* (Adjective, modifies *I.*)

But to describe the action of the verb, use an adverb.

> She looked *happily* at him. (Adverb, modifies *looked.*)
>
> He felt *carefully* for his key. (Adverb, modifies *felt.*)

G-5-c. Adverbs that are negative in meaning should not be used with negatives.

> Anne *scarcely* had time to finish the report.
>
> NOT: Anne *hadn't scarcely* time to finish the report.

G-6. Prepositions

A preposition is a word used to connect a noun or a pronoun with some other word in the sentence.

> Jorge asked *about* the current financial condition *of* the store.

G-6-a. The noun or pronoun following a preposition is called the *object of the preposition.* A preposition and its object, called a *prepositional phrase,* may be used as a noun, an adjective, or an adverb. The object of a preposition must be in the objective case.

> Trisha sat between *him* and *me.*

G-6-b. Do not use superfluous prepositions.

> Where has he gone?
>
> NOT: Where has he gone *to?*

G-6-c. Do not omit necessary prepositions.

> Alex is interested *in* and excited *about* the trip.
>
> NOT: Alex is interested and excited about the trip.

G-6-d. Certain words are always followed by certain prepositions.

> Noah is angry *about* the mix-up. (Angry *about* or *at* something.)
>
> Noah is angry *with* me. (Angry *with* a person.)

If you are unsure, look up the word in a dictionary or a reference manual.

G-6-e. Ending a sentence with a preposition is acceptable for emphasis. Short questions often end with prepositions.

> These are the questions I want answers *to.*
>
> Which files are you finished *with?*

G-7. Conjunctions

A conjunction is a word that connects words, phrases, or clauses.

G-7-a. A conjunction may be *coordinate* or *subordinate.* A *coordinate* conjunction connects words, phrases, or clauses of equal grammatical construction. A *subordinate* conjunction connects dependent words, phrases, or clauses to the main, or independent, clause.

> Ten applications have been received, *and* more are still coming in. (Coordinate.)
>
> We have not received the desk, *although* we ordered it six weeks ago. (Subordinate.)

G-7-b. *Correlative* conjunctions are a type of coordinating conjunctions used in pairs to connect two or more words, phrases, or clauses. They should immediately precede the words, phrases, or clauses that they connect, which should be parallel in form.

> You may order *either* now *or* when our sales representative calls.
>
> NOT: You may *either* order now *or* when our sales representative calls. (Note that *now* and *when* are in parallel form; both are adverbs.)

G-7-c. Do not use prepositions such as *without, except,* and *like* to introduce a subordinate clause.

> The package looks *as though* it has been tampered with.
>
> NOT: The package looks *like* it has been tampered with.

Using Words in Sentences

To convey your meaning successfully in letters or in conversation requires expertness in putting words together. A successful letter is made up of strong, well-constructed sentences and paragraphs.

G-8. Kinds of Sentences

A sentence must contain a subject and a verb (predicate) and express a complete thought. A *simple* sentence contains a subject and a predicate. A *compound* sentence contains more than one independent clause. A *complex* sentence contains one independent clause and at least one dependent clause in either the subject or the predicate. A *compound-complex* sentence contains two or more independent clauses and one or more dependent clauses.

> SIMPLE: The vice president left yesterday and will return on Thursday. (This simple sentence contains two verbs joined by the conjunction *and.* A simple sentence may also contain two or more subjects joined by conjunctions.)
>
> COMPOUND: The survey has been completed, and the results will be available in a few days.
>
> COMPLEX: Results of the survey, which has just been completed, will be announced tomorrow.
>
> COMPOUND-COMPLEX: Our Chromex model aroused much interest, and we believe it will appeal to a new

market because its price is lower than that of any other model.

G-9. Sentence Fragments

A group of words that does not express a complete thought is not a sentence. Occasionally such an incomplete thought may stand alone for emphasis. Experienced writers sometimes use this device—but sparingly. In business correspondence, this technique is generally limited to sales writing.

South Padre Island. *The* place to spend your vacation this summer.

Please check these figures carefully and return them to me as soon as you have finished.

NOT: Please check these figures carefully. Returning them to me as soon as you have finished.

G-10. Run-On Sentences

A sentence containing two or more complete thoughts loosely strung together without proper punctuation is called a *run-on* sentence. The remedy for this sentence error is either to place each complete thought in a separate sentence or to retain the several thoughts in a single sentence by the use of proper subordination and punctuation.

RUN-ON: The meeting had to be canceled and the chairperson asked me to notify each of you and she regrets any inconvenience this cancellation may have caused you.

BETTER: The chairperson asked me to notify you that the meeting had to be canceled. She regrets any inconvenience this cancellation may have caused you.

G-11. Sentence Length

The length of the sentences in any written message is an important factor in catching and holding the reader's interest. Avoid monotony by varying sentence length. However, very long sentences are suitable for business letters only if they are used sparingly and if they are carefully constructed.

In letter writing, as in cooking, too much of anything is not good. Avoid too many short words, too many short sentences, too many long words, too many long sentences. Avoid also too many similar sounds or too many sentences of similar construction.

G-12. Sentence Rhythm

To achieve good sentence rhythm, learn to place words carefully in the sentence. Vary the length and emphasis of the sentences. Use—but do not overuse—intentional repetition of sounds, words, and phrases.

Cultivate an ear for the sound of a sentence. Read your sentences aloud, emphasizing the important words. If the sentences sound awkward, choppy, or involved, rewrite them until they are pleasing to listen to.

Constructing Paragraphs

Combining sentences into paragraphs requires an understanding of the work a paragraph should do in any written message. A paragraph is made up of one or more sentences that together make a single point or relate to one aspect of a central theme.

G-13. Topic Sentence

A paragraph should usually contain a topic sentence that summarizes the main idea of the paragraph. The topic sentence is usually at the beginning of the paragraph, but it may be at the end or in the body of the paragraph. In business letters made up of short paragraphs, the topic sentence may be only implied.

G-14. Transition

One paragraph should lead naturally into the next, to guide the reader from one central thought or point to the next. To achieve this continuity, use transitional words or phrases, such as *however, therefore, for example, in addition, as a result.*

G-15. Paragraph Length

A paragraph may be of any length as long as it treats only one point or one aspect of the central thought. Business communications, particularly sales and advertising letters, tend to have fairly short paragraphs so as to keep the reader's interest. Technical communications often contain longer paragraphs.

G-16. Paragraph Rhythm

Like sentences, paragraphs should be pleasing to the ear when read aloud. Avoid a succession of very long or very short paragraphs. Vary the placement of the topic sentence. Avoid starting successive paragraphs in the same manner, such as with a participial phrase.

G-17. Unity, Coherence, and Emphasis

In addition to applying the fundamentals of grammar, a good business writer will be sure to observe the principles of unity, coherence, and emphasis.

G-17-a. To secure *unity,* include only relevant material and exclude all that is irrelevant. Ask yourself, "Is this word, this sentence, this paragraph, essential to the development of my main thought?"

G-17-b. *Coherence* is the result of an orderly presentation of your message. Main points should follow each other in logical order. To achieve coherence you should plan your message carefully before you begin to write.

1. One enemy of coherence in the sentence is the *misplaced modifier.* Be sure to place every modifier where it clearly modifies the word it is intended to explain or qualify. Put phrases as close as possible to the words they modify. Placement of participial and infinitive phrases needs special care in order to avoid the dangling modifier with its often ludicrous distortion of meaning.

> After examining the encyclopedias in your home, you may return them if you are not completely satisfied.
>
> NOT: After being examined in your home, you may return the encyclopedias if not completely satisfied.

2. Another enemy of coherence is *unclear antecedents.* Be sure every pronoun has a clear antecedent.

> The letters should be checked for errors and *the errors* should be neatly corrected.
>
> NOT: The letters should be checked for errors, and *they* should be neatly corrected.

G-17-c. *Emphasis* means giving the important points in your message special prominence to show the reader that they are important. Ways to achieve emphasis include:

1. Position. Put the important word, phrase, or clause at the beginning or the end of a sentence, of a paragraph, or of the whole message.

2. Proportion. The most important point in the message should usually occupy the most space. Don't clutter a letter with trivial details.

3. Repetition. You gain impact by careful use of the same construction. Like all good things, intentional repetition should not be overdone.

> By using the new vocabulary builder, *you will discover how* to find the right word and *how* to avoid hackneyed words. *You will discover how* to increase your word power and *how* to put that power to profitable use.

4. Balance. You gain emphasis by balancing words, phrases, clauses, or sentences. But don't strain for this effect or your writing will sound forced.

> The more words you know, the better you can express your ideas.

If you heed the following warnings, you will not weaken the emphasis you intend in your messages:

1. Avoid generalizations and other vague expressions.

> POOR: As a rule, we ordinarily make an exception for such circumstances as yours.
>
> BETTER: Your circumstances merit our making an exception.

2. Change passive constructions to active.

> WEAK: Your check must be mailed to us immediately in order to avoid legal action.

> STRONGER: To avoid legal action, you must mail your check to us immediately.

3. Eliminate general, unemphatic sentence openings.

> POOR: There are several new features planned for our next issue.
>
> BETTER: Among the new features in our next issue will be . . .
>
> OR: Featured in our next issue will be . . .

4. Watch the placement of transitional expressions. They are usually more effective after, rather than before, an important word, phrase, or clause.

> If you have a particular problem, however, please write to me about it.

Punctuation

P-1. Period

The period is used at the end of a declarative sentence (one that makes a statement) and at the end of an imperative sentence (one that gives a command).

> Half a million people are employed by this organization. (Declarative.)
>
> Take these books to the library. (Imperative.)

P-2. Question Mark

The question mark is used at the end of an interrogative sentence (one that asks a question). Even if the question is part of a declarative statement, the question mark is used. Even though a question does not form a complete thought, it may be set off if it logically follows the preceding sentence.

> How should we introduce our new product? On a television show? At a press conference?

> Do not use a question mark at the end of a courteous request; use a period.

> Will you please send us your latest price list.

P-3. Exclamation Point

The exclamation point is used at the end of an exclamatory sentence to indicate strong feeling, surprise, or enthusiasm. An exclamatory sentence is seldom appropriate in business messages except in sales and advertising letters.

> Yes! You can save $100 *today only!*

P-4. Comma

A comma indicates a short break in thought within a sentence. Used properly, a comma ensures clarity by conveying the writer's exact meaning. Commas are not, however, to be used in a sentence simply because a speaker might normally pause. Rather, commas are to be used according to well-established rules. For a fuller discussion of comma usage, consult a handbook of English grammar and usage.

P-4-a. Separate the principal clauses of a compound sentence by a comma before the coordinate conjunction *(and, but, or).*

> A new computer will be installed, and a computer programmer will be hired.

P-4-b. Set off nonrestrictive elements by commas. A nonrestrictive element is not essential to complete the meaning of the sentence.

> The annual report, *which is published in April,* shows our financial condition. (Nonrestrictive.)

P-4-c. Do not use commas to set off a restrictive element, that is, one which limits the meaning of the sentence.

> The bank cannot honor checks *that are improperly signed.* (Restrictive.)

P-4-d. Use a comma after an introductory participial phrase. (Avoid overuse of this construction in letters.)

> *Having committed ourselves to this plan,* we are not backing down now.

Use a comma after an introductory dependent clause.

> *Since this assignment is due tomorrow,* I must finish it tonight.

Use a comma after an introductory prepositional phrase unless the phrase is very short or very closely connected to what follows.

> *In the five years following our merger with Dynamo Sales Corporation,* our sales increased 50 percent.

P-4-e. Use a comma after an introductory inverted phrase or clause.

> *Because it was improperly signed,* the check was not honored by the bank.

P-4-f. Parenthetical (or interrupting) words, phrases, and clauses should be set off by commas.

> We, *like all unions,* must protect the interests of our members. (Interrupting phrase.)
> We cannot, *as you will agree,* make such an exception. (Interrupting clause.)

P-4-g. Transitional words, phrases, and clauses should be set off by commas.

> We must, *therefore,* change our plans.
> *Therefore,* we must change our plans.

P-4-h. Set off appositives by commas. An appositive has the same meaning as the word or phrase it follows.

> Heather Frazee, *the new manager,* telephoned today.

P-4-i. A comma is used to set off a direct quotation from the rest of the sentence.

> The speaker said, *"I agree with your recommendation."*

P-4-j. A comma should precede and follow such expressions as *for example, that is, namely,* when they introduce explanatory words or phrases.

> Homonyms, *that is,* words that sound alike, are often confused.

P-4-k. A comma should precede *such as* only when it introduces a nonrestrictive expression. When *such as* introduces a restrictive expression, do not use a comma.

> All stationery, *such as* letterhead, second sheets, memorandum forms, as well as envelopes, is ordered from A.R. Taylor Stationers. (Nonrestrictive.)
> An office *such as* this is every executive's dream. (Restrictive.)

P-4-l. Items in a series should be separated by commas. If each member of a series is connected by *and* or *or,* no comma is needed. If a comma is used within any item of a series, a semicolon separates the items.

> The chairs, desks, and tables were all refinished.
> Attending last week's conference in Williamsburg were David Rice, marketing director; Vicki Fuentos, advertising manager; and John Holmes, sales promotion manager.

P-4-m. A comma should precede and follow *etc.* (unless it closes the sentence).

P-4-n. Two or more adjectives modifying the same noun should be separated by commas if each alone modifies the noun *(simple, well-designed letterhead).* But if the first adjective modifies the combination of the noun and the second adjective, the comma is not used *(fireproof metal container).*

P-4-o. Indicate by a comma the omission of a word or words in a parallel construction.

> Model 101 will be available June 1; Model 109, July 1.

P-4-p. Separate repeated words by commas to make the sentence easier to read.

> The fire spread very, very quickly.

P-4-q. Use a comma to prevent misreading a sentence.

> Soon after, the strike ended.

P-4-r. Use a comma to separate thousands, millions, etc., in numbers of four or more digits, except years, page numbers, addresses, telephone numbers, serial numbers, temperatures, and decimal amounts.

P-4-s. Separate consecutive unrelated numbers by a comma.

> In 1986, 15 new plants were built.

P-4-t. Separate by commas the parts of a date and of an address *(May 5, 1978; 3412 Lincoln Avenue, Riverside, California).*

P-4-u. The name of a state, when it follows the name of the town, is set off by commas.

> Our restaurant in Decatur, *Alabama,* burned last week.

P-4-v. A comma follows the complimentary closing of a letter unless open punctuation is used throughout.

P-5. Dash

A dash is used to indicate a stronger break in thought than is shown by a comma. The word or phrase enclosed in dashes is grammatically separate from the sentence and not necessary to the meaning.

P-5-a. A parenthetical expression or an appositive that already contains a comma may be set off by dashes.

> All large appliances—microwave ovens, ranges, refrigerators, washers, dryers—will be drastically reduced this weekend.

P-5-b. When an introductory word is only implied, a dash is used to set off a following word or phrase.

> New inventions are patented every month—hundreds of them.

P-5-c. A dash is used to separate a summarizing word from a preceding enumeration.

> M.A., M.S., M.B.A.—all are graduate degrees.

P-5-d. No other punctuation is used with a dash. When an expression set off by dashes ends a sentence, omit the closing dash and use the appropriate sentence-end punctuation.

> See our dealer in your area—today!

P-6. Semicolon

The semicolon indicates a stronger break in thought than the comma.

P-6-a. Separate the principal clauses of a compound sentence by a semicolon when no connective is used.

> Meeting notices were sent yesterday; today the agenda was prepared.

P-6-b. When the principal clauses of a compound sentence are connected by a conjunctive adverb (such as *consequently, therefore, however*), use a semicolon.

> Budget requests were received late; *therefore,* the preparation of the final budget was delayed.

P-6-c. When either of the principal clauses in a compound sentence contains one or more commas, use a semicolon to separate the clauses if using a comma before the conjunction would cause misreading.

> We ordered letterhead stationery, carbon packs, envelopes, and file guides; but plain paper, carbon paper, and file folders were sent to us instead. (The semicolon is necessary to prevent misreading.)

P-6-d. When *for example, that is, namely,* or a similar transitional expression links two independent clauses or introduces words, phrases, or clauses that are added almost as afterthoughts, use a semicolon before the expression and a comma after it.

> Amy K. Shelby is a leader in many professional organizations; *for example,* she is president of the National Secretaries Association, a member of the board of directors of the Medical Secretaries Association, and program chairperson of the Business and Professional Women's Club.

P-7. Colon

A colon is the strongest mark of punctuation within the sentence.

P-7-a. A colon introduces an explanation or an amplification following an independent clause.

> The organization has one objective: to satisfy its customers.

P-7-b. A formal listing or an enumeration is introduced by a colon.

> David's qualifications are these: honesty, dependability, and sincerity.

P-7-c. If the list or enumeration grammatically completes the sentence, omit the colon.

> David's qualifications are honesty, dependability, and sincerity.

P-7-d. A colon introduces a quotation of more than one sentence.

> Dr. Truemper said: "The fate of Velasco's chemical discharges will be determined by the judge. There are, however, two possible alternatives to the procedure now used."

P-7-e. A colon follows the salutation in a business letter unless open punctuation is being used.

P-7-f. A colon separates hours and minutes *(11:15 a.m.).*

P-7-g. A colon separates the main title of a work from the subtitle *(Africa: Continent in Turmoil).*

P-7-h. At the end of a letter a colon may separate the dictator's initials from the transcriber's *(HWH:me).*

P-8. Parentheses

Within a sentence parentheses set off explanatory words, phrases, and clauses that are not essential to the meaning of the sentence. No punctuation is used preceding an opening parenthesis, but the appropriate punctuation follows the closing parenthesis. If the material enclosed in parentheses requires a question mark or an exclamation point, that punctuation should precede the closing parenthesis.

Sales have increased (about 20 percent) despite the weather.

He expected to stop overnight in Chicago (or was it Detroit?).

Parentheses also have the following uses:

P-8-a. To cite authority.

"Happiness lies in the joy of achievement and the thrill of creative effort" (Franklin D. Roosevelt).

P-8-b. To give references and directions.

Insert key at A (see Operating Manual, page 10).

P-8-c. To verify a spelled-out number in legal material.

The sum of Fifteen Hundred Dollars ($1500) . . .

P-8-d. To enclose figures and letters of enumerated items that do not begin on separate lines.

The reasons are these: (1) rising labor costs, (2) inadequate space, and (3) shortage of personnel.

P-8-e. To indicate subordinate values in an outline.

1. Operating procedure
  a. Open switch A.
    (1) Hold switch A open and turn valve B.
      (a) Check flow at nozzle C.

P-9. Brackets

Brackets are seldom used in business letters but are sometimes required in formal reports (1) to enclose material in a quotation that was not in the original; (2) to enclose *sic*, which indicates that an error in quoted material was in the original; (3) to enclose material within a parenthesized statement.

P-10. Quotation Marks

Quotation marks are used to set off direct quotations. A quotation within a quotation is set off by single quotation marks.

P-10-a. Consecutive quoted paragraphs each begin with quotation marks, but only the final paragraph closes with quotation marks.

P-10-b. The comma and period are placed inside closing quotation marks. The colon and the semicolon are placed outside. A question mark or an exclamation point precedes closing quotation marks only if the quoted material is in the form of a question or an exclamation.

P-10-c. Quotation marks are also used to enclose titles of chapters, parts, sections, etc., of books; titles of speeches, articles, essays, poems, short musical compositions, paintings, and sculpture; and slogans and mottoes.

P-10-d. Quotation marks are not used for names of books, newspapers, and magazines. In business letters the main words of such titles are usually capitalized and the complete titles are underscored; or the titles may be typed in all capitals as an alternative to underscoring.

P-11. Apostrophe

The apostrophe is used to form the possessive of nouns (see G-1-b). The apostrophe also has the following uses:

P-11-a. To indicate a missing letter or missing letters in a contraction *(can't, wouldn't)*.

P-11-b. To form the plural of letters, figures, and symbols, if the omission of the apostrophe would cause misreading (see G-1-a-15).

P-11-c. To indicate the omission of the first part of a date *(class of '86)*.

P-11-d. As a single quotation mark.

Capitalization

Capitalize parts of business letters as follows:

C-1. Each word of the inside address and the envelope address, including main words of titles of persons.

C-2. The main words in subject and attention lines when these lines are underscored (use all capital letters when these lines are *not* underscored).

C-3. The first word of the salutation, plus titles.

C-4. The first word of the complimentary closing.

C-5. Main words of titles following the writer's name.

Capitalize the first word of:

C-6. A sentence or a group of words used as a sentence. *(Sales have skyrocketed. No wonder we need help.)*

C-7. Items in an outline.

C-8. Separate-line itemizations.

C-9. A direct quotation. *(Howard W. Newton said, "People forget how fast you did a job—but they remember how well you did it.")*

C-10. Lines of poetry.

C-11. An explanatory statement following a colon if it is a complete sentence that states a formal rule or principle or requires special emphasis. *(He made this point: Build your speech to a climax.)*

C-12. An independent question within a sentence. (The question is, *How much would such a procedure save us?*)

Capitalize the first word and the main words of:

C-13. Titles and subtitles of publications, musical compositions, motion pictures, plays, paintings, sculpture (*Sports Illustrated; Official Airline Guide; "A Midsummer Night's Dream"*).

C-14. Titles of speeches, lectures, addresses. (The title of his speech was *"How to Double Your Income."*)

Capitalize the following:

C-15. Proper nouns—names of particular persons, places, and things—and proper adjectives derived from them (*Jefferson, Jeffersonian; Latin America, Latin American; Discovery II*).

C-16. Words that are used in place of proper names (*the Lone Star State*).

C-17. Common nouns when substituted for specific proper nouns (*the Territory*, meaning *Indian Territory; the Zone*, for *Canal Zone*).

C-18. Exact titles of courses of study. (*He enrolled in Accounting II and Business Communication.*)

C-19. Titles of persons—business, professional, military, religious, honorary, academic, family—when preceding the name (*President James Kusyk; Lieutenant Beatty; Judge Watts; Cousin George*).

C-20. Titles following a name only if they refer to high government officials (*Frank Bates, Associate Justice;* but *Priscilla Cartmell, mayor of Cordova*).

C-21. Official names of organizations, such as associations, bureaus, clubs, commissions, companies, conventions, departments (*National Sales Executives Association; Dallas Chamber of Commerce*).

C-22. Names of governments and subdivisions of government, whether international, national, state, or local (*Soviet Union; Commonwealth of Australia; the Supreme Court; the Port of New York Authority*).

C-23. Common nouns substituted for a specific organization or for a government agency (*the Company; the Association; the Council; the Department; the Commission;* but *our company; that department*).

C-24. Names of streets, buildings (*Broadway; Chrysler Building*).

C-25. Religious names and pronouns referring to the Deity (*the Bible; the Heavenly Father; First Baptist Church*).

C-26. Military services, branches, and divisions (*the Navy; the Armed Forces; the 101st Airborne; the Seventh Regiment*).

C-27. Trademarks, brand names, names of commercial products, proprietary names, and market grades. Manufacturers and advertisers often capitalize the common noun following the trade name (*Xerox; Dictaphone; Coca-Cola, Coke; Midas Mufflers*).

C-28. *State* only when it follows the name of the state or is part of an imaginative name (*New York State; Volunteer State;* but *state of New York*); and *States* only when it stands for *United States*.

C-29. A particular geographic area (*Great Plains; the Far East; the West Coast; to visit the South;* but *southern agriculture; drive south two miles; southern Illinois*).

C-30. Days of the week, months, holidays.

C-31. Personifications (*"O Truth, where art thou?"*).

C-32. Races, peoples, languages (*French; Orientals; Spanish;* but *blacks* and *whites*).

C-33. Historical events and documents (*Vietnamese War; Declaration of Independence*).

C-34. Nouns followed by a number referring to parts, divisions, or sequence (*Column 2; Volume II; Room 17; Car 16788;* but *page 15; paragraph 3; note 2*).

C-35. Every word in a compound title that would be capitalized if standing alone, but only the first word of a compound not used as a title (*UN Aid to Non-Self-Governing Territories*).

C-36. Certain important words in legal documents such as the name of the document, references to parties, special provisions, and spelled-out amounts of money may appear in initial capitals or all capitals: (*WHEREAS, RESOLVED, THIS AGREEMENT, Notary, SELLER, WITNESS*).

C-37. Emphasized words in sales and advertising material (Don't miss our famous *End-of-the-Year Sale!*).

Do *not* capitalize the following:

C-38. Names derived from proper nouns but no longer identified with them (*diesel engine; india ink; manila envelope*). If in doubt consult the dictionary or a reference manual.

C-39. *The* unless part of the official name (*the Denver Post; the First National Bank;* but *The New York Times*).

C-40. *The* when the name is used as a modifier. (*I find the New York Times foreign news complete and informative.*)

C-41. *City* unless part of a name (*Kansas City; Sioux City*).

C-42. *Ex, former, late* preceding titles (*former President Ford, the late Senator Mann*).

C-43. Names of subjects of study. (*I enjoy psychology more than I do history.*)

C-44. The words *federal, government, nation, union,* and *commonwealth* in ordinary business writing. Capitalize *union* and *commonwealth* only when they refer to a specific government.

Numbers

In business correspondence, numbers are more often expressed in figures than in words, both for clarity and for quick reference. The following rules reflect acceptable business practice.

Use words to express the following:

N-1. Exact numbers up to and including ten (*seven sales*).

N-2. Indefinite numbers (*several thousand; few hundred*).

N-3. Ages unless expressed in exact years, months and days. (*He has a twelve-year-old son; he is 12 years, 5 months, 11 days old.*)

N-4. A number at the beginning of a sentence. Or, better, recast the sentence. (*Seventy-five applications were received today.* OR: *We received 75 applications today.*)

N-5. Approximate designations of time. (*The meeting will begin about eleven o'clock.*) But use figures if exact time is given with *a.m.* or *p.m.* (*Our hours are from 8:30 a.m. to 4 p.m. daily.*) Use words also to express periods of time except in discount and credit terms and interest periods (*for the last fifteen years; a 60-day note; 2% 10 days, net 30 days*).

N-6. Ordinals, except dates and street numbers (*our eighth anniversary*).

N-7. Fractions used alone (*one-third of the coupons*).

N-8. Numbers in legal documents, usually followed by the amount in figures in parentheses.

N-9. Political and military divisions; sessions of Congress (*Thirty-first Regiment; Ninety-first Congress; Thirty-third Congressional District*).

Use figures for the following:

N-10. Numbers above ten when used alone (*450 miles*).

N-11. Exact amounts of money, no matter how large (*an increase of $55,000,000*). For very large amounts the word *millions* or *billions* may be used with figures (*$55 million* or *55 million dollars*); be consistent within a piece of writing. In a series repeat the dollar sign before each amount (*$10 to $15 deductions*). Do not use the decimal point or zeros with whole-dollar amounts (*$6; $250*); do use them in tabulations if any of the amounts include cents. Do not use the symbol ¢ except in such technical material as price lists.

N-12. Population figures unless very indefinite. (*Over 50,000 people visited the festival;* but *several hundred thousand are expected next year.*)

N-13. Mixed numbers, including stock quotations (*an average of 5½ errors per page; IBM closed at 31⅛*).

N-14. Numbers in a series of related items (*5 local men, 15 from Nashville, and 20 from neighboring states*).

N-15. One of two adjacent related numbers. The first should be in figures (*75 two-cent stamps*) unless the second is longer and more awkward to write. (*fifty 25-cent stamps*).

N-16. Measurements. Use the unit of measure only with the last figure of a series (*6 by 9 by 13 inches;* technical style: *2" × 3½" × 4"*).

N-17. Ratios, proportions, and percentages (*outnumbered 3 to 1; 22 percent*).

N-18. House numbers over one, street names over ten, and all ZIP Code numbers (*77 West 34th Street, Los Angeles, California 90017*).

N-19. Highway numbers, pier and track numbers, page numbers, policy and other serial numbers (*Route 75; Pier 88; WA 5-7770*).

N-20. Dates (*March 5, 1986; your order of May 15; shipped on the 7th of June*).

N-21. Decimal amounts (*savings of 0.812 mills; an increase of 12.3 per day*).

N-22. Votes (*defeated by a vote of 12 to 5*).

N-23. References to parts of publications (*Figure 17; Chapter 23; Plate VI; Table 41*).

N-24. Statistical material, including ages, time, etc.

Abbreviations

Abbreviate the following:

A-1. These titles when used with personal names: *Dr., Mr., Messrs.* (plural of *Mr.* and pronounced "messers"), *Mrs., Mme.* (short for *Madame*), *Ms.* (pronounced "mizz"), and *Mses.* or *Mss.* (plural form of *Ms.*). The plural of *Mme.* may either be spelled out (*Mesdames,* pronounced "may-dahm") or abbreviated (*Mmes.*). The titles *Miss* and *Misses* are not abbreviations.

A-2. These titles following personal names: *Esq., Jr., Sr.;* also, academic and honorary degrees such as *M.D., O.D., Ed.D.* (used when *Dr.* does not precede the name).

A-3. Names of government agencies, without periods (*FCC* for *Federal Communications Commission*).

A-4. Names of well-known business organizations, labor unions, societies, and associations. When these abbreviations consist of all capital initials, they are typed without periods or spaces *(IBM, AT&T, AFL-CIO, NAACP, YMCA)*.

A-5. *B.C.* and *A.D.* in dates *(350 B.C.; A.D. 440)*.

A-6. *a.m.* and *p.m.* Designations of time *(6:15 a.m.)*.

A-7. *No.* for *number* preceding a figure *(No. 189)*.

A-8. Common business terms, according to usage in a particular field *(c.o.d.; f.o.b.; e.o.m.)*. Such terms are often capitalized, without periods *(COD, FOB, EOM)*.

Do *not* abbreviate the following except as indicated:

A-9. Personal, professional, religious, and military titles when used with a surname only *(Professor Jensen; Vice President Maxon)*. When both first name and last name are used, the title may be abbreviated in business correspondence but not in formal usage *(Lt. Col. Robert E. Morris)*. **EXCEPTION:** The title *Doctor* is usually abbreviated *Dr.*

A-10. Any part of the name of a business firm unless the abbreviated form appears in the firm's letterhead or other official usage *(Hammond Steel Corporation; Marz Brothers Inc.)*.

A-11. *Honorable* and *Reverend* except in addresses, lists, and notices. And, except in these usages, use *The* preceding the title.

A-12. Names of days and months, except in columnar work if space is limited.

A-13. Geographical names—cities, counties, countries—except for states and possessions of the United States, which may be abbreviated in lists, addresses, and tabulations, according to the forms recommended by the United States Postal Service.

A-14. Units of measure except in invoices, lists, and tabulations. Be consistent in using abbreviations in a particular piece of work *(15 inches, or 15 in, or 15")*.

A-15. Note that no periods are used in the following: ordinals *(5th)*; letters referring to a person or a thing *(Mr. X)*; radio and TV station letters and broadcasting systems *(WMCA; CBS)*; mathematical symbols *(tan)*; chemical symbols *(NaCl)*; and such symbols as *IOU, SOS*, which are not abbreviations.

Abbreviations: (1) States, Territories, and Possessions of the United States; (2) Canadian Provinces

Alabama	AL	North Carolina	NC
Alaska	AK	North Dakota	ND
Arizona	AZ	Ohio	OH
Arkansas	AR	Oklahoma	OK
California	CA	Oregon	OR
Canal Zone	CZ	Pennsylvania	PA
Colorado	CO	Puerto Rico	PR
Connecticut	CT	Rhode Island	RI
Delaware	DE	South Carolina	SC
District of		South Dakota	SD
Columbia	DC	Tennessee	TN
Florida	FL	Texas	TX
Georgia	GA	Utah	UT
Guam	GU	Vermont	VT
Hawaii	HI	Virgin Islands	VI
Idaho	ID	Virginia	VA
Illinois	IL	Washington	WA
Indiana	IN	West Virginia	WV
Iowa	IA	Wisconsin	WI
Kansas	KS	Wyoming	WY
Kentucky	KY		
Louisiana	LA	Alberta	AB
Maine	ME	British Columbia	BC
Maryland	MD	Labrador	LB
Massachusetts	MA	Manitoba	MB
Michigan	MI	New Brunswick	NB
Minnesota	MN	Newfoundland	NF
Mississippi	MS	Northwest	
Missouri	MO	Territories	NT
Montana	MT	Nova Scotia	NS
Nebraska	NE	Ontario	ON
Nevada	NV	Prince Edward	
New Hampshire	NH	Island	PE
New Jersey	NJ	Quebec	PQ
New Mexico	NM	Saskatchewan	SK
New York	NY	Yukon Territory	YT

Dividing Words

Whenever possible, avoid dividing a word at the end of a line. If a word must be divided, insert a hyphen at the point of division, according to the following generally accepted rules.

Divide a word:

D-1. Only if it is more than one syllable and more than five letters and can be divided so that more than a two-letter syllable is carried over. Divide between syllables (if unsure of syllabication, consult the dictionary) (knowl-edge, **NOT:** know-ledge; prod-uct, **NOT:** pro-duct; passed, **NOT:** pas-sed; strength, **NOT:** streng-th).

D-2. By retaining a single-vowel syllable preceding the hyphen *(cata-log)*.

D-3. Between two one-vowel syllables *(situ-ation)*.

D-4. After a prefix or before a suffix (rather than within the root word) *(inter-national;* **NOT:** *interna-tional)*. Avoid divisions that could confuse a reader.

D-5. Between double consonants not ending a root word *(begin-ning)*, and following other double consonants *(bluff-ing)*.

D-6. Before a suffix that has three or more letters *(compensa-tion)*.

D-7. Preferably, only between the elements of a compound word (air-conditioning).

D-8. Avoid dividing the following: proper nouns; titles with proper names; abbreviations; contractions; numbers, including dates and street addresses.

D-9. Do not divide words at the ends of more than two consecutive lines.

D-10. Do not divide the last word on a page.

Spelling

Misspelling is perhaps the most prevalent as well as the most irksome smog that can cloud up your letters. Here are three simple suggestions to help you produce letters free from misspellings: (1) check each word carefully; (2) when in doubt, consult a dictionary; (3) keep an up-to-date list of your personal spelling demons and memorize the correct spelling of each word on your list.

To correct some of your own spelling problems, review Unit 2—especially the section "Appropriate Words"—and study the following words that many business people find troublesome.

Words Frequently Misspelled in Business Communications

absence	cancellation	debtor	finally	noticeable	recognize
accommodate	capital	decide	formerly	occasion	recommend
accompanying	career	deductible	freight	occurrence	referred
accumulate	casualty	defendant	further	offering	requirement
achievement	catalog	definitely	general	omission	responsibility
acknowledgment	circumstances	dependent	government	omitted	restaurant
adequate	collateral	depreciation	grateful	opportunity	salary
advertisement	commercial	desirable	guarantee	ordinary	satisfactorily
advice	commitment	develop	incidentally	overdue	separate
advisory	committee	director	independent	pamphlet	sincerely
affidavit	comparable	disappear	interest	parallel	stationery
all right	competent	disappoint	itinerary	partial	statistics
analysis	competitor	discrepancy	its	particular	succeed
announcement	complement	dissatisfied	judgment	permanent	successful
apologize	concede	economical	liaison	permitted	superintendent
apparently	conceivable	effect	library	personal	supervisor
appearance	concurred	eligible	license	personnel	surprise
appropriate	confidential	eliminate	lose	practically	temporary
approximately	congratulate	embarrass	magazine	precede	their
associate	conscience	emphasize	maintenance	preliminary	there
attendance	conscious	employee	management	principal	thorough
authorize	consistent	envelope	material	principle	transferred
available	continuous	especially	memorandum	privilege	transit
believe	convenience	exceed	merchandise	proceed	typing
beneficial	cooperative	excellent	miscellaneous	professor	unfortunately
benefited	corporation	except	mortgage	quantity	unnecessary
brochure	correspondence	exercise	necessary	questionnaire	usually
business	correspondents	existence	negligible	quite	vendor
calendar	counsel	expense	negotiate	receipt	warehouse
campaign	creditor	experience	ninety	receive	yield

Revision Symbols

Using standard revision symbols when editing and proofreading helps the typist make necessary changes quickly and correctly. Study the following list, and refer to it until you have memorized the symbols.

REVISION SYMBOLS

Revision	Edited Draft	Final Copy
Delete stroke	qua~~l~~lity	quality
Delete word	~~very~~	
Change	document ~~letter~~	document
Let it stand	~~however~~	however
Transpose	th̸a̸t	that
Move as shown	(to aid the reader)	
Insert word	timely a ˄fashion	a timely fashion
Insert space	all#right	all right
Close up space	key‿board	keyboard
Insert period	sentence⊙	sentence.
Insert comma	clause˄	clause,
Underscore	<u>Proofreading</u>	<u>Proofreading</u>
Hyphenate	9=by 12=inch envelope	9- by 12-inch envelope
Spell out	(Ave.)	Avenue
Capitalize	<u>c</u>ouncil	Council
Lowercase	/Monthly	monthly
Begin new paragraph	¶ He agreed	
No new paragraph	no¶ To accomplish this	
Align horizontally	Thomas	Thomas arrived at
	_arrived at	
Align vertically	‖Thomas arrived at	Thomas arrived at
	the office early	the office early
	‖to finish the report.	to finish the report.
Single-space	Thomas arrived at	Thomas arrived at
	the office early] ss	the office early
Double-space	Thomas arrived at	Thomas arrived at
	the office early] ds	the office early

INDEX